THE ANASAZI OF MESA VERDE
AND THE FOUR CORNERS

/// \\\ /// \\\ /// \\\ /// \\\ /// \\\ /// \\\ /// \\\ ///

THE ANASAZI OF MESA VERDE
AND THE FOUR CORNERS

// \\\ /// \\\ /// \\\ /// \\\ /// \\\ /// \\

WILLIAM M. FERGUSON

PHOTOGRAPHS BY WILLIAM M. FERGUSON

UNIVERSITY PRESS OF COLORADO

/// \\\ /// \\\ /// \\\ /// \\\ /// \\\ /// \\\ ///

Published by the University Press of Colorado
P.O. Box 849
Niwot, Colorado 80301
303-530-5337

The University Press of Colorado is a cooperative publishing enterprise supported, in part,
by Adams State College, Colorado State University, Fort Lewis College, Mesa State College,
Metropolitan State College of Denver, University of Colorado, University of Northern Colorado,
University of Southern Colorado, and Western State College of Colorado.

The paper used in this publication meets the minimum requirements of the American National
Standard for Information Sciences—Permanence of Paper for Printed Materials. ANSI Z39.48–1984

Library of Congress Cataloging-in-Publication Data

Ferguson, William M.
The Anasazi of Mesa Verde and the Four Corners / William M. Ferguson.
p. cm.

Includes bibliographical references and index.
ISBN 0-87081-375-7 (casebound : alk. paper). — ISBN 0-87081-392-7 (paper : alk. paper)
1. Pueblo Indians—Antiquities.   2. Pueblo Indians—Antiquities—Pictorial works.
3. Mesa Verde National Park (Colo.)   I. Title.
E99.P9F39   1996
978.8'01—dc20

95-53089 CIP

10   9   8   7   6   5   4   3   2   1

/// CONTENTS

/// ILLUSTRATIONS

HOVENWEEP

/// MAPS

/// PREFACE

During the mid-1960s, another Kansas lawyer, John Q. Royce, and I developed an interest in the art and architecture of the Maya Indians of Mesoamerica. At that time we found there were no published books for the general reader that described and illustrated the important Maya sites. So we photographed a number of Maya sites in Mexico and published in 1977 *The Maya Ruins of Mexico in Color*. Since then, with the help of John Royce and Arthur Rohn, I have published three more illustrated volumes—two on Mesoamerica and one on the Anasazi of the Southwest. These books and *The Anasazi of Mesa Verde and the Four Corners* have all been labors of love—for Precolumbian Indians and their accomplishments.

As with my previous projects, this book is meant for the general reader: everyone who has an interest in the American Southwest and the Anasazi. I have avoided as much jargon as possible to make the book readable. I have not, however, avoided the assistance of professionals. This story of the Anasazi was prepared after consultation with and review by Anasazi archaeologists with special expertise, rock art experts, ancient-pottery specialists, and museum curators. The information in this text is accurate and current.

The Anasazi left no written records. What is known about them comes primarily from the study and analysis of their architecture, pottery, rock art, and other artifacts. Much, too, has been learned from their descendants, the modern Pueblo Indians. With photographs, captions, text, and illustrations, this volume presents tangible evidence of the way of life of the Anasazi Indians when they lived in the Four Corners region.

The photographs tell the Anasazi story. Ancient ruins viewed from the ground often appear to be little more than a pile of rocks. From the air, however, you can see what the buildings and settlements looked like, and the sites become understandable.

When planning an aerial photograph, the photographer imagines building a platform from which to take the photograph and determines the platform's best location and height. The airplane is then used as a substitute for the imaginary platform. The photographs are made by shooting the picture from the plane's open window (not through the glass) at exactly the right altitude and position during the fly-by.

I have learned from more than twenty-five years of photographing ruins in Mexico, Central America, and the American Southwest that the best system is to use a 1/1500-to 1/2000-second exposure, usually with the lens wide open. The airspeed of the plane should be reduced to between 100 and 120 miles per hour. Since it is not possible to both fly the plane and shoot the photograph with a handheld camera, in my work on this book I would fly the plane and have a passenger operate the camera. Before his death, John Royce (a U.S. Navy fighter pilot during World War II) and I worked together. He would fly and I would photograph, then I would fly and he would shoot the picture.

The problem, particularly if the site is in a canyon or surrounded by trees, is to shoot the picture in that split second when the plane is in exactly the right position. If you miss that moment, you need to go around to get into position to make the pass again. Many times, just before reaching the site, I would say to the passenger, "Get ready to shoot!" and then "Shoot now!"—sometimes only to hear, "Sorry, I missed it." So we would have to go around again.

I have endeavored to take photographs that portray as accurately as possible the actual color and hue of the ruins or artifacts. It is important to have a good camera with a good set of lenses. Telescopic lenses are very important for reaching cliff dwellings across canyon or for photographing other ruins that cannot be seen close-up. A tripod is advisable to ensure a crisp, sharp negative. A thin-overcast day is best for cliff dwellings, to cut the deep shadow in the back of the cave.

The setting of *The Anasazi of Mesa Verde and the Four Corners* is that spectacular area of southwestern Colorado and southeastern Utah that is bounded by Sleeping Ute Mountain, the San Juan River, Comb Ridge, and the Abajo Mountains. Along the road west from Pleasant View, Colorado, toward the Hovenweep ruins, you will be impressed by the special quality of the sunlight, particularly if you are a photographer or a landscape painter. The light radiates from the red-hued bean fields and the brown and white canyon walls. The masonry buildings and towers of the Hovenweep sites are a camera buff's dream. To follow this back road across the Great Sage Plain to Blanding, Utah, is an adventure in itself.

The photographs become more meaningful when placed in their geographic context. The sites in this book may be located by referring to the book's regional maps, and most may be easily visited.

The three museums covered in this book—those at Mesa Verde, the Anasazi Heritage Center, and Edge of the Cedars State Park—are open at reasonable times and are free. Their exhibits are interesting and educational. For example, the Anasazi Heritage Center has a reconstructed and furnished Anasazi pithouse so real it appears that the Ancient Ones have just moved out. The Heritage Center Museum also contains a wonderful collection of Anasazi artifacts and a number of hands-on displays of Anasazi tools.

The following sites are on public land and are prepared for visitors: Mesa Verde, Hovenweep, Escalante, Lowry, Little Westwater, the Butler Wash cliff dwelling, Edge of the Cedars State Park, the Arch Canyon ruins, and Mule Canyon Pueblo.

Mesa Verde National Park contains examples of Anasazi culture from early Basketmaker through Pueblo III times. All of the Mesa Verde sites that are open to the public can be visited during the summer. Paved roads make them easily accessible. Portions of the park are open during the winter. Spruce Tree House is always open and other sites along Ruins Road are open depending on the snowfall. At Hovenweep National Monument, the Hovenweep Square Tower site and the outlying sites—Holly, Horseshoe, Hackberry, Cutthroat, and Cajon—can also be visited by car and without a guide. The condition of the roads to the outliers needs to be checked at the monument headquarters in wet weather.

For the more adventurous, the Three Kiva Pueblo in Montezuma Creek Canyon, south of Monticello, Utah, can be reached by driving down the spectacular canyon road toward the Hatch Trading Post. By floating down the San Juan River in Utah, from the town of Montezuma Creek to Mexican Hat, you can see some of the most spectacular ancient rock art in the Southwest, or anywhere in the world. Many of the photographs of the cliff dwellings and rock art of the San Juan River, Butler Wash, and Comb Ridge are published here for the first time.

Other sites are less accessible. A visit to the Ute Tribal Park requires a guide provided by the Ute Mountain Utes. The Comb Ridge, Butler Wash, and Cannonball sites, on federal land administered by the Bureau of Land Management, are difficult to find and prospective visitors should arrange to be accompanied by someone who knows the way.

Wherever you go, I have endeavored to provide coverage of the fascinating and beautiful Anasazi sites of the Four Corners region, coverage that will serve well whether you travel by car, by raft, by foot, or simply by armchair.

William M. Ferguson

/// ACKNOWLEDGMENTS

Each of the sections of this book has been reviewed by archaeologists and curators whose expertise includes the Northern San Juan Anasazi. Others have contributed to the maps, drawings, and photographs. This volume would not have been possible without their contributions.

Arthur H. Rohn, author of *Cultural Change and Continuity on Chapin Mesa* and *Mug House, Mesa Verde National Park, Colorado,* and a co-author with me of *Anasazi Ruins of the Southwest in Color,* read the Introduction and the sections on Mesa Verde, Yellow Jacket, Lowry and Pigg, Hovenweep, and the San Juan River.

Sally J. Cole, author of *Legacy on Stone: Rock Art of the Colorado Plateau and the Four Corners,* reviewed all the illustrations of, and references to, rock art.

Norman T. Oppelt, who wrote *Earth Water and Fire: The Prehistoric Pottery of Mesa Verde,* selected pottery sherds from his collection for many of the photographs in this book and reviewed my comments on Anasazi pottery.

Douglas Bowman, for several years the Ute Mountain Tribal Park archaeologist and now the director of the University of Colorado's Cortez CU Cultural Museum and Center, toured the Ute Tribal Park Anasazi ruins with me and reviewed the Tribal Park section and the Introduction.

Dale Davidson, archaeologist with the Bureau of Land Management at Monticello, Utah, who codirected the excavation of Old Man Cave and is an authority on ancient road segments in southeastern Utah, added the known ancient road segments to the large map of the Mesa Verde–Northern San Juan region. In addition, he read and commented on the text and captions in the section on southeastern Utah.

Susan Thomas, curator of the Anasazi Heritage Center Museum, identified the artifacts from the museum that appear in the photographs.

Victoria Atkins, archaeologist for the Anasazi Heritage Center, reviewed and edited the section on the Escalante and Dominguez sites.

Crow Canyon archaeologists Bruce A. Bradley, Ricky Lightfoot, and Kristin Kuckelman furnished the data and reviewed the text on the McElmo section, including the treatment of the Castle Rock, Sand Canyon, and Duck Foot excavations.

I also received assistance from Robert C. Hyter, former superintendent of Mesa Verde National Park; Elizabeth Bauer, curator of the Mesa Verde National Park Museum; Jack E. Smith, former chief archaeologist of Mesa Verde National Park; Stephen J. Olsen, manager of Edge of the Cedars State Park in Blanding, Utah; Gary G. Parker, assistant manager of Edge of the Cedars State Park; Nancy B. Lamm, who created the reconstruction and schematic drawings; Tom McMurray, who helped with the mapmaking; and Lovenia Villarreal, who lent her skills as a photographic librarian.

These people have each made an enormous contribution to the *Anasazi of Mesa Verde and the Four Corners* for which I am most grateful.

W.M.F.

THE ANASAZI OF MESA VERDE
AND THE FOUR CORNERS
/// \\\ /// \\\ /// \\\ /// \\\ /// \\\ /// \\\ /// \\\ ///

/// Introduction

Sleeping Ute Mountain is sacred to the modern Utes and Navajos and was probably sacred to the Anasazi as well. Situated almost on the Four Corners, it is visible from nearly all the ancient Anasazi sites in the Montezuma Valley to the north and in southeastern Utah to the west. From the Mesa Verde side, it appears to be a giant lying on his back with a feathered headdress flowing to the north. His arms are folded across his chest. It is an extraordinary mountain in that its silhouette is almost the same from every direction—both from the ground and in the air. Here is a winter view from the northeast.

Mesa Verde National Park in southwestern Colorado is known worldwide as the location of Anasazi cliff dwellings. The high Mesa Verde plateau affords a view of most of the Four Corners region, which the Anasazi once occupied. The region is so named because it contains the only spot in the United States where four states join together. The term *Mesa Verde* is also used to refer to the architecture, masonry, and pottery of the Four Corners area.

Sleeping Ute Mountain, to the west of the plateau, is sacred to the Ute Mountain Utes, the Navajos, and the Zuni, as it probably was to the Anasazi. The Joan Foth painting shows the sweep of canyons and flatlands from Mesa Verde to the Abajo Mountains in the northwest and to Comb Ridge in the west, where the Kayenta and Mesa Verde Anasazi cultures overlapped. The Dolores Valley lies north of the plateau and the Mancos and San Juan rivers lie to the south.

The larger of these rivers, the San Juan, flows from the San Juan Mountains above Pagosa Springs, Colorado, into northern New Mexico, then west to the Four Corners and into southern Utah, where it joins the Colorado River in Glen Canyon. The Anasazi who lived north of the San Juan—on Mesa Verde, in the Ute Mountain Tribal Park, in McElmo Canyon, in southwestern Colorado west of the McPhee Reservoir (part of the Dolores River), and in southeastern Utah south of Monticello and east of Comb Ridge and to some extent on Cedar Mesa, west of

The Mesa Verde Anasazi lived in the region from Mesa Verde to Comb Ridge in Utah, north of the San Juan River and south and west of a line from Mesa Verde to the Abajo Mountains near Monticello, Utah. The region includes the Montezuma Valley in southwestern Colorado, and southeastern Utah. This book is a guide to the Anasazi ruins in this region. Five geographic landmarks mark the perimeters of the region: Mesa Verde, Sleeping Ute Mountain, the San Juan River, the Abajo Mountains, and Comb Ridge.

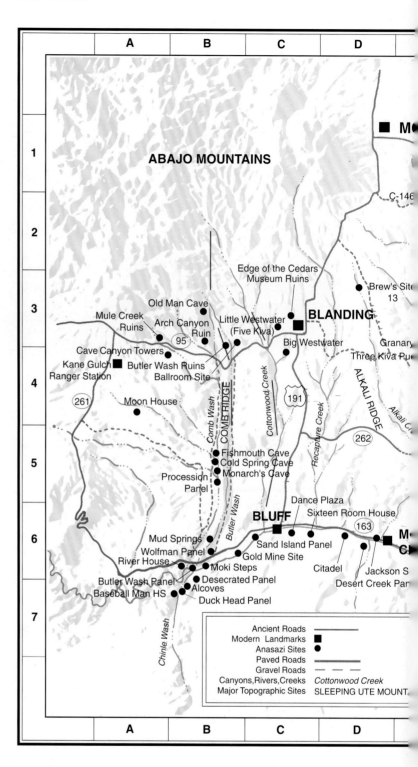

Comb Ridge—are referred to as the Northern San Juan Anasazi. Archaeologists include the pueblos at Salmon and Aztec, New Mexico, and Chimney Rock, Colorado, in the Northern San Juan region. The other Anasazi regions of the Southwest are Kayenta, Chaco Basin, Little Colorado River, and Rio Grande. This volume will discuss the Anasazi of the Four Corners area, or the western portion of the Northern San Juan region. Southwestern archaeologist Douglas Bowman has an illustrative saying: "If there were a stake in place for every Anasazi site in the Four Corners, one could see thousands of stakes in every direction!" On Mesa Verde alone there would be some twelve thousand markers.

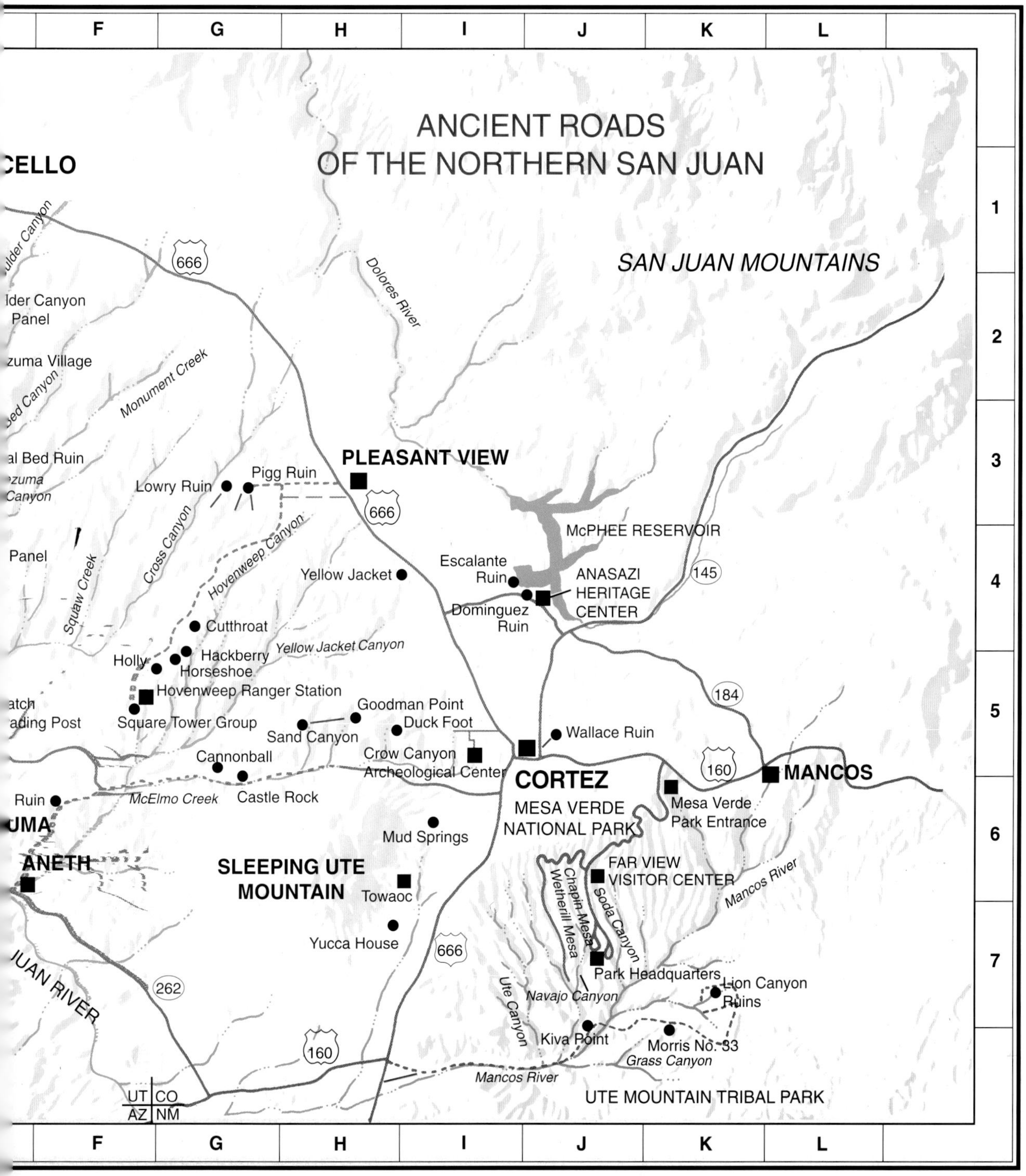

ANCIENT ROADS
OF THE NORTHERN SAN JUAN

SAN JUAN MOUNTAINS

F G H I J K L

1 2 3 4 5 6 7

CELLO

der Canyon

Ider Canyon
Panel

zuma Village

ed Canyon

al Bed Ruin

zuma
Canyon

Panel

atch
ading Post

Ruin

UMA

ANETH

666

Dolores River

Monument Creek

Squaw Creek

Cross Canyon

Hovenweep Canyon

McElmo Creek

PLEASANT VIEW

666

Lowry Ruin   Pigg Ruin

Yellow Jacket ●

Cutthroat ●

Holly ●   Hackberry
Horseshoe
● Hovenweep Ranger Station
Square Tower Group

Yellow Jacket Canyon

Cannonball   Castle Rock

Escalante
Ruin ●

Dominguez
Ruin

McPHEE RESERVOIR

ANASAZI
HERITAGE
CENTER

Goodman Point ●
● Duck Foot
Sand Canyon ●

Crow Canyon
Archeological Center

Wallace Ruin ●

CORTEZ

MESA VERDE
NATIONAL PARK

Mud Springs ●

SLEEPING UTE
MOUNTAIN   Towaoc ●

Yucca House ●

JUAN RIVER

262

160

666

145

184

160   MANCOS ■

Mesa Verde
Park Entrance

FAR VIEW
VISITOR CENTER

Chapin Mesa
Wetherill Mesa

Soda Canyon

Mancos River

Park Headquarters   Lion Canyon
Ruins

Navajo Canyon

Ute Canyon

Kiva Point   Morris No. 33
Grass Canyon

Mancos River

UTE MOUNTAIN TRIBAL PARK

UT | CO
AZ | NM

The Anasazi, like all other Native American tribes, were descendants of Asian hunters who began to cross from Siberia to Alaska at least ten thousand, and perhaps twenty thousand, years ago. For thousands of years, these Asian nomads came in waves across the narrow Bering Sea—on a dry land bridge during the ice ages—and spread across North, Central, and South America. Paleo-Indian people occupied Colorado and the Four Corners as early as 10,000 B.C. The oldest known evidence indicates that Archaic hunter-gatherers who had adopted agriculture were in the region by around 500 B.C. Some archaeologists suggest the Archaic people were present as early as 700 B.C.

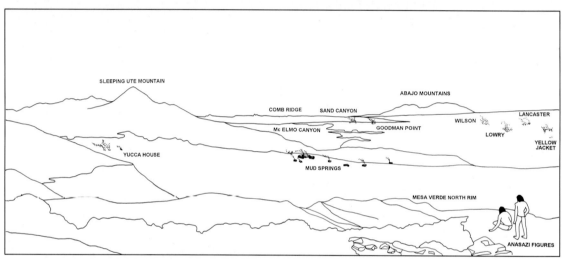

The Montezuma Valley and southeastern Utah as they would have appeared in the A.D. 1200s. From the cliffs of Mesa Verde, these two Anasazi men could see the pueblos in the region bounded by Mesa Verde, Sleeping Ute Mountain, the Abajo Mountains, and Comb Ridge. This view assumes that all the Pueblo III settlements were occupied at the same time. They were all abandoned by 1300. Painting by Joan Foth.

The Anasazi, too, became farmers, evolving from roving bands of hunters. Their unique way of life was developed without an elite class or hereditary chiefs. There was warfare and killing, of course, but little evidence points to the veneration of warriors. Except for a few instances, Anasazi burials do not indicate differences in economic or social status.

The egalitarian aspect of the ancient Anasazi character did not mean they were a peaceful people. They were as human or inhuman as any others. They took scalps, massacred each other, and engaged in ritual killings involving defleshing and mutilation. But like other peoples, they had a humorous side, which can be seen in their rock art and pottery.

The pueblo way of life—the way of life of the Anasazi—has survived for more than two thousand years. The modern Pueblo Indians of New Mexico and Arizona still cling to some of the traditions handed down from their Anasazi ancestors.

Studies of the many skeletons and mummified bodies of the Anasazi conclude that these ancient people probably resembled the modern Pueblo Indians. Evidence indicates that the Anasazi had

The Abajo Mountains (B-2) mark the northwestern corner of the Mesa Verde–Northern San Juan Anasazi region. They lie at the apex of a rough triangle of land that is bordered by Sleeping Ute Mountain, the San Juan River, and Comb Ridge. The Abajos were visible from all the ancient Anasazi villages down to the San Juan. This is a view from near U.S. 666, just east of Monticello, Utah.

Here Comb Ridge (B-4–6) is seen from near the San Juan River. This massive natural wall extends from the San Juan north to the part of Utah 95 that runs west from Blanding. The side shown here, the east side, is made up of many canyons eroded into the gray sandstone slickrock. Butler Wash follows the east side of Comb Ridge and Comb Wash follows the west side. There were settlements in the east-side canyons in prehistoric times, extending over a period of three thousand years, from Archaic times (2000 B.C.) to the Anasazi migrations of A.D. 1300.

The part of the San Juan River that runs from the Four Corners to Comb Ridge is roughly the base of the triangle that encompasses the region that was once the home of the Mesa Verde Anasazi. The Anasazi who lived in what is now southwestern Colorado and southeastern Utah displayed sufficiently similar characteristics that they can be said to have shared a cultural identity.

somewhat Asiatic features—brown eyes, black hair, high cheekbones, and brown skin—and that they were of medium height and were moderately sturdy, the men averaging about five feet six inches tall, and the women five feet.

Archaeologists have divided the Anasazi phases of occupation of the Northern San Juan region into five main periods: Basketmaker II, Basketmaker III, Pueblo I, Pueblo II, and Pueblo III. These periods followed, and to some extent coincided with, the non-Anasazi phases known as Paleo and Archaic. The following chronological chart (p. 8) shows the dates of ancient occupation of the Northern San Juan with examples of ruins and rock art panels from the various periods.

ARCHAIC PEOPLE

The Archaic people consisted of roving bands of hunters and gatherers of wild foods. They used *atlatls* (throwing sticks) with darts and spears. Their shelters were crude. These people coexisted with the Basketmaker II Anasazi, who were more advanced. Douglas Bowman has found evidence that Archaic settlements existed in the mountains adjacent to Lizard Head as late as A.D. 500. The Archaic people are discussed in the short section on Old Man Cave at the end of this volume.

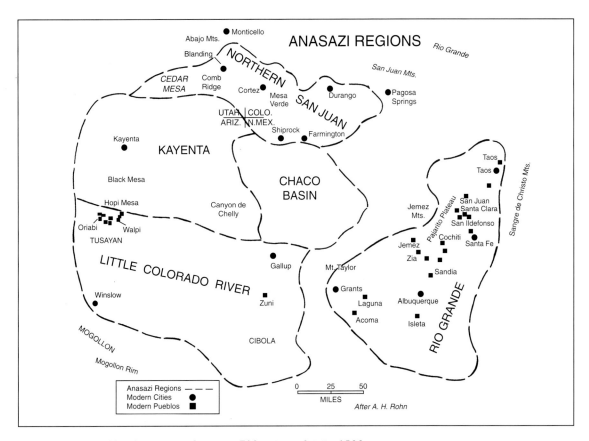

Regions occupied by the Anasazi between 700 B.C. *and* A.D. *1500.*

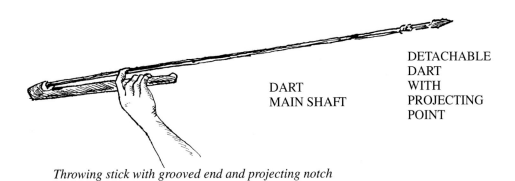

Throwing stick with grooved end and projecting notch

The atlatl (pronounced AT-lat-l) was a stick used for throwing spears or darts. It was employed as a weapon prior to A.D. *500, before the bow and arrow. Drawing by Joan Foth.*

Dates	Ruins and Rock Art
Paleo: 10,000 to 6500 B.C.	
Early Archaic: 6500 to 3500 B.C.	Old Man Cave, rock art at Sand Island and Butler Wash
Middle Archaic: 3500 to 1500 B.C.	
Late Archaic: 1500 B.C. to A.D. 500	
Early Basketmaker II: 1500 B.C. to A.D. 50	
Late Basketmaker II: A.D. 50 to 500	Rock art at Sand Island
Basketmaker III: A.D. 500 to 750	Mesa Verde Earth Lodge B, Step House, Wetherill Mesa rock art, Comb Ridge Procession Panel, Mesa Verde Badger House Community, Wolfman Rock Art Panel
Pueblo I: A.D. 750 to 900	Brew's Alkali Ridge Site 13, Mesa Verde Deep Pithouse, Badger House Community, Duck Foot site, Sand Island rock art
Pueblo II: A.D. 900 to 1100/1500	Mesa Verde Far View ruins, Mesa Verde Site 16, Badger House Community, Butler Wash Rock Art Panel, Sand Island rock art, Lowry Pueblo
Early Pueblo III: A.D. 1100/1500 to 1200	
Late Pueblo III: A.D. 1200 to 1300	Mesa Verde cliff dwellings (Spruce Tree House, Cliff Palace), Comb Ridge (Monarch's Cave), Montezuma Creek (Three Kiva), Hovenweep ruins, Johnson Canyon ruins

BASKETMAKERS

The Basketmakers were the early Anasazi farmers of corn and squash, gatherers of wild seeds, and hunters of small game. They lived in caves and rock overhangs. The early Basketmakers hunted with atlatls, made stone and bone tools, wove sandals and baskets, and had cotton cloth. Baskets played an important role in the culture of the Anasazi before they learned to make pottery. Explorers named these people Basketmakers for the number of baskets found at the sites they occupied. Baskets served the functions later served by pottery. For example, the Basketmakers cooked by dropping very hot rocks into water-filled, tightly woven baskets.

The early Basketmakers, those who lived before A.D. 500, were builders and farmers even though they moved around in pursuit of game. They built *pithouses* (houses dug partially into the ground) and made storage chambers for food. Corn was stored in slab-lined cists to protect it from rodents while the families moved about. As they became better farmers, the Basketmakers farmed more and traveled less. By Basketmaker III times, they lived year-round in small villages of pithouses with aboveground storage rooms, and they farmed nearby fields.

About A.D. 500, the Basketmakers acquired the ability to make pottery, use the bow and arrow, and plant and harvest beans acquired from the south. These were giant steps forward. These later Basketmakers had an improved diet, in part because pottery gave them greater freedom of movement (pottery canteens were used to carry water) and a more effective way of cooking (pottery replaced the use of hot stones in baskets), and the bow and arrow made game easier to kill. Thus, meat was easier to come by, and food was much easier to store and cook. The addition of beans greatly enhanced the diet of the Anasazi, who now had the four basic staples that would serve them for hundreds of years: meat, corn, beans, and squash.

PUEBLOANS

During the early Pueblo stage (Pueblo I times/A.D. 700s), rooms aboveground had walls of interwoven branches laced with brush and filled and faced with mud, a technique called *jacal* (pronounced *ha-CALL*). Later, rows of single-story masonry rooms were built for storage and living quarters. Pithouses were used as shelters during bad weather and as places for weaving, teaching, tool making, and family gatherings. The Spaniards called the Indian settlements in New Mexico *pueblos*, the Spanish word for *towns*. We still refer to ancient Anasazi settlements and to the settlements of the modern Indian descendants of the Anasazi as *pueblos*. The Puebloans lived in villages and nearby settlements.

The Pueblo II period (A.D. 900 to 1100/1150) was a time of marked influence on Mesa Verde and the Northern San Juan region by the brilliant Chacoan Anasazi civilization to the south. Evidence of the Chacoan cultural influence can be seen at Far View in Mesa Verde and at the Escalante, Chimney Rock, Aztec, and Lowry sites. Chaco Canyon, in northern New Mexico, was the center of the Chacoan Pueblo II culture. These Anasazi built *great houses*—multistory edifices, the most spectacular of which is Pueblo Bonito. Chaco Canyon was a center for trade with Mexico and the American Southwest. Roads radiated from the canyon to satellite villages called *outliers*. Lowry may have been an outlier of Chaco. There is no question that Chaco's influence was felt in the Northern San Juan during Pueblo II times, but how much and in what way is still the subject of much speculation. During the late 1000s and early 1100s, the Chacoans began to leave the Mesa Verde region and northwestern New Mexico for the Rio Grande area near Santa Fe. The Chaco Canyon pueblos were abandoned by 1150. This movement has been considered the second Anasazi migration. The first came late in the Pueblo I period (mid-800s), when many Anasazi of the Northern San Juan moved south into the Chaco region.

During Pueblo II, Anasazi villages had the kinds of buildings that have been restored at Far View in Mesa Verde National Park: rectangular masonry structures with side-by-side rooms, common walls, and interior kivas. Another basic type of village orientation was developed during Pueblo I and continued during Pueblo II. Known as the *unit pueblo*, it featured masonry storage rooms in the back of the pueblo, on the north side; residential rooms in the front, facing south; *ramadas* (pole-and-roof structures that resembled modern carports) in front of the residential rooms; and, in the courtyard, kivas that had developed from Anasazi pithouses. Beyond the courtyard was a trash dump. Pithouses and kivas, though different in design, served the same functions.

The kiva is a hallmark of the Anasazi, although the term has been applied to Mogollon structures as well. It is generally considered a key architectural element that distinguishes the Anasazi from the Hohokam and Mogollon Indians of the Southwest, who were also farmers and pueblo builders and lived at about the same time. The kiva evolved from the pithouse about A.D. 750. Kivas were built underground, in a courtyard or inside *room blocks* (aboveground groups of adjoining rooms). Generally, access was by ladder through a hole in the roof. Inside the kiva was a fire pit, a ventilator for bringing in fresh air, and a *sipapu*, a small sacred hole in the floor near the center of the kiva. The sipapu symbolized the Anasazi belief that their ancestors came from below the surface of the earth. In Pueblo III times, family groups built kivas in the cliff dwelling plaza, near their room block, creating a comfortable family gathering place.

During Pueblo II times (A.D. 900 to 1100/1150), villages were generally built in the open on the mesas and were surrounded by farmland. These pueblos were not fortified. Recent research has shown that some Mesa Verdeans had begun living in cliff dwellings during Pueblo II times. But for the most part, Pueblo II ended with a movement from the mesas and into the cliffs. There probably was enough rainfall during Pueblo II, and times were good. We know from tree-ring data, however, that by the 1200s the weather had become drier, and European records indicate that the weather became colder. Kenneth L. Peterson calls it the "Little Ice Age." He suggests cooler temperatures coupled with drought reduced the corn-growing season and consequently the productivity of the land during Pueblo III.

By the mid-1100s, stressful things were happening to the Anasazi. They moved closer together and built pueblos in defensive positions with walls, peepholes, and limited access. In these ways, the pueblos were like smaller versions of the medieval castles of Europe. The Pueblo III period (A.D. 1100/1150 to 1300) was the age of the cliff dwellers. They built Spruce Tree House and Cliff Palace at Mesa Verde, which consisted of two- and three-story masonry buildings and paved courtyards that contained many kivas. Cliff dwellings were built all over the Four Corners region—in the canyons of Comb Ridge, on the banks of the San Juan River, in the Ute Mountain Tribal Park, and at Hovenweep. Because the cliff dwellings are better preserved than other living quarters, they give the impression that most of the Anasazi lived in the cliffs during Pueblo III. Actually, many Anasazi lived in settlements other than the cliff dwellings. Such settlements were around canyon heads (as at Hovenweep), on canyon rims, and on mesas.

WHAT THE ANASAZI ATE

Corn, beans, and squash, plus meat from wild game, were the staples of the Anasazi diet. Small game was the chief source of meat. Game included deer, rabbits, squirrels, raccoons, wood rats, turkeys, and sometimes elk, mountain sheep, and grouse. Domesticated turkeys, which at first were used primarily as a source of feathers—probably by A.D. 1000—were eaten as well. But the primary meat staples were rabbits and deer, killed or captured with atlatls, bows and arrows, nets, and snares.

Meat stew simmered on the fire much of the time. In season, greens, piñon nuts, wild seeds, fruits, and berries became part of the bill of fare. Squash and beans, and sometimes fruits and berries, were added to the meat stew for flavor. Corn was made into meal by stone grinding. The never-ending, tedious task of the women was to grind corn on the *metate* (flat stone receptacle) with the *mano* (handheld stone). Cakes of cornmeal were part of almost every meal. Corn was roasted in the husk, and meat was cooked over the open fire. The men did the hunting and farming. Gathering and cooking were women's chores.

HOW THEY LIVED

In warm weather the women wore an apron and sandals, and the men wore a breechcloth and sandals. The sandals were made of twined or twisted yucca-leaf cords. In the winter they wore robes of deer or elk hides, rabbit fur, or turkey down. The feather-cloth robes were light, fluffy, and warm. In later times, the Anasazi made cotton cloth.

The Anasazi had jewelry, including necklaces and pendants made of bird bones, snail shells, lignite, turquoise, and hematite. Jewelry was traded, and some made from olivella and abalone shells came from the Pacific Coast. A few tiny copper bells have been found. Feathers, of course, were important items of personal adornment.

The Anasazi were outdoor people. They lived and worked in the open, on the roofs of the room blocks or in the plazas. In bad weather, people worked in the kivas because the masonry rooms were small and unventilated and used primarily for sleeping. Over the centuries, the Anasazi tended to *aggregate* (move together) and then *disperse* (separate). Even during the periods of aggregation, however, the villages and their outlying settlements never exceeded about two thousand to twenty-five hundred people. Arthur Rohn suggests that this is as large an assemblage as the Anasazi social structure could accommodate. Large villages existed during Pueblo I (A.D. 800s) and again in late Pueblo II and in Pueblo III.

In Europe from the A.D. 800s to the 1000s, people built great Gothic churches. During that same period in the American Southwest, the Anasazi built structures known as great kivas. These large, partially underground buildings developed from the large pithouses built in Basketmaker times. Great kivas were much larger than other kivas—which are known as *kin kivas*—and could accommodate many more people. Kin kivas were used only by an extended family. Great kivas were community centers. Other community or ceremonial buildings included stone towers, shrines, and tri-walled and D-shaped structures.

Roads fanned out from some of the villages and connected some of the Anasazi settlements with one another. These ancient roads are more difficult to identify in the Northern San Juan region than around Chaco because of decades of modern farming; but the Anasazi built them, and a number have been located.

The Anasazi were independent and self-sufficient farmers. They made their own clothing, shelter, and tools. Some archaeologists believe they must have had markets where they traded such personal items as jewelry, tools, clothing, pots, and baskets with other members of their village or with people from other villages. But there is no evidence that Anasazi markets were as common as they were in the villages and cities of the Maya and Aztecs. Nevertheless, we do know there was trade, because so many trade items have been found.

WATER

Water was always a key concern to the Anasazi. It was a protected resource and vital to life. The cliff dwellings and canyon-head pueblos were usually built near a dependable spring. The Anasazi supplemented the springs by damming runoff water above the pueblo, knowing that the pond created by the dam would seep through the porous rock and feed the spring below during dry weather. They built other dams for domestic water and for garden plots.

Settlement location involved the question of water. The mesa-top pueblos were close to the farming fields, but water for cooking, drinking, and building had to be carried up from the bottom of the canyons. The cliff dwellings and canyon-head settlements were much closer to water, yet farther from the fields.

ROCK ART

Ancient figures carved on cliff walls are called *petroglyphs*. Painted figures are *pictographs*. Together, these two types of figures are referred to as *rock art*. The Anasazi had no system of writing. The rock art is as close as they came. Many of the figures have been interpreted as representing such things as water sources, trail markers, kachina masks, scalps, and migration routes. Other figures are still a mystery. Rock art from each period—from pre-Anasazi to Pueblo III—has definite characteristics. For example, the broad-shouldered, narrow-waisted figures are Basketmaker, while the "lizard men" or "stick men" are Puebloan. Archaic and early Basketmaker rock art is more plentiful and elaborate because it was those peoples' primary medium for artistic display. After pottery became available, Anasazi art appears on pottery as well as on cliff faces.

BASKETS AND POTTERY

The basic shallow band baskets made by *twilling* (over two, under two) or *plaiting* (over one, under one) split yucca leaves or willow into a mat and then attaching the mat to a willow ring have been made by the Anasazi and their descendants for two thousand years. Pottery making probably came to the Anasazi from Mexico by way of the Hohokam and Mogollon peoples of the Southwest. In early 1995, pieces of broken pottery resembling Mogollon Brown sherds, perhaps as old as A.D. 300—Basketmaker II times—were found in the Bluff, Utah, region. Their discovery indicates not only that the early Anasazi traded with the Mogollon but also that the Basketmaker II Anasazi knew about fired pottery. The Basketmakers themselves made highly fired pottery by A.D. 500. The pots were made by rolling strands of moist clay and coiling the strands one upon the other to make the bottom and sides of the vessel. The pots were then smoothed, decorated, dried, and fired.

Great kivas were large covered buildings used for ceremonial purposes. Most were partially underground and circular, although some were rectangular. These photographs show the exterior and interior of a restored Anasazi great kiva at Aztec, New Mexico. Some great kivas were entirely aboveground and uncovered. Fire Temple in Fewkes Canyon is one of these. The uncovered great kivas are sometimes referred to as dance plazas.

Women probably made the pottery. Each piece was distinctive, but general patterns enable modern archaeologists to determine the period during which each pot was fired and where it was made. Anasazi pottery included a wide variety of items: cooking and storage vessels, dippers, canteens, ceremonial objects, cups, and vases. Some pieces were beautifully decorated works of art; others were simple corrugated cookware. Pottery styles persisted for generations and then gradually changed. Pottery and architecture are the two most reliable keys to Anasazi history because there was no written language and thus no written record.

SPIRITS AND RITUALS

Almost everything said about the Anasazi way of life must be inferred from knowledge gained from modern Pueblo people. The customs and culture of the Pueblo Indians have been handed down, generation to generation, by storytellers of the pueblos. The origin myth tells of the upward migration of the people through the spirit world inside the earth until they reach the surface through a sipapu. Spirits and *kachinas* came from the spirit world to teach the people. The supernatural kachinas left masks and instructions for dances and rituals that would produce fertility, rain, crops, and other things beneficial to the people. The Pueblo Indians believed that animals and objects had spirits and could do good or evil. Life and death were governed by ritual—that is, by the proper and correct way of doing things.

The Anasazi had a whimsical side to their character. In their pottery and rock art, lighthearted figures are portrayed—for example, a dancing sheep playing a flute. All sorts of funny little creatures are shown in their rock art and pottery.

The timing of rituals was probably governed by the movement of the sun from winter to summer and back again. The pueblos had solstice and equinox markers by which the changes of the seasons could be precisely noted. At Hovenweep's Holly Pueblo, for example, the "Sun Dagger" pierces a carved circle on the canyon wall with a narrow shaft of light on the summer solstice, about June 21. Ancient rituals probably were passed down for centuries to the people of the modern pueblos. In Anasazi times, as now, the conduct of rituals, together with the power of custom, governed the lives of the Indians. There were no chiefs or nobles—no ruling class.

ANASAZI ARCHITECTURE

Several archaeological terms are used to describe structures built by the Anasazi. Following is a description of some of the most important ones.

Pithouses were partially or totally underground structures built in Basketmaker and early Pueblo times. They served initially as living quarters and later as family gathering centers.

Kin kivas were family units built into the pueblo room blocks or underground during Pueblo times (A.D. 750 to 1300). These kivas served as the center of Anasazi domestic and religious life.

Great kivas were ceremonial and community centers built by the Basketmakers and the Puebloans. Generally they were large, round, covered buildings that lay partially underground. Some were rectangular, or horseshoe-shaped, and uncovered. Recently the uncovered great kivas have been referred to as *dance plazas*.

Pueblos each consist of numerous rooms that are arranged in single or multiple stories and are used for living and storage. Pueblo rooms and kivas were built by individual families, but they were joined to rooms built by other families. Pueblos were not preplanned.

Great houses were planned, multistory structures with large rooms and enclosed kivas. Their style and design resembled those of buildings constructed in Chaco Canyon in the 1000s.

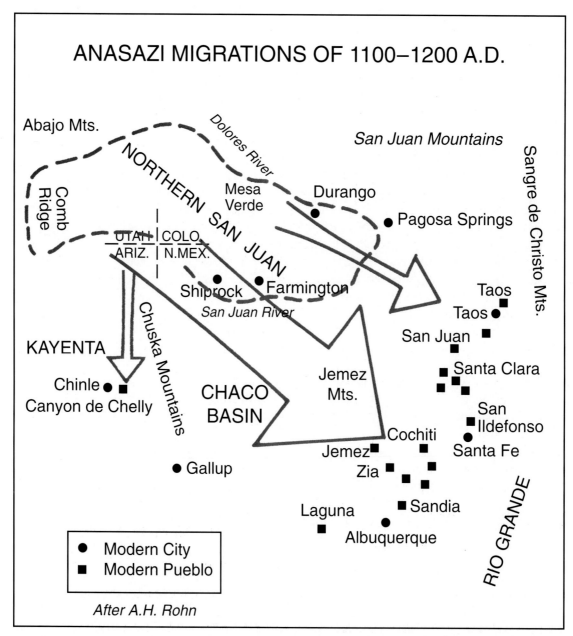

The Pueblo III Anasazi migrated out of the Four Corners region and into the Rio Grande Valley and Canyon de Chelly during the A.D. 1100s and 1200s, leaving the Northern San Juan region empty of people by 1300.

Towers were built by the Anasazi all over the Four Corners area. They stood several stories high and had rooms and peepholes. In most cases, there was a single door at the base. Some towers served as lookouts, and others were ceremonial. Many were part of a kiva-tower combination.

MIGRATIONS

Homo sapiens have been migrating for millions of years. The Precolumbian residents of the New World migrated from Alaska to the tip of South America. The evidence now indicates that the

Pueblo I Anasazi dispersed in the A.D. 800s, moving out of their old pueblos and villages. Some sought new land. Others may have migrated out of the Northern San Juan area to the Chacoan region of northwestern New Mexico. The Chacoan Anasazi left Chaco Canyon and its surrounding area in the late 1000s and early 1100s, and the Pueblo III Anasazi had abandoned the Northern San Juan by 1300. This last was the greatest of three migrations from the Northern San Juan.

The Anasazi, for reasons not entirely agreed upon, began to migrate out of the Northern San Juan region in the 1200s. Reasons proposed for the migration include colder weather, drought, religious omens, pressure from raiding Indians from the north, troubles with other Anasazi villages, and overpopulation. The Indians moved in small groups southeast to the Rio Grande Valley (around what is now Santa Fe), south to the Zuni region, and southwest to Canyon de Chelly and the modern Hopi lands. They left behind sparkling rock art, ruins of ancient pueblos, and cliff dwellings.

After fifteen hundred years of land use and a series of droughts, there were too many people and too little food. The weather became colder, making it difficult to farm at higher elevations. There was terror from outside the pueblos in the form of raids by marauding tribes or other Anasazi. Interpueblo raids and killing must have triggered the defensive building that began during the 1100s and accelerated in the 1200s. Some twenty-four ritual killings in the region have been documented.

Excavations at Castle Rock have demonstrated that battles were fought there after 1250. Perhaps the priests told the people that the gods had said they should raid and kill, and later that they should leave. Or perhaps the people, even if they did not believe it necessary to move, felt they could live better and more safely with their old neighbors in the Rio Grande Valley. In any event, the Anasazi abandoned Mesa Verde and the Northern San Juan region by 1300.

For an overview of the Anasazi, see Ferguson and Rohn's *Anasazi Ruins of the Southwest in Color*, which gives readable coverage.

VISITING ARCHAEOLOGICAL SITES

The archaeological sites in Mesa Verde National Park are well protected and preserved by the National Park Service. The outlying sites in Colorado and Utah that are dealt with in this book are not as carefully regulated and protected. This means that the visitor must take personal responsibility for making sure that these archaeological sites are protected so their scientific and cultural value will be preserved. It is illegal to damage an archaeological site located on public land. This includes land administered by the National Park Service, the Bureau of Land Management (BLM), or the U.S. Forest Service. There are severe penalties for excavating, collecting from, or damaging archaeological sites on public land. Permission should be obtained before visiting sites on private land. A guide provided by the Utes is required for visits to the Ute Tribal Park.

Hovenweep is managed by the National Park Service. However, most of the public-land sites in southeastern Utah are on lands managed by the BLM. The BLM suggests the following guidelines for people visiting remote archaeological sites:

1. Be respectful of the land. You are walking on land and in the former homes of people Native Americans consider to be "alive." Consider yourself to be a guest in another's home.

2. Learn about the site. Before you go to an area and while you are in it, talk to park rangers, local citizens, and archaeologists. The more you know, the more respect you will have for the Anasazi that built and lived in these villages and pueblos—and the better sense you will have of how old and fragile these ruins are.

3. Use care in visitation. Before entering a site, stop and plan how you will visit it. Stay off the walls and follow existing trails. Be careful of the *midden* (trash) areas. They are unstable underfoot.

4. Do not pick up pieces of pottery or arrowheads or other stone points. Collecting these artifacts violates the law. Even moving them destroys some of their "in place" value for scientific study. Photograph them in place. If you find something that looks particularly unusual, contact the BLM.

5. Do not camp in an archaeological site.

6. Be very careful to preserve rock art. Take photographs only. Do not touch the surface or make rubbings. These ancient pictographs and petroglyphs are of great artistic value and cannot be restored or replaced.

7. Be alert to make sure that others protect these sites. Pot hunting and vandalism destroy our precious heritage. They are also illegal. If you observe suspicious activity, contact the BLM.

MESA VERDE NATIONAL PARK

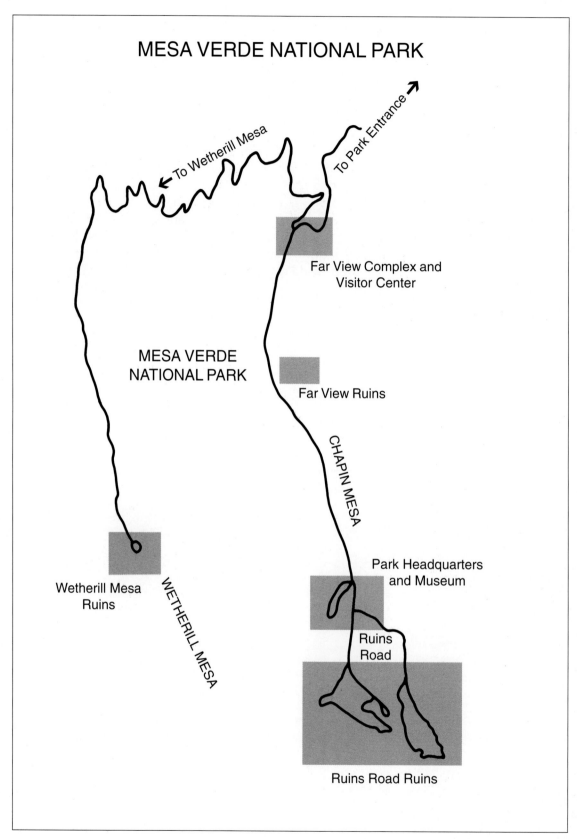

To Wetherill Mesa

To Park Entrance

Far View Complex and
Visitor Center

MESA VERDE
NATIONAL PARK

Far View Ruins

CHAPIN MESA

Wetherill Mesa
Ruins

WETHERILL MESA

Park Headquarters
and Museum

Ruins
Road

Ruins Road Ruins

Mesa Verde National Park

Chapter One

✪ *Mesa Verde*

MESA VERDE NATIONAL PARK

Mesa Verde! Cliff dwellers! Words familiar to millions of people all over the world who have visited Mesa Verde National Park in Colorado. This national and world park, strikingly beautiful in its setting with high piñon and juniper forests and numerous canyons, is unique among our national parks because it is dedicated to the display and preservation of the ancient Anasazi Indian culture. One of the first national parks, Mesa Verde opened in 1906 and has always functioned as a source of information on the lifestyle of the ancient Anasazi. It has also been a place of cultural display, allowing the people of the world to see, feel, and understand traces of six hundred years of the Anasazi culture in its original setting.

Mesa Verde, left, and Sleeping Ute Mountain, right, from U.S. 160, near Mancos, Colorado. The road that climbs to the mesa top begins at the Mesa Verde National Park entrance and angles up the side of the mesa from the valley below. In this photograph, the modern road entering the park forms a visible line one-half to two-thirds of the way up the face of the cliff. The entrance road winds up the side of the escarpment, across canyons, and down Chapin Mesa to the national park headquarters, about twenty miles from the entrance. In this photo, the highest point of the mesa is more than eighty-five hundred feet above sea level and marks the mesa's north end. The Anasazi didn't enter the mesa from the north side as the modern road does, but rather used the relatively easy southern access, up the canyons from the Mancos River Valley.

The park sits on a high plateau with a north escarpment rising nearly two thousand feet from the valley below. The mesa is shaped like a horseshoe with the rounded part to the north and the open portions bounded by the Mancos River to the south. High cliffs surround all of the mesa except the south side. More than twenty canyons serrate Mesa Verde from north to south. The park is bounded on the east and south by the Mancos River Valley, and on the west and south by land of the Ute Tribal Park.

From the entrance, the drive up the park road to Far View and the park headquarters winds up, down, and across canyons and the smaller mesas into which Mesa Verde is divided. The road was an abomination in the 1920s and 1930s. Even today, with a better route, engineers constantly monitor the cut across the east face of Mesa Verde. It may slip at any time, though the road is well maintained and there is no danger to visitors. How did the Anasazi get in and out from this side? They probably didn't. They came up the canyons from the Mancos Valley. In fact, an ancient road has been found along the Mancos River there. The defensive towers placed by the Anasazi look down canyon to the south.

The national park takes up only a portion of Mesa Verde, a "green table" so named by early Spanish explorers. The Ute Mountain Tribal Park, to the west and south of Mesa Verde National Park, occupies the rest of the mesa. The circle drive that passes Cliff Palace on the way to Balcony House briefly passes through a portion of the Ute Mountain Ute Reservation. This anomaly resulted from the park's boundaries being drawn by someone, in Washington, D.C., we presume, who had never visited Mesa Verde.

The mesa, a part of the Colorado Plateau, resulted from the uplifting of the San Juan Mountains. During the Middle Cretaceous Period, about one hundred million years ago, the region was periodically covered by shallow seas. Over millions of years, fine sediments settled to the bottom of the seas and were compacted to form what is called Mancos shale. Later, coarse sands covered the shale and hardened into what is known as Point Lookout sandstone. Still later, a finer deposit called Cliff House sandstone covered the first two strata. The seas retreated about sixty million years ago and the process of uplift began. The flat mesa, formed about one million years ago, tilted upward from south to north, showing at the higher elevations the Cliff House sandstone, below that the Point Lookout sandstone, and below that the Mancos shale. Erosion cut the canyons that now drain into the Mancos River. The two top strata are porous, allowing moisture from rain and snow to percolate down to solid rock, where it follows the hard surface of the shale to the canyon walls, resulting in seeps and springs. Alternate freezing and thawing of this water created the overhangs by loosening the lower sandstone slabs and causing them to break away from the cave ceilings. In these overhangs, the Anasazi built the cliff dwellings.

Mesa Verde National Park is part of the Four Corners region, where Colorado, Utah, New Mexico, and Arizona join. The park entrance is off U.S. 160, about ten miles east of Cortez, Colorado. Twenty-one miles of surfaced, winding mountain road stretch between the entrance and the park headquarters. At various points along this road, visitors can see the magnificent La Plata Mountains to the east. The striking Sleeping Ute Mountain dominates the west side, and across the valley to the northwest are the Abajo Mountains. Shiprock, too, can usually be made out through the smog almost directly south of the park.

Chapin Mesa, in the center of the park, contains the principal park facilities: Far View Visitor Center, the museum, the park headquarters, and many of Mesa Verde's most spectacular Anasazi ruins. The ruins of Wetherill Mesa, which lies west of Chapin Mesa, may be visited only in summer.

Mesa Verde was one of the first U.S. national parks—and the only one dedicated to the preservation of an ancient culture, that of the Anasazi. In 1978 it was designated a World Heritage Cultural Site by UNESCO. Because of its location far above the surrounding region, the Anasazi ruins were not detected by early explorers and travelers.

In the 1880s what is now Mesa Verde National Park was part of the Ute Mountain Ute tribal lands. Benjamin K. Wetherill and his sons, by agreement with the Utes, ran cattle in the Mancos River Valley and in the canyons to the north. The discovery of the first of the large cliff dwellings is the stuff of which legends are made. Around Christmastime in 1888, Richard and Al Wetherill and their brother-in-law Charles Mason rode out of the canyon from the south onto the mesa top looking for stray cattle. They looked across Cliff Canyon and there beneath the overhang was a huge string of masonry buildings! Mason and the Wetherills were so impressed that they named the cliff dwelling Cliff Palace. On the same day, Richard Wetherill and Mason discovered another large cliff dwelling to the west of Cliff Palace, and they named it Spruce Tree House. The trees were Douglas fir, but no matter, it is still called Spruce Tree House.

The park has been a focal point for research over the years. On Chapin Mesa, where the park headquarters and the principal cliff dwellings are located, there are about 1,000 listed sites, including the mesa-top ruins, agricultural check dams, and shrines. On Wetherill, there are about 800 more, and it is estimated that there are a total of as many as 5,000 sites within the park and from 8,000 to 12,000 sites on the entire mesa. By using the tree-ring dating system and pottery fragments, and by comparing masonry and the design of structures, archaeologists can now trace the development of the Anasazi culture from the beginning of Basketmaker III times, around A.D. 500, to the cliff dwellings in the 1200s. The park's visitors have an opportunity to see evidence of eight hundred years of Anasazi occupation—pithouses, pueblos, great kivas, kin kivas, village settlements, spectacular rock art, and cliff dwellings. The dry climate has preserved artifacts such as clothing, baskets, tools, weapons, cradle boards, and foodstuffs, some of which are now on display in the park's museum. An interested visitor can see how the Anasazi culture changed and advanced over time—how and where the people built shelters, farmed, made clothing, designed tools, obtained water, and held ceremonies. It's all available at Mesa Verde.

Splendid facilities are provided for park visitors. There is a large campground at Morefield Village. The Far View complex includes a visitor center building with displays designed as an introduction to Mesa Verde, a restaurant, a service station, and the Far View Motor Lodge. Farther down the road are the park headquarters, another restaurant, rest rooms, a research center, and the museum. At Wetherill, a free minitrain reaches the Kodak House and Long House overlooks. At the parking area for the overlooks, about twelve miles from Far View, rest rooms and food and beverage services are available.

SPRUCE TREE HOUSE

A surfaced trail beginning between the museum and the park headquarters descends into Spruce Tree Canyon. At several points along the trail are slabs of slickrock that afford an excellent opportunity to photograph Spruce Tree House, one of the gems of the Anasazi builders. During the A.D. 1200s, Spruce Tree House was the center of a Pueblo III community in the canyon.

On its way to Spruce Tree House, the trail loops to the north and passes near a spring that served the canyon community. Water was fundamental to the Anasazi, whose communities always were located near a reliable source. Along the canyon walls are a number of masonry buildings that belonged to the Spruce Tree House Community. These buildings range in size from one to fifteen rooms.

Spruce Tree House itself contains 114 rooms and 8 kivas, and it probably housed about 100 people. It is the third-largest cliff dwelling in the park. The pueblo was built under an overhang about 216 feet long and 89 feet from front to back.

Visitors enter the cliff dwelling at the north end onto a plaza containing two restored underground kivas whose entrances are at plaza level. Around this plaza are masonry rooms that housed the families whose kivas were located in the plaza. The rooms were very small by our standards: six feet by eight feet with a ceiling only about five and one-half feet high. The Anasazi were, however, smaller in stature than the average American. The restored kivas here were reconstructed with cribbed roofs following the design of an intact kiva found at Square Tower House.

In this plaza, with a little imagination, you can reconstruct the daily lives of the Anasazi. The room blocks were built by individual families—Spruce Tree House was not a planned project like a modern apartment complex. Each section was constructed by the members of a particular family. However, there must have been cooperation between families because the rooms closely adjoin each other, either side by side or one above the other. The folks above were not necessarily part of the same family group as the folks below. The back rooms were probably used for storage. The front rooms were sleeping rooms for both children and adults. This basic building plan was employed in the other cliff dwellings. The restored courtyard with its kivas is typical of the Pueblo III Anasazi period. Note the number of intact original roofs—Spruce Tree House is one of the best preserved of all the cliff dwellings.

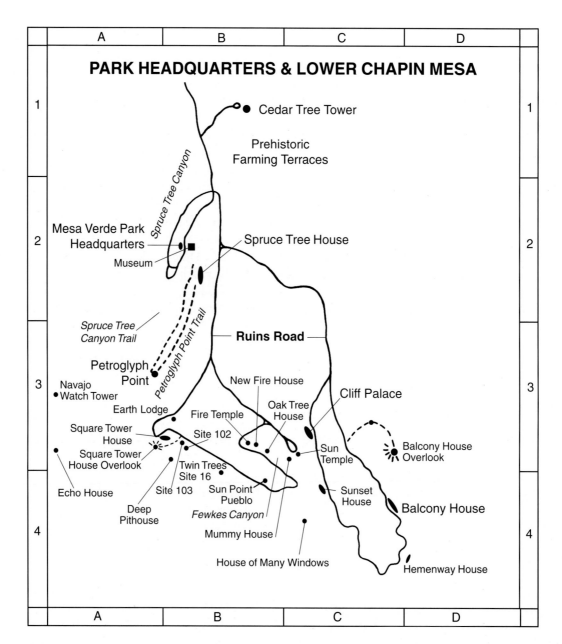

PARK HEADQUARTERS & LOWER CHAPIN MESA

Cedar Tree Tower

Prehistoric Farming Terraces

Spruce Tree Canyon

Mesa Verde Park Headquarters

Museum

Spruce Tree House

Spruce Tree Canyon Trail

Petroglyph Point Trail

Ruins Road

Petroglyph Point

Navajo Watch Tower

New Fire House

Cliff Palace

Earth Lodge

Fire Temple

Oak Tree House

Square Tower House

Site 102

Balcony House Overlook

Square Tower House Overlook

Sun Temple

Twin Trees Site 16

Echo House

Site 103

Sun Point Pueblo

Sunset House

Deep Pithouse

Fewkes Canyon

Balcony House

Mummy House

House of Many Windows

Hemenway House

The rooms of the pueblo were poorly ventilated, smoky, and cold in winter. Fires were kept burning in the back of the cliff dwelling during cold weather, but there were few fire pits inside individual rooms. The blackening of the cave ceiling was caused by the smoke. The Anasazi lived and worked outdoors on the plaza when possible. Cooking was done in fire pits in the plaza. Rectangular corn-grinding bins lay side by side in a corner of the courtyard. Corn grinding was an arduous daily task done by the women. Other work was done in the kivas, on rooftops, or on balconies.

The Spruce Tree House cliff dwelling faces southwest and is nestled under a huge rock overhang that gives it maximum sunshine in winter and shade in summer. The underground kin kivas were fairly comfortable year-round. They were warm and well ventilated. Here family ceremonies were held, weaving was done, children were instructed, and tools were made. The people also gathered in the kivas when the weather was at its worst.

All the large openings in the walls of the cliff dwelling are doors, not windows. Some of these doors are square, some are T-shaped, and others are rectangular. The few visible small openings were beam sockets or holes for ventilation. Some of the doors could be closed from the inside with stone slabs or animal skins. There were no interior stairways. All the second- and third-story

Spruce Tree House (located at B-2 on the map), a spectacular Pueblo III (A.D. 1200s) cliff dwelling, sits under a cliff overhang across Spruce Tree Canyon from Mesa Verde National Park headquarters. Discovered by Richard Wetherill and Charlie Mason in 1888, it was misnamed Spruce Tree House for the Douglas firs that were then—and are still—growing in the canyon. Spruce Tree House is probably the most visited Precolumbian ruin in the Americas.

rooms were entered by way of the openings in the outside walls. Second-story roof timbers can be seen extending from one of the buildings. On these timbers, a balcony was constructed to give access to the rooms. Balconies were reached by ladder.

Near the center of the ruin is a three-story building with a collapsed third-story wall. On the back wall, just under the horizontal roof timber, is an abstract wall painting. The Anasazi painted the interiors of many of their rooms and kivas. In the back of the cliff dwelling, under the overhang, is a space that was used for refuse and for toilet purposes. Trash also was discarded in front of the pueblo, on the talus slope. Burials were common in the talus slopes because digging there was easier than it was elsewhere. Archaeologists search these talus-slope refuse dumps for broken, discarded tools, for weapons, and particularly for broken pieces of pottery. Refuse dumps tell the period of occupancy. Pottery sherds do not disintegrate and clearly reflect the time and place of firing.

Spruce Tree House could be entered in ancient times by trails from the mesa top. One of the trails begins at the south end of the ruin and leads to the top. Across the canyon, on the west side, are a series of hand- and toeholds that are cut into the canyon wall and lead to the canyon rim.

The restored courtyard at Spruce Tree House covers two kivas that served the people living in the dwellings adjoining the courtyard. The side rails of ladders protrude from the entrances to the kivas. The restoration shows the original building methods of the Anasazi.

The hand- and toeholds in the rock surface at the center of this picture lead out of Spruce Tree Canyon to the mesa top. They were one of two ways to get in and out of Spruce Tree House in ancient times. This toehold trail can be seen from the modern path to the cliff dwelling.

Petroglyph Point Panel (A-3) consists of late Pueblo II and early Pueblo III (A.D. 1100s and 1200s) rock art carved on the east wall of Spruce Tree Canyon, about a mile down the trail that leads out of Spruce Tree House. The depictions here were created over a period of several hundred years. Members of the Hopi tribe have suggested that the line winding through the panel represents the Anasazi migration route from the Grand Canyon to Mesa Verde. Anasazi petroglyphs depicted mountain sheep, turkeys, and other animals, humanlike figures, handprints, and more abstract designs, such as spirals and wavy and zigzag lines.

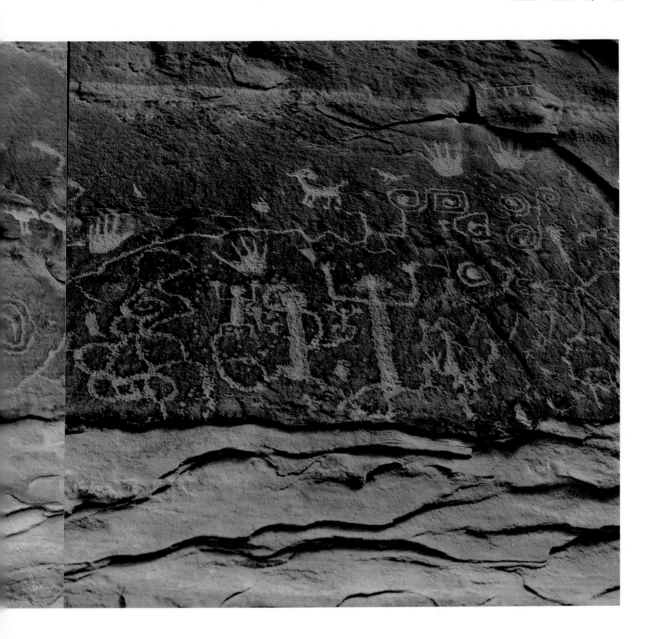

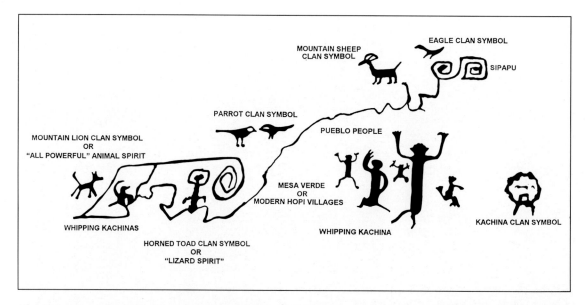

The Hopi interpreted the Petroglyph Point Panel as showing the people emerging from the Grand Canyon (represented by the sipapu) to begin their migrations. From time to time during the migration, groups split off, forming the Eagle Clan, the Mountain Sheep Clan, the Parrot Clan, the Horned Toad Clan, and the Mountain Lion Clan. The Whipping Kachinas gave direction and guidance to the people during the migration.

PETROGLYPH POINT

A trail to Petroglyph Point leads out of the south end of the Spruce Tree House ruin. The Park Service makes available a splendid nature-trail guide that identifies the trees, plants, animals, and insects as well as some of the geological outcroppings along the canyon wall. This loop trail is about a three-mile round-trip.

The Petroglyph Point Panel is one of the finest, best preserved, and most easily reached displays of Anasazi rock art in Anasaziland. Certainly it is well worth seeing, both because of the beautiful trail down the canyon and because of the close-up view that visitors can get of these ancient pecked figures. The panel is not as old as much of the rock art of the Southwest. Most if not all of the Petroglyph Panel was done during the 1100s and 1200s. The sticklike figures are characteristic of Pueblo times. A number of individuals made the figures over many generations.

The rock artists created the petroglyphs by pecking into the canyon face, cutting away the *desert varnish* to reveal the sandstone beneath. Desert varnish, the coloration, or patina, on the rocks, is seen throughout the Southwest. It is caused by iron oxide and manganese oxide that are dissolved in runoff water that pours over the canyon walls. When the water evaporates, the chemicals leave a stain on the rock surface.

Archaeologists, art historians, and rock art specialists have not been able to interpret the symbols left by these ancient people. The Anasazi had no written language. The rock art is a tantalizing written record of sorts, and it could tell us much more than it currently does if we only knew what the symbols meant. Some symbols are found in many places and are associated with trails, water, and sacred places. Other drawings, such as the stick men, tell us the era in which they were drawn or cut. We know the stick men were carved in late Pueblo II and early Pueblo III times.

In 1942 four members of the Hopi tribe of northwestern Arizona visited Petroglyph Panel and interpreted portions of it for Mesa Verde National Park. Their interpretation is published in the park's *Petrograph Trail Guide*. These Hopis suggested a theme of emergence by the people from the underground at the Grand Canyon. The long line that meanders from one end of the panel to the other represents a migration trail. The point of emergence, the sipapu, is in the upper right-hand

Two stone ax heads and one hafted stone ax.

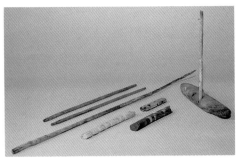

These drills were twirled between the hands and into the soft piece of wood to create enough heat to ignite a small piece of tinder.

This basket was made with yucca leaves of two colors. The black leaves were dyed prior to weaving. Modern Pueblo Indians weave similar baskets.

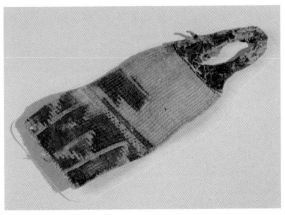

This small sack is made of cotton. Cotton was grown and made into cords for weaving during Pueblo III times (A.D. 1200 to 1300).

A cradle board used by the Basketmaker Anasazi. It was soft and did not modify the shape of the child's head. The board was lined with fibers and the child was bound to the board with fur straps. The hard surface of pine boards used during Pueblo times flattened the back of the child's head—a characteristic then carried for life. It was the absence of the flattened cranium that first enabled explorers to distinguish between the remains of the Basketmaker people and those of the Pueblo people. The study of skeletons has enabled us to re-create the life and physical features of the Anasazi: their size, appearance, life expectancy, diseases, and tribal affiliations.

part of the panel. As the migration proceeded, groups separated and formed individual clans along the way: first the Eagle Clan, followed by the Mountain Sheep, Parrot, Horned Toad, and Mountain Lion clans. *Whipping Kachinas* are depicted performing their function of influencing and directing the people during the migration. The concentric circle at the end of the trail may represent the end of the migration at Mesa Verde, or possibly the modern villages on the three Hopi mesas in Arizona.

MESA VERDE MUSEUM

The park buildings and excavations show the evolution of the Anasazi culture from Basketmaker times to the end of Pueblo III: pithouses, pueblos, kivas, great kivas, and cliff dwellings. Over the years thousands of sites in Mesa Verde have been studied as part of the archaeological investigation of the Anasazi culture. The climate of Mesa Verde is dry. This dryness has preserved, in the cliff overhangs, such otherwise perishable items as clothing, fabrics, wooden objects, and foodstuffs. In the museum, which is operated by the Mesa Verde Museum Association, Inc., visitors can see displays of many of the artifacts that have been discovered and preserved over the years as a result of careful research and investigation.

The museum displays items used by the Anasazi in their daily lives. Near the entrance is a series of five excellent dioramas re-creating scenes of Indian life from 8000 B.C. to A.D. 1300. The first diorama shows hunters of 8000 B.C. ambushing now-extinct bison. Next are early Basketmakers living and working beneath a cliff overhang before A.D. 450. After that come the later Basketmakers with pithouses similar to those reconstructed at Step House on Wetherill Mesa. The fourth diorama displays a scene from Pueblo I and II times (A.D. 750 to 1100/1150). It shows the construction of single-story masonry rooms on a mesa top. The last diorama is a model of an occupied cliff dwelling. In it are displayed turkeys, a bow and arrow, multistory buildings, and a round tower. These dioramas are a wonderful way to catch glimpses of the lives of the Indians, from the early hunters to the Anasazi who lived at Mesa Verde.

As you go through the museum, stop to realize that the Anasazi were Neolithic—that is, people of the late stone age. They had no metal, no wheels, and no beasts of burden. Yet they were self-sufficient farmers who grew or killed their own food and made their own weapons, tools, utensils, and clothing. From animal bone they made fleshing tools, awls, and needles. From stones they made axes, chipped out cutting tools, made manos and metates for grinding corn, and shaped blocks for building. From plant and animal fibers they made sandals, clothing, bags, bowstrings, and baskets. From clay they made cooking vessels, mugs, dippers, and beautifully painted ceramics. Trees were made into ceiling beams, bows and arrows, spears, and digging sticks. As you walk through the museum, you can see that nearly everything the Anasazi had was made by hand, and they made it themselves. A few trade items were obtained, such as jewelry and pots.

MESA-TOP RUINS

Earth Lodge B

Ruins Road circles by pithouse excavations, a Pueblo III cliff dwelling that can be seen from a mesa overlook, and a partially restored Pueblo III kiva and tower. The visitor needs a dedicated imagination to make the pithouse excavations come alive. One visitor at Earth Lodge B, the first stop on Ruins Road, was overheard to say, "We've got better hog wallows than this in Arkansas."

To make Earth Lodge B understandable, we have to be able to feel the presence of people living at this spot on this mesa around A.D. 600. This was not long after the fall of the West Roman Empire and was during the time the Angles and Saxons were taking over England.

When you look at the excavation of Earth Lodge B, remember that these Anasazi were Basketmakers. They were just moving out of the stage in which they hunted with an atlatl and cooked with baskets. Now they had the bow and arrow, pottery, and substantial permanent shelters like

Ruins Road South on Chapin Mesa, begins at the right fork of Ruins Road in Mesa Verde National Park. Along the route are open pithouses, Square Tower House, Sun Point Pueblo, an excellent view of Cliff Palace and Sunset House across Cliff Canyon, all the cliff sites along the wall of Fewkes Canyon, and Sun Temple. Anasazi structures that can be seen on this drive cover a time span from A.D. 600 to the late 1200s. A detailed discussion of the archaeology of Chapin Mesa can be found in Cultural Change and Continuity on Chapin Mesa, *by Arthur H. Rohn.*

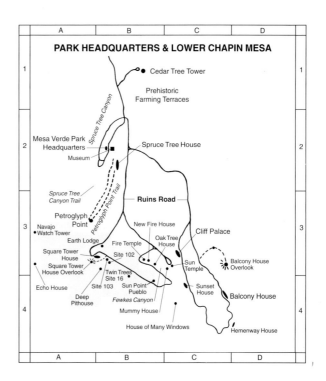

this one. The partially reconstructed pithouses at Step House on Wetherill Mesa make the excavation here at Earth Lodge B easier to visualize. Unlike Earth Lodge B, the Step House reconstructions do not have a storage-room entrance. Instead, they show a type of rooftop entrance that the Anasazi would use for seven hundred years. In Earth Lodge B, four upright posts supported cross members that were covered with brush, juniper bark, and mud to form the roof. Other poles were leaned against the cross members, laced with brush, and sealed with mud to form the side walls above ground level. The pithouse was dug about fourteen inches into the ground.

When you look at the excavation of Earth Lodge B, remember that these Anasazi were Basketmakers. Each pithouse was probably home to several related people: parents and children, certainly, but probably also grandparents, aunts, and uncles, or the spouse and children of an adult child.

Even though the Anasazi had permanent shelters, they lived and worked outdoors, in the courtyards or on the roofs of their houses. These practices are followed by the Pueblo people today.

Navajo Canyon Overlook

The next stop on Ruins Road is the Navajo Canyon Overlook. Across the canyon is Echo House. Farther up the canyon the remains of an Anasazi tower called Navajo Tower can just barely be seen.

Square Tower House

A mesa-top trail that leaves Ruins Road south of the Navajo Canyon Overlook takes visitors to another overlook, above Square Tower House. From this point, the visitor can look down on the ruins of this Pueblo III cliff dwelling. Built in the A.D. 1200s, Square Tower House had seven kivas and more than seventy rooms. Two of the kivas still have portions of their original roofs. These cribbed-roof kivas were used as models for the reconstruction of kivas at Spruce Tree House. A roofed kiva lies between the four-story "square tower" and a building to the right of the tower. The tower, which stands in the center of the ruin, was a four-story dwelling constructed against the back wall of the cliff. In front of the tower (and the top room) was a three-story room block, and in front of that were two rooms, the first at plaza level and the second just above it. Together, these structures made up a nine-room, multistory residence. The two- and three-story room blocks are gone, leaving only the tower.

Two trails led into the cliff dwelling. One is a hand- and toehold trail that leads down the cliff face near the overlook. This trail entered the cave on the south side. The other trail came down near the Little Long House cliff dwelling (which is around the bend in the canyon wall to the northwest), then followed the cliff base and entered Square Tower House from the north. A hand- and toehold trail led to a spring at the bottom of the canyon that served both cliff dwellings.

Little Long House had twenty-four rooms and four kivas, as well as a reservoir constructed in a nearby gully. Altogether, the Square Tower–Little Long House Community contained 7 cliff dwellings, 111 rooms, and 17 kivas. Arthur Rohn estimates there may have been 120 to 150 people living in the community at any one time. A total of four cliff dwelling communities stood at the lower, southern end of Chapin Mesa: Spruce Tree House, Square Tower–Little Long House, the Cliff–Fewkes Canyon group, and Balcony House. We will discuss these last two communities a little later.

Twin Trees Village

Deep Pithouse at Twin Trees Village represents one hundred years of Anasazi progress since Earth Lodge B was built. The two pithouses at Deep Pithouse were the new and improved version. How were they different? They were dug deeper, about twenty-four inches into the ground, and were built with a bench around the walls. The anteroom was eventually eliminated, and the residents got in and out by ladder through a hole in the roof. In place of the anteroom, these pithouses had a ventilator—a shaft that was dug into the ground to floor level on the south side of the dwelling and that was connected by a small tunnel to the pithouse room, thus providing outside air. A stone-slab deflector was placed in front of the ventilator shaft to keep the outside air from blowing across the fire. The Anasazi used this system of ventilation for the next six hundred years.

At first sight, the Deep Pithouse excavation can be confusing because it appears to be one big pithouse. Actually, the site contains two pithouses, one larger than the other. The larger one burned and was replaced a few years later by the smaller one. Both were part of a village that was occupied around A.D. 700.

The next great leap forward for the Anasazi is represented by the long excavation at Site 103, where the Indians had begun living in rooms constructed aboveground. This excavation once formed the base of an aboveground string of rooms built in Pueblo I times, around A.D. 830. The shallow slab-lined pit seen at the site was also lined with tall vertical poles interlaced with sticks and small branches. This framework was then filled with mud to form jacal walls. A deep pithouse lies in the courtyard next to the rooms.

Also at Twin Trees is a third group of structures, known collectively as Site 102. They were built about A.D. 950, in Pueblo II times, more than a hundred years after the string of rooms at Site 103. By this time, the Anasazi had begun using masonry for the walls of their one-story, aboveground rooms, which they continued to build in a row, side by side. They also continued to utilize the pithouses, though they had converted them into kivas, using them as extended family living space, particularly in cold weather. A kiva at Site 102 resembles a pithouse. Like other kivas, however, the roof was held up by timbers that rested on stone pilasters built on an earth bench inside the structure.

Site 16 Villages

The Site 16 villages consist of three partially excavated communities built one above the other over a period of more than two hundred years. They include an early Pueblo II unit pueblo, a late Pueblo II pueblo, and a Pueblo III village. Together, these three villages cover about the same

The Wetherill brothers named this Pueblo III cliff dwelling Square Tower House (A-3). What appears to be a tower with three windows was in fact a four-story group of rooms built against the cliff wall. The "windows" were doors. In front of this four-story building was a three-story residence, and in front of that a two-story building. In ancient times these buildings would have had a stair-step-like appearance. Each of the buildings was accessible from the others. Two hand- and toehold trails led to Square Tower House. One came down the cliff face to the base of the cliff and then led to the southeast corner of the cliff dwelling. The other came down by Little Long House, a cliff dwelling north of Square Tower House, and approached the buildings from the north.

This excavation at the Deep Pithouse site at Twin Trees Village (B-3) displays two pithouses. The portion in the foreground was built in the late A.D. 600s with the traditional small entrance room. Later, during the early 700s, the entrance room was rebuilt to form the deep pithouse in the background. That pithouse was built after the original two-room dwelling had been abandoned.

amount of time as does the period that stretches from the days of Colonial America to the present. The earliest of the three villages, built in the early 900s, had jacal walls and was L-shaped with a kiva in a plaza in front. The second village, built about 1000, consisted of a string of one-story rooms built of single-coursed masonry. West of the foundations of these rooms lies a large excavated kiva that was part of the third village.

Tree-ring dates indicate the third village was built about A.D. 1075. This village includes two circular rooms and a circular tower that were built over the second village. The tower may have been a lookout, which indicates a time of disturbance—disturbance that contributed to the Anasazi's decision to abandon the mesas for the cliffs. Nearby is a kiva that was part of the third village. Larger than the earlier kivas, it had eight pilasters to support the roof, and trenches next to the fire pit that probably were covered and used as foot drums.

Sun Point Pueblo

Sun Point Pueblo, a Pueblo III village, was one of the last of the mesa-top developments. The Anasazi built it around A.D. 1200, just before they moved to the cliffs. Probably about fifty people lived at the pueblo. A kiva was built in the central plaza of the village with rooms all around it.

CLIFF-FEWKES CANYON RUINS/BALCONY HOUSE

Sun Point Overlook

Sun Point Overlook, where Ruins Road turns back toward the northwest, affords one of the most spectacular views at Mesa Verde. The overlook is located where the paved road across the mesa reaches the junction of Cliff and Fewkes canyons. Cliff Canyon runs north and south and is

The visible portion of Sun Point Pueblo (B-4) consists of an excavated kiva connected by an ancient tunnel to the base of a round tower. Here we have an early Pueblo III (A.D. 1100s) kiva-tower complex. The tower was not a watchtower, but was used in connection with kiva ceremonies. The tunnel from the tower would allow the priest to appear in the kiva without descending down the ladder from the opening in the kiva roof. The kiva and tower were the core of a twenty-room pueblo. Not long after Sun Point Pueblo was constructed, the Anasazi began to move off the mesa top and build cliff dwellings in the canyon walls.

joined at the overlook by Fewkes Canyon from the northwest. Sun Point offers beautiful and striking views of a number of cliff dwellings.

The Pueblo III Anasazi built rooms in these canyons like swallows nesting on barn doors. Across the canyon from the overlook are Sunset House and Cliff Palace. In the canyon walls were numerous structures built for living and storage. In earlier times, the Anasazi built mesa-top villages near the land they farmed. In the Pueblo III period, they built groups of small masonry rooms in recesses in the canyon walls. The view from the top of the sheer canyon wall makes it evident that transporting people, food, fuel, water, and building materials up and down these cliff faces must have been a never ending task!

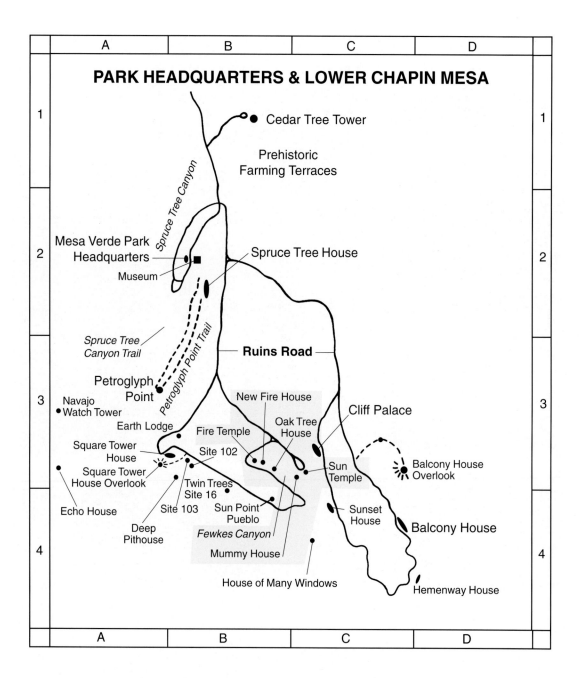

Assume you were entering these canyons on an extended camping trip—one that would last a lifetime. Suddenly you realize that you didn't bring many of the things you ordinarily take camping: toilet paper, soap, insect repellent, aspirin, sleeping bag, and a towel! Winter will be coming on, and you have no gloves or heavy boots. There is no dentist or doctor available. What about warm clothes for the toddler and how about the baby that is on the way? The Anasazi coped with these problems for generations and survived.

From the overlook you can see the two-tiered Sunset House directly across Cliff Canyon, and on the same canyon wall, north of Sunset House, sits the grandest cliff dwelling of them all, Cliff Palace. The walls of Sun Temple are directly north of the overlook, on the mesa top. The rooms of Mummy House are strung along the ledge below Sun Temple.

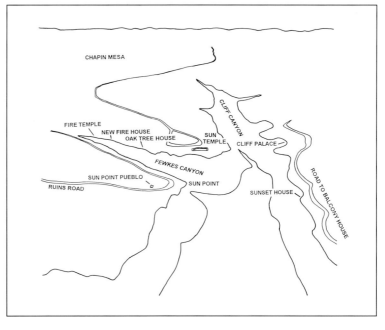

Fewkes and Cliff canyons as seen from the south. You can see Ruins Road as it reaches Cliff Canyon, where it swings by Sun Temple. From the lookout point where South Canyon Road curves back to the west along Fewkes Canyon, Cliff Palace and Sunset House lie across Cliff Canyon to the east. Across Fewkes Canyon to the north sits Sun Temple. Mummy House is directly below Sun Temple. In the cliffs along Fewkes Canyon, the Anasazi built Oak Tree House, New Fire House, and Fire Temple. Fire Temple and Sun Temple served as ceremonial buildings for the residents of the cliff dwellings in the Cliff-Fewkes Canyon Community, and possibly for Anasazi from as far away as the Mancos Valley.

Cliff-Fewkes Canyon Community

The Pueblo III period, from A.D. 1100 to 1300, is the Anasazi cliff dwelling era. Beginning in the mid-1100s, the Anasazi began moving off the mesas and into the cliffs. They abandoned the mesa-top villages and re-established communities in the canyons, tearing down the mesa-top pueblos and using the materials to build cliff dwellings. The Cliff-Fewkes Community consisted of thirty-three cliff dwellings, sixty kivas, one great kiva, and Sun Temple. The community contained more than five hundred living and storage rooms. Its two ceremonial centers were Sun Temple, capping the promontory across from Sun Point, and the great kiva called Fire Temple, on the north wall of Fewkes Canyon. Kin kivas were centers for family ceremonies and other family activities. Great kivas were community centers and probably used largely for religious activities.

Springs at the head of Fewkes Canyon and below Sun Temple were the community's reliable water sources. The cleared mesa top, on both sides of the canyons, was planted with corn, beans, and squash, as they had been for hundreds of years. The farmland, water sources, ceremonial buildings, residential rooms, kin kivas, storage rooms, and connecting access trails were all part of the Cliff-Fewkes Canyon Community.

Fewkes Canyon Cliff Dwellings

Farther down Fewkes Canyon are two additional overlooks that give good views of Oak Tree House, Fire Temple, and New Fire House.

Oak Tree House

In the Fewkes Canyon wall west of Mummy House sits Oak Tree House, a sizable cliff dwelling with fifty-two rooms and six kivas built on two ledges located one above the other. The upper ledge is much smaller than the bottom one. The rooms of the upper ledge were used primarily for storage. If you look closely, it appears that the upper rooms would have been inaccessible from the lower level. In ancient times, however, the rooms on the lower ledge had multiple stories, and the upper ledge could be reached by ladders from the roofs below.

In Anasaziland, jacal walls were used at first—in the 700s—but were generally replaced later with masonry walls. A well-preserved jacal wall still stands at Oak Tree House, which is a Pueblo II and Pueblo III cliff dwelling.

Recent work at Oak Tree House has demonstrated that the pueblo was occupied almost continuously from A.D. 1000 to 1300, indicating that the Anasazi lived in cliff dwellings during Pueblo II times. This finding has required re-examination of the concept that outside pressure forced the Pueblo people off the mesas and into the cliffs in Pueblo III times.

In the summer, cliff dwelling would have been pleasant. Archaeologists have recently theorized that many Mesa Verde residents lived on the mesa and in the canyons in the summer and moved to the Mancos Valley in the winter. The snow is often hip deep on the mesa, but it seldom snows in the Mancos Valley. Evidence that pueblos were built in the valley, which is now part of the Ute Tribal Park, supports this concept. Also, it is very hot in the valley in the summer, with lots of insects, and corn doesn't grow well there.

Fire Temple and New Fire House

Fire Temple and New Fire House sit side by side. Fire Temple was built as a ceremonial center and New Fire House as a residential complex.

Fire Temple is a rectangular great kiva containing an encircling bench that served as seating for those who attended the ceremonies. Also inside the structure is a raised circular fire box flanked by two masonry floor vaults. Behind the fire box stands a wall painted red and white. Because the great kiva was under the overhang and thus partially protected from the elements, it may not have been roofed. Rooms are attached on both sides. The left group of rooms contains a raised, squarish

When Fewkes Canyon was occupied by the Anasazi, its cliff dwellings formed part of a community. Some of the buildings were residences, and others were community meeting places. From the A.D. 700s and perhaps earlier, the Anasazi built what we now refer to as great kivas, *which served as meeting places for the people who lived nearby. Ordinarily, great kivas were round and roofed, but not always. Fire Temple (B-3), shown here under a cliff overhang and to the left of New Fire House, was a rectangular great kiva. It was the meeting place for the people who lived in Mummy House, Oak Tree House, and New Fire House, and probably for those who lived in Cliff Palace, Sunset House, and other cliff dwellings in Cliff Canyon.*

masonry altar. Fire Temple served as a ceremonial center for the Cliff-Fewkes Canyon Community and probably for many of the other Pueblo III inhabitants of Mesa Verde.

New Fire House, which has twenty rooms and three kivas, exemplifies the access problems faced by the Anasazi. The upper structures could only be reached from the lower level by a combination of a rooftop ladder and hand- and toeholds cut into the cliff. Look closely between the two larger buildings on the upper level. There a vertical row of hand- and toeholds can still be clearly seen. A ladder resting on a rooftop below extended upward to the lowest of the hand- and toeholds.

New Fire House (B-3) sits in Fewkes Canyon northwest of Oak Tree House and is visible from an overlook above the canyon. New Fire House was constructed on two levels, both of which had residential rooms. Rooms could be built one above the other on the upper level, but the vertical space of the lower level was so short that only small rooms and kivas could be wedged in. Note the vertical line of hand- and toeholds in the cliff face between the two largest structures of the upper level.

Jesse Walter Fewkes, who excavated and stabilized many of the Chapin Mesa cliff dwellings during the 1910s and 1920s, conjectured that New Fire House was occupied by the priests who presided in the great kiva. Here, he thought, they lighted the new fire for the New Fire Ceremony, a Hopi kachina ceremony. Later archaeologists, however, have discounted the priest-residence concept.

Sun Temple

Sun Temple, begun at the start of the 1200s, was an Anasazi counterpart of the great cathedrals of Europe that were built about the same time. The Anasazi never finished Sun Temple, however,

This photograph is of Sun Temple (C-3). The aerial view was taken looking toward the west. Fewkes Canyon is on the left. This spectacular Anasazi building crowns the point where Fewkes Canyon joins Cliff Canyon. It is a Pueblo ceremonial center or gathering place. Its masonry resembles that of the cliff dwellings. Sun Temple was central to a thriving community of more than thirty cliff dwellings in Cliff and Fewkes canyons. It is D-shaped like the ceremonial buildings at Hovenweep but was never finished. There were three large kivas inside the structure and, on the outside to the southeast, an adjoining free-standing tower. Sun Temple was not designed for habitation. The function of the rooms that surround the kiva at the west end, and of the narrow rooms encircling the inner court and the other two kivas, is not known. They probably played a role in the ceremonial activities conducted at the temple.

and abandoned it around 1276. The D shape of this ceremonial building is not unique. A temple at Horseshoe ruin in Hovenweep is very similarly shaped, though it is not so grand. Sun Temple was a huge enterprise. The walls stood nearly fourteen feet high. Between the walls were narrow rooms connected by doorways.

At the east end of the temple, double, concentric, D-shaped rubble-core walls enclose two large kivas. The kivas were probably roofed and aboveground. Outside the temple walls at the east end was a free-standing tower. At the west end of the temple stands another D-shaped structure with several rooms and a kiva. Next to this kiva is a small circular room that was probably the base of a tower. Next to the outer wall at the west end is a stone with sundiallike markings that were used to note the seasonal movements of the sun.

Sun Temple crowned the hill above a strong spring where Cliff and Fewkes canyons join—an imposing, sacred, and beautiful site. It was built with cooperative labor (not exactly the norm for the highly individualistic Anasazi), and was dedicated to the spiritual well-being of the community. Sun Temple ranks among the greatest achievements of the ancient Anasazi.

Cliff Palace

Cliff Palace is the largest and most spectacular of all the Mesa Verde cliff dwellings. It contains 220 rooms and 23 kivas. Tree-ring dates show that this Pueblo III dwelling was constructed between A.D. 1210 and 1273. It was abandoned, as was the entire region, by 1300.

Archaeologists' estimates of the number of Anasazi living at any one time in Cliff Palace vary from 200 to 350. Estimating how large the population was at any given time over a seventy-five-year period is difficult. One method is to multiply the number of kin kivas by an estimated number of persons likely to have used each kiva. Ten or twelve persons is one estimate of the size of a typical extended family using a kin kiva. Other estimates are based on the number of residential rooms.

Tiny masonry rooms sit on the narrow ledge just under the overhang. Along the ledge were fourteen storage rooms measuring only a little over three feet in height. Entrance to these rooms was by ladder from a rooftop at the north end of the pueblo. The isolation of this storage area protected the foodstuffs kept there from rodents and dogs. Also on this ledge is a *dry wall*—that is, a wall constructed without mortar. In Anasaziland, segments of dry walls appear often in conjunction with mortared masonry walls.

Although there were two refuse spaces in the back of Cliff Palace, most of the trash was thrown over the retaining wall at the front of the pueblo, where it mixed with the soil and rock debris being eroded off the cliff. Still standing at the south end of the ruin is a four-story building containing wall paintings. The paintings form three segments. The lower portion of the room wall was plastered and painted red with a number of triangles jutting from the top of the red panel. Note the series of red dots between two sets of the triangles. Above the red panel, the wall is covered with white paint on which appears an abstract textile design in red. There were floors on each of the four stories. Although the building now appears to be a tower, it originally served as living quarters. Access to the upper stories was by hatchways through the ceilings of the lower rooms. The larger opening on the outside of the tower's base and the T-shaped opening at the top of the tower were outside entrances. Beneath the T-shaped entrance was probably a balcony. The other openings were for ventilation. The rooms in this structure measured about six feet by eight feet.

To the south of the tower are two kivas joined by a tunnel. One of the kivas was also connected to a room by an underground tunnel. Conjecture has it that these tunnels were designed to allow the priests to make a dramatic appearance during kiva ceremonies as if they were rising from the earth!

The large multistory building at the north end of Cliff Palace was labeled, by J. W. Fewkes, Speaker Chief Tower. Most likely, however, this building contained ordinary residential rooms.

Cliff Palace has kivas set into the courtyard at the front of the pueblo. These kivas conformed to the general style of Mesa Verde kivas—that is, they were oval with *banquettes* (benches) around the walls, and rising from the benches were stone *pilasters* (columns). These pilasters supported logs that were laid from pilaster to pilaster and formed the base of a cribbed roof. Most Mesa Verde kivas had ventilators positioned in a southerly direction to bring fresh air inside. To block incoming cold air, a low wall called a *deflector* was placed between the ventilator opening and the fire pit. Usually there was a small hole in the kiva floor—the sacred *sipapu*, or entrance from the underworld. Access to the kiva was by ladder through a hole in the roof. The plaza above the kivas served as a work area for the cliff dwellers and a play area for the children.

The residents of Cliff Palace drew water from a strong spring in the canyon floor just beneath Sun Temple. Access to the canyon floor and to the mesa above was by hand- and toeholds cut into the cliff face.

Two sets of ruins can be seen across the canyon from the visitors' trail that enters Cliff Palace. These ruins, known as Sites 501 and 502, each consist of three to five rooms, and each site housed a family group. These sites are in the cliffs to the north of the mouth of Fewkes Canyon.

House of Many Windows

The House of Many Windows, one of many small cliff dwellings in the canyons of Mesa Verde, can be seen in the west wall of Cliff Canyon, from an overview just south of Cliff Palace. The ruins consist of a row of buildings constructed on a very narrow ledge. Several additional one-, two-, and three-room units are nearby. These habitations were all a part of the Cliff-Fewkes Canyon Community, which was centered on Sun Temple and Fire Temple.

Balcony House

Balcony House, also called Site 615, was the largest cliff dwelling in the Soda Canyon Community. It had forty-four rooms and two kivas. The two kivas were dug into the bedrock at the south end of the pueblo's plaza. Site 515, located in Soda Canyon north of Balcony House, contained only eleven rooms but had three kivas and an ancient reservoir next to a strong spring. It was a part of a larger community to which Balcony House also belonged. Perhaps Balcony House shared kiva space with Site 515. The entire community that contained Balcony House and Site 515 consisted of 12 cliff dwellings, 6 kivas, and some 81 rooms. Ten tree-ring dates cover the period from A.D. 1096 to 1272, indicating nearly 200 years of occupation.

Balcony House is divided into two sections by a wall that separates the north part of the pueblo from the south part. Arthur H. Rohn suggests that this physical division of Balcony House probably came about because of a duality in the community, a duality similar to the one that exists in some modern pueblos between the Winter People and the Summer People.

The Anasazi had no hereditary chiefs, no nobles, and no hereditary elite class. In this respect, they resembled the modern Pueblo people. When the first arriving Spaniards asked, "Who are your chiefs?" they were surprised to hear the Pueblo people reply that they had none. But the Anasazi did have ceremonial leaders, and war leaders when necessary. We may assume that at Balcony House, responsibility for these activities passed back and forth between the "North of the Wall" people and the "South of the Wall" people.

Balcony House also shows in its construction the Pueblo III Anasazi's concern for defense. The only passage in and out of the cliff dwelling was behind a huge sandstone boulder that slipped from the cliff face thousands of years ago, leaving only a narrow passage between it and the cliff face. The Balcony House residents made this narrow crevice even narrower with a thick masonry wall, leaving only a small crawl space. No enemy could enter here as long as the passageway was guarded.

The trail from this restricted entranceway led south along the cliff to the end of the ledge. There, the Anasazi built a small circular tower and hand- and toeholds leading down the cliff to the top of the talus slope. The trail then went north along the talus slope to turkey pens and a spring. Several hundred yards farther on, the Anasazi cut a hand- and toehold trail to the top of the canyon. There was also a very steep hand-and-toe route from the south block of rooms to the mesa top. Access to Balcony House was so difficult that supplies were probably lowered into the pueblo with ropes from the top of the canyon.

Balcony House gets its name from the still-intact balcony on the four-room structure at the north end of the cliff dwelling. The balcony was laid on beams that supported, and extended out from, the first-floor ceiling. Sticks and small poles were laid on the beams and topped by several

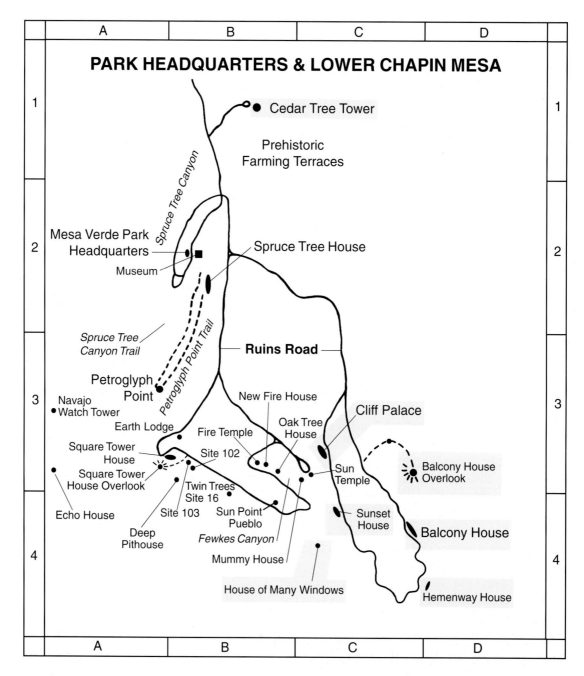

PARK HEADQUARTERS & LOWER CHAPIN MESA

Cedar Tree Tower

Prehistoric Farming Terraces

Spruce Tree Canyon

Mesa Verde Park Headquarters

Museum

Spruce Tree House

Spruce Tree Canyon Trail

Petroglyph Point Trail

Ruins Road

Petroglyph Point

Navajo Watch Tower

New Fire House

Cliff Palace

Earth Lodge

Oak Tree House

Fire Temple

Square Tower House

Site 102

Square Tower House Overlook

Twin Trees Site 16

Sun Temple

Balcony House Overlook

Echo House

Site 103

Sun Point Pueblo

Sunset House

Balcony House

Deep Pithouse

Fewkes Canyon

Mummy House

House of Many Windows

Hemenway House

inches of juniper bark and mud. The balcony gave access to the doors of the second-story rooms. Another interesting feature of the north end of Balcony House is a small room with an intact roof. Across the inside of the room extend poles from which foodstuffs and other things were hung for drying and storage.

The north portion of Balcony House also has a retaining wall across the front of the plaza. This was an unusual feature for cliff dwellings but certainly a delight for those pueblo mothers!

Balcony House is unique in several ways: it was built in a defensive posture; it could be reached only with much difficulty; it had a spring at the back of the cave, which would have helped the residents resist a siege; it faces east (most of the other big cliff dwellings face west or southwest); and at the time of abandonment, its northern part was sealed off from its southern part by a dividing wall, except for a very narrow passage in the back of the cave.

The Park Service has arranged for visitors to go though Balcony House in groups. The trail at the north end of the parking area leads down the canyon wall to a path that takes you to a thirty-foot ladder. The ladder leads up to the north end of the ruin. The tour then passes through the cliff dwelling and leaves by way of the defensive entrance on the south. Then it returns up a ladder to the top of the mesa. Often there is a wait involved before the tour begins—but be patient, it is an exciting tour!

The Cliff-Fewkes Canyon ruins, as well as all the other ruins on Chapin Mesa, are discussed and analyzed in Arthur Rohn's Harvard doctoral dissertation, which has been published as *Cultural Change and Continuity on Chapin Mesa*. His book contains detailed discussions of all aspects of the Mesa Verde Anasazi culture: architecture, pottery, food, clothing, petroglyphs, tools, shrines, settlement patterns, and agriculture, from the Basketmakers to the cliff dwellers. It contains photographs of artifacts, site plans of the pueblos, maps, drawings, and tables. But most of all it is a detailed and scholarly work that demonstrates, with evidence found on Mesa Verde, the evolution of the Anasazi from Basketmaker times to the abandonment of the mesa at the end of the Pueblo III period. In the present book, all population estimates for Chapin Mesa communities have been taken from Rohn's dissertation.

CEDAR TREE TOWER AND CHECK DAMS

Cedar Tree Tower was a Pueblo III ceremonial complex, a shrine with no living quarters nearby. Its ruins sit on the rim of Soda Canyon, at the end of a short access route off the Headquarters–Far View Road, about three-fourths of a mile north of the place where the two branches of Ruins Road meet. The nearly round masonry tower probably was originally twice as high as it is now. It has double-coursed masonry walls, the stones of which were dressed by carefully pecking them to fit them together. Inside the tower is a sipapu carved into the bedrock of the tower's base.

A crack in the sandstone foundation of the tower forms a passage to a tunnel that was dug under the tower's south wall. The tunnel divides, one fork going to a kiva and the other to a hidden underground room to the west of the tower and kiva. The tunnel enters the kiva at bench level near one of the pilasters. The kiva itself has almost all the Mesa Verde characteristics: ventilator, deflector, fire pit, bench, six pilasters, and wall niches. The sipapu, however, is in the tower floor and not in the kiva. The masonry of the complex is peck faced.

From the Cedar Tree Tower complex, a trail leads south to a series of masonry dams built by the Anasazi to collect and hold topsoil and water for gardens. There are more than sixty such series of dams in the park. The Anasazi used water management and soil management to offset the dry times in the summer.

FAR VIEW AND BATTLESHIP ROCK

The Far View pueblos are an enigma! They were designed and built during Pueblo II times, yet they were occupied through the Pueblo III period. Why did the people living at the south end of Chapin Mesa, on Wetherill Mesa, and on the present-day Ute reservation move into the cliffs at the beginning of the 1100s, while the Anasazi of Far View stayed in pueblos on the mesa?

A village was built in the Far View area during the early Pueblo II period. More than a hundred years later, in late Pueblo II times, another village was built over the earlier one. Far View House, Pipe Shrine House, and Site 820 were part of this construction. Later still, in Pueblo III times, structures with double-coursed masonry walls were erected over these earlier buildings. By early Pueblo III, the Far View villages had about 375 rooms and 32 kivas and could have housed 400 to 500 people.

The Far View Community lies just off the park headquarters–Far View road at the northern end of Chapin Mesa and next to Soda Canyon. The pueblos of this mesa-top community were

This panorama shows in detail the buildings that make up the best-known pueblo in the Southwest. So impressed were the Wetherills that they gave it the name Cliff Palace (C-3). It is the jewel of cliff dwellings and one of the most photographed structures in the world. The pueblo was discovered by Charles Mason and Richard Wetherill in December 1888. Constructed under a southwest-facing cliff overhang, it was sunny in winter and shady in summer. In Pueblo III times, Cliff Palace contained some 220 rooms and 23 kivas and housed from 250 to 350 people. Families built stone living quarters and storage rooms near and around family kivas. Trails led to the mesa top and down into the canyon. A big spring at the base of the cliff, just below Sun Temple, was the main source of water for the pueblo.

**J.W. FEWKES
"SPEAKER CHIEF TOWER"**

**MULTISTORY
ROOMS AND DOORWAYS**

**VISITOR ENTRANCE
(NORTH)**

Cliff Palace

LKWAY   ROUND TOWER
AND TWO RESTORED
KIVAS   MULTISTORY
ROOM BLOCKS   FOUR-STORY
BUILDING WITH
PAINTED INTERIOR   VISITOR EXIT
(SOUTH)

The Anasazi painted the interiors of many of their kivas and buildings. This is the interior of the four-story, towerlike building at the south end of Cliff Palace. The bottom of the wall is red and the top portion cream-colored. The triangles at the top edge of the red panel probably represent mountains. Red dots are painted between the peaks. The rectangular box above the mountains, red over cream, appears to contain a textile pattern.

This room block at the north end of Cliff Palace is a spectacular example of an Anasazi residential building. Each family constructed its own house block and kiva. The openings are doors, not windows. The folks who lived on the top level reached their rooms by using ladders that led from rooftop to rooftop. There were no interior stairways. J. W. Fewkes called this room block Speaker Chief Tower, suggesting that the community sun watcher might have used it to make announcements to the community.

surrounded by cultivated fields. Corn, beans, and squash were the basic crops. Production of foodstuffs may have been enhanced by a sophisticated water system around Mummy Lake, a body of water built during the early Pueblo II period. For many years, some archaeologists have believed Mummy Lake was originally used to store irrigation and domestic water. It held half a million gallons of water when full. Irrigation water may have been diverted to the mesa-top fields by a series of ditches. Recently, some archaeologists have doubted that there really was an irrigation system, raising two questions: Did the ditches carry water into or out of Mummy Lake? and Where did the water come from?

Far View House

A driveway off the main road leads to a cul-de-sac parking area next to Far View House and Pipe Shrine House. A footpath circles around Far View Tower, Mummy Lake, Site 820, and back to the parking area.

An aerial photograph of Far View House reveals its basic layout. It was built originally with room blocks two and three stories high. Far View House was begun in Pueblo II times, when the Anasazi of the Northern San Juan were feeling the influence of the Chaco Canyon Anasazi culture. Four of the five kivas were constructed within the room blocks, following the Chaco

The courtyard wall at Balcony House is an unusual feature for cliff dwellings. It must have been appreciated by the elderly and by mothers with toddlers. With only hand- and toehold access to cliff dwellings, small children, people with injuries, pregnant women, and senior citizens would have had difficulty getting in or out—particularly in winter. They would have been confined to the pueblo unless they were hoisted in or out by ropes. Cliff dwellings must have been a pleasant place to live in summer but cold and inaccessible in winter. For this reason, some archaeologists suggest many of the Mesa Verdeans built pueblos in the Mancos Valley—where it is warmer and seldom snows—and lived there in the winter, returning to Mesa Verde in the summer to live and plant their crops.

tradition. An unanswered question is: Were these pueblos built by Chacoans, or did the Mesa Verdeans borrow Chacoan techniques?

The Chaco Canyon civilization flourished from the mid-1000s to the mid-1100s in the Chaco Basin of northwestern New Mexico. These Anasazi built the structures known as great houses. Pueblo Bonito, in Chaco Canyon, was the largest and is the best known. The Chacoans also were road builders. Their roads connected the Chaco Canyon settlements with outliers in every direction. Some archaeologists argue that the Chacoans were traders, others argue that they were

Kivas were a hallmark of Anasazi building and culture. This one at Cliff Palace is a typical Mesa Verde–type kiva. It is about fifteen feet in diameter. Warm in winter and cool in summer, kivas were used for weaving, toolmaking, education, storytelling, and family gatherings. Visualize this excavated kiva as having a roof with a hole in the top. The Anasazi entered the kiva by a ladder that led down to the floor through the hole in the roof. The little wall next to the fire pit served to deflect from the pit fresh air coming in through a ventilator tunnel. The interior of the kiva was encircled by a bench. The square stone columns on the bench supported logs that held up the roof. The top of the kiva was flush with the surface of the courtyard.

missionaries, and still others say they spread their culture by military force. There is evidence of Chacoan influence at Lowry, Escalante, and other places in the Mesa Verde region. The Chacoan culture began to wane by the 1100s, at the beginning of the Mesa Verde cliff dwelling period.

The rooms at Far View have Chacoan characteristics: they are regularly spaced and have larger doors and higher ceilings than those of the cliff dwellings. The kivas, too, are Chacoan in size, location, and style. Mesa Verde kivas were ordinarily built in a plaza in front of the room blocks. At Far View, four of them were built into the room blocks. When the second and third stories were in place, the kiva roofs served as courtyards for the second-story rooms. The high walls and low pillars of the kivas are also Chacoan characteristics. The central kiva is different from the others—it is larger and has eight pillars and two rectangular vaults in the floor. It may have been used as a kin kiva, as the other four were, or as a smaller version of the great kivas at Fire Temple and Long House. The Chacoans built great kivas within great houses.

Most Anasazi structures were built by individuals. Walls were shared, but there was no preplanning. The Chacoan great houses were an exception. They were preplanned, two-story masonry buildings with large rooms and built-in kivas. Far View House is considered to have been a great house. Defining the architecture of great houses is not difficult, but archaeologists disagree about

In ancient times, Balcony House was divided into two segments by a wall, possibly to separate the Summer People from the Winter People. Balcony House had forty-four rooms and only two kivas—relatively few kivas compared with other cliff dwellings. However, it formed a larger community with nearby smaller cliff dwellings that also had kivas. The two Balcony House kivas are set in the plaza of the south section.

their function. Were the great houses power bases for Chacoan troops, missionaries, or traders? Here at Far View are three excavated pueblos that fit the archaeological description of a great house. But were any or all of them power bases for Chacoan groups, or were they simply residential units built in the Chacoan tradition?

Pipe Shrine House

J. W. Fewkes excavated Pipe Shrine House in the 1920s. He gave it its name because of a dozen decorated clay tobacco pipes he found there. Stories here conflict: one says the pipes were found in a small pit in the floor of the central kiva; the other says they were found in a small masonry shrine south of the pueblo.

At Pipe Shrine House, visitors can see Pueblo II single-coursed masonry walls and Pueblo III double-coursed walls in the same structure. The two rows of rooms on the north were the early ones. They are built of single-coursed, loaf-shaped stones. The walls of the rest of the structure, built in Pueblo III times, are two or more stones thick and made of sandstone blocks. The single kiva is enclosed within the room blocks and its roof served as a plaza inside the pueblo. There may have been a tower next to the kiva. In front of both Far View House and Pipe Shrine House, the Anasazi built a plaza that was encompassed by a low retaining wall.

Site 820

Site 820 was excavated in 1969. The site spans a hundred years, 1050 to 1150, a period that stretches from late Pueblo II to early Pueblo III times. The rooms at the back were arranged in three stories and overlooked a plaza containing five kivas and a ceremonial tower. When the pueblo was occupied, each of the kivas was probably used by a family group for family activities and ceremonies. Each family's rooms probably were next to its kiva. In good weather, the families lived and worked in the open on the plaza.

The Anasazi blocked much of the narrow passage between the boulder and the cliff at the south end of Balcony House, leaving only a very small and easily defended tunnel.

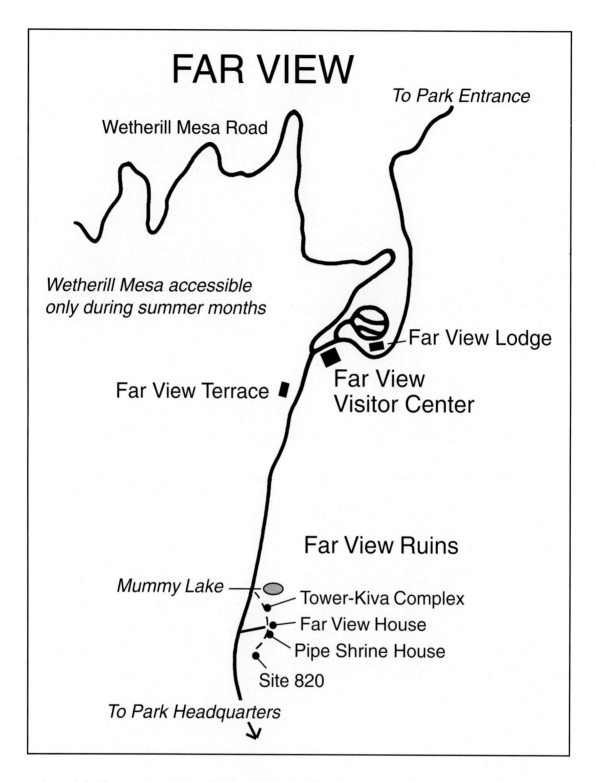

One of the kivas is round, in Chacoan fashion. The four others are keyhole-shaped with stone pilasters rising from banquettes. The pilasters supported a cribbed roof. In the kiva to the south-east there are poles set between each pair of pilasters. These were for decoration or to hang items such as clothing, jewelry, or corn husks. The people sat on mats around the fire pit.

The kivas were built inside the pueblo and were surrounded by rooms, in Chacoan fashion. Although the architecture shows Chacoan influence, there is little evidence of pottery from the

Cedar Tree Tower (B-1) and its associated kiva were part of a ceremonial complex and not of a residential pueblo. The complex, built in Pueblo III times, consists of a tower, a kiva, and an underground room. The three structures are interconnected by tunnels.

Chaco Canyon region. Pottery ordinarily is a key to determining who occupied a site and when. The same situation exists at Chimney Rock Pueblo, near Pagosa Springs, Colorado. There, on a high narrow ridge, Chacoans built a pueblo in the late 1000s but left no Chacoan pottery. Frank Eddy, who dug that site, suggests that the Chimney Rock Pueblo was built by migrant priests from Chaco who were not accompanied by women. Pottery making is a skill generally attributed to the women.

One very interesting feature of the pueblo at Site 820 is the grinding-bin room. It stands next to the kiva at the southwest corner of the pueblo. In each of six bins there would have been a *metate* (sandstone block with a recessed center), upon which kernels of corn were placed for grinding. The women of the pueblo used a handheld stone slab called a *mano* to grind the corn on

A circular trail built by the Park Service leads into the trees west of Cedar Tree Tower and goes to a series of check dams. These stair-step masonry dams, erected in a draw, were designed to hold water and collect soil for gardens. The dams were built where rainwater runs off the mesa and into the canyons. Behind each dam was several feet of rich topsoil. Every time it rained, runoff water was held behind the dams to water the garden plants. There are more than sixty such impoundments in the park.

the metates into meal for cooking. The metate was set at an angle so that as the corn was ground, the meal would dribble down to the lower end, where it could be scooped up for cooking. The six bins located side by side indicate that corn grinding could be a social affair—it was backbreaking work that had to be done on almost a daily basis, and the social exchange must have been welcome.

Far View Tower

Far View Tower was probably not an observation tower, but a Pueblo III ceremonial tower built on top of a Pueblo II residential site. Just north of the tower is the outline of an older, sixteen-room site. The pueblo beneath Far View Tower has walls of single-coursed masonry. One of the kivas next to the tower was part of the pueblo. It was built in the courtyard, on the south side of the masonry rooms, in typical Mesa Verdean style. The other kiva at the site was built in Pueblo III times as part of the kiva-tower ceremonial complex. This complex is similar to the Cedar Tree kiva-tower complex down the road to the south.

The Anasazi built more than fifty towers in the Mesa Verde region. Archaeologists often say they were "ceremonial," which may be translated as, "We don't know why they were built." Lone towers built on a promontory, such as Navajo Tower, were watchtowers. Towers that were part of a kiva-tower complex, or those down in a canyon next to a spring, probably were ceremonial.

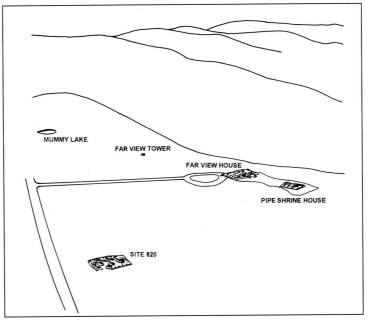

Here is a February view of the Far View area of Mesa Verde, with a schematic drawing of the area. The schematic identifies Far View House, Pipe Shrine House, Site 820, Far View Tower, and Mummy Lake. Walking trails connect these sites with the parking area.

The Anasazi lived in Far View House and other mesa-top pueblos in the A.D. 1000s and 1100s, during late Pueblo II and early Pueblo III times. When occupied, Far View House was three stories high. It had some fifty rooms and, as you can see, five kivas. The rooms surrounded four of the kivas. The fifth kiva was next to the pueblo, in a terrace bordered by a retaining wall. All of the kivas had roofs. The roof of the one in the terrace would have been level with the ground. The architectural design of this pueblo resembles that of a Chacoan great house.

Battleship Rock

Across Soda Canyon from the Far View area, you can see Battleship Rock, with a sandstone outcropping visible at its crest. Along the south ridge below the peak is a spectacular panel of rock art that includes a fine Pueblo I "lizard man." This panel, reachable only by a steep trail down into Soda Canyon and another up Battleship Rock Mountain, is closed to the public.

WETHERILL MESA RUINS

Two large mesas, Chapin and Wetherill, together with their adjoining canyons, contain most of the Mesa Verde ruins open to visitors. On Chapin Mesa, on the east side of the park, are the park headquarters, the visitor center, the Far View area, and the spectacular cliff dwellings Spruce Tree House, Cliff Palace, and Balcony House.

Wetherill Mesa, on the west side of the park, is open only in the summer and is reachable by a winding, narrow, surfaced road. This road begins at Far View and winds west across canyons and mesas for about eight miles and then turns south on Wetherill Mesa. The first stop on the mesa is the Rock Canyon Overlook. Across Rock Canyon, in the Ute Tribal Park, you can make out a small cliff dwelling with three or four masonry buildings.

At the ten-mile marker is a turnout with a surfaced path leading to the canyon edge. Across the canyon, on the mesa top, you can make out with binoculars a sizable Anasazi tower.

In the trees northwest of the Far View and Pipe Shrine pueblos is a small complex made up of a tower, two kivas, and the walls of some room blocks. This group was ceremonial, not residential. The Anasazi built it in early Pueblo III times on top of older rooms that date from the 1000s. The site is often referred to as Far View Tower.

The parking area for the Wetherill ruins is just over twelve miles from the entrance at the Far View complex. Here you will find a ranger station, rest rooms, an information kiosk, a boarding area for a minitrain, and a food and beverage facility.

From the parking area, one trail leads east to the Step House cliff dwelling, and another goes south to the Badger House Community. The north minitrain makes a ten-minute circuit, making a stop at the Badger House Community and other sites and connecting with the south minitrain. The south train circles the Badger House Community and makes stops at the Kodak House and Long House overlooks—a thirty-minute circuit with stops. Each train has two open-air cars. The driver serves as a tour guide.

For a one-hour, ranger-conducted tour of Long House, the train offers a drop-off-and-pick-up service. The same system is used for trips to the Nordenskiold Ruin 16 Overlook trail.

Wetherill Mesa was occupied from around A.D. 500 (the beginning of Basketmaker III times) to the late 1200s (the end of Pueblo III times). The Wetherill Mesa Archeological Project, carried out between 1958 and 1964 by the National Park Service and the National Geographic Society, revealed nearly a thousand Anasazi sites on the mesa.

Kodak House Overlook

Kodak House cliff dwelling is not accessible to visitors, but there is a splendid view of it from an overlook. This overlook, about a mile south of Long House, is reachable by a paved road. The cliff dwelling was named Kodak House by Gustaf Nordenskiold, a Swedish nobleman who explored Mesa Verde with the Wetherills in the early 1890s. In 1893 he published *The Cliff Dwellers of the*

Here is a photograph of Pipe Shrine House. Just below the steps leading down from the terrace in the foreground was a shrine that, according to one story, contained a dozen tobacco pipes. According to another story, the pipes were found in a kiva. In any case, because of the discovery of the pipes, J. W. Fewkes named the pueblo Pipe Shrine House. The north side of the pueblo, background, was built in the 1000s, during Pueblo II times. The walls were only one stone thick. The other rooms, and a round tower, were added in the 1100s, during the Pueblo III period. These later parts utilized double-coursed masonry.

A trail from the parking area next to Far View House leads southwest to Site 820. In this aerial view, the "keyhole" design of the typical Mesa Verde kiva shows clearly in the shape of four of the five kivas. These kivas were roofed, and the pueblo's rooms were built around them. Next to the kivas in the lower left corner of the pueblo are a number of stone grinding bins that were originally enclosed in a small grinding room. Here the women ground corn into meal. Although it was hard work, the activity provided social time. The tower in the foreground was a ceremonial structure, not a lookout.

WETHERILL MESA

Mug House
Step House
Parking Area
Basketmaker Pithouse
Two Raven House
(*Stockaded Village*)
Nordenskiold's
Ruin #16 Overlook
Ruin #16
Badger House
Long House
Pueblo I Room Blocks
and Great Kiva
Long House Overlook
Wetherill Mesa
Kodak
House
Kodak House
Overlook

Mesa Verde, which has been reprinted and gives an excellent description of his exploration. Nordenskiold stirred up a substantial local brouhaha by shipping Mesa Verde artifacts to Europe—a local reaction that was part of the awakening of America's consciousness respecting its Precolumbian heritage.

Kodak House sits in a tributary of Rock Canyon and faces southwest. The pueblo fills two caves and originally contained some seventy rooms. At the east end of the lower ledge is a spectacular four-story house block that originally extended from plaza level to the overhang above. Unfortunately this pueblo was ruthlessly looted during the late 1800s. Some of the ancient buildings were razed by vandals looking for salable artifacts.

Long House

Long House overlooks a finger canyon that joins Rock Canyon on the west side of Wetherill Mesa. The pueblo was built beneath a huge overhang about one-half mile from the Wetherill Mesa parking area. Because Long House contains a great kiva, it probably was the center of the Wetherill community of settlements in Pueblo III times. The aerial photograph shows Long House and a view to the northeast across Mesa Verde to the north rim.

The Mesa Verde Park Service allows ranger-conducted visits to Long House. Steps descend from the cliff above and enter at the west end of the ruin, near a triangular building. As Nordenskiold put it in 1891,

> A triangular tower, one wall of which is formed by the cliff, and which still stands to its full height of four stories, is the first object to attract our attention in this part of the ruin. One cannot help admiring the skill with which it has been erected. The building material consists of the same soft sandstone as the vault of rock. The stones, generally a little larger than ordinary bricks, seldom too large to be lifted without difficulty, are rough-hewn and cemented with mortar.

Kodak House can be seen from a cliff on the south side of Rock Canyon, but it is not open to visitors. It lies in an alcove off the canyon about a mile south of Long House. It was named Kodak House by Gustaf Nordenskiold in 1891 because he stored his camera there while doing archaeological research. This photo displays a three-story dwelling, right foreground, that extended from the cave floor to the roof overhang. The residential rooms and kivas were built on the lower ledge and the storage rooms on the narrow upper ledge. During Pueblo III times, from 1100 to 1300, droughts often occurred, so surplus food—corn mostly—was stored for use in dry spells as well as in winter. Ladders from the rooftops of the lower buildings reached the storage level.

Long House was built on three levels. Most of the 150 rooms and all 21 kivas are on the lower levels. Along the upper level is a crude wall, with several openings, built along the front of the narrow ledge under the overhang. In most cliff dwellings upper-ledge structures were used for storage alone. Here, however, there is only a long, single enclosed space with peepholes—not a series of small storage rooms as is usually the case. Perhaps the wall served as a fort of last resort in case of attack, as a curtain wall similar to those in the cliff dwellings at Comb Ridge. This top ledge was reachable only with ladders from the roofs of the residential rooms below.

East of the triangular tower that stands at the west end of Long House, and on the lowest of the three levels, the same level as the tower, the Anasazi built three kin kivas. One of them has six holes in the floor that were used as loom anchors, and a wall painting similar to the designs found on Mesa Verde pottery. Below the tower notice a huge split boulder that fell in ancient times.

A striking aspect of Long House is the rectangular great kiva. This great kiva, or dance plaza, has the standard features: a raised masonry fire box in the center, floor vaults on the east and west sides of the fire box, benches at both ends of the kiva, and a sipapu next to the fire box. The floor vaults may have been covered to serve as foot drums. Adjoining the great kiva on the west is a group of rooms that may have been part of the ceremonial complex. This great kiva was in a beautiful open-air setting that allowed the spectators and participants to look down the canyon to the southwest.

Wetherill Mesa from the southwest, overlooking Long House, with Rock Canyon in the foreground and the north rim of Mesa Verde National Park to the north. This February photograph shows how the Anasazi designed their cliff dwellings to receive maximum sunlight during the winter months. Here you can see bright sunlight reaching into the back of the pueblo.

Visitors can climb a set of ladders to the second level of Long House. You can almost feel the presence of the ancient people in the group of residential rooms there. One of the rooms has a partially preserved flat roof. From this level in the cliff dwelling, a rectangular kiva next to a round kiva can be seen on the ledge below. Most Mesa Verde kivas were round, but not all of them. In ancient times, of course, these kivas would have been roofed, as would the rooms next to them, providing a level plaza.

In the back of the cave is a spring. Little grooves were cut in the rock in front of the spring to allow the water to flow out and into depressions in the bedrock, where it could be ladled out. The spring was stimulated by a dam above the overhang. This dam held back rainwater so that it could percolate down through the sandstone to bedrock and then seep out into Long House cave.

The rectangular great kiva at Long House, shown here in the plaza foreground, was not walled or roofed. It has a raised stone fire box in the center and a stone-lined sipapu next to the fire box. Floor vaults flank the fire box. Benches at both ends of the kiva, an altar room in the foreground, and an open space—probably for ceremonial dancing—complete the kiva. Living quarters were erected on both sides of the kiva. This may be evidence of a division between Pueblo III Winter and Summer people. The division of ceremonial duties between Winter People and Summer People that we find in modern pueblos may also have been characteristic of the Anasazi.

This kiva at Long House still has a portion of its log-and-mud roof intact. The roof was laid on top of the kiva walls.

Step House

The trail to Step House begins at the parking area at the Wetherill Mesa Visitor Center and works its way down the Long Canyon wall to the Step House ruin. The trail descends next to the ancient masonry steps from which Step House takes its name. These steps are unusual because the cliff dwellings were usually reached only by hand- and toeholds. A visit to Step House is especially rewarding because it includes the remains of habitations constructed six hundred years apart. On the west side of the cave are four excavated Basketmaker III pithouses. Two additional pithouses were covered by the small cliff dwelling that was built on the east side of the cave in the 1200s.

The Park Service has partially reconstructed three of the pithouses. The Anasazi dug the base of the pithouse a few feet down and lined the sides of the excavation with upright sandstone slabs. A bench encircled the pithouse above the slabs. Four posts were set in the floor to provide support for rafters. Against these rafters leaned poles whose bottom ends rested against the bench. Additional poles were laid across the rafters to make the roof. The poles on the sides and roof were covered first with a matting of sticks and then with mud. A ladder extended from the floor to a hole in the roof. In the center of the pithouse was a fire pit. Smoke went out through the hole in the roof. These pithouses were constructed about A.D. 600.

The little Pueblo III cliff dwelling, across the cave to the east, consisted of three kivas and of residential and storage rooms. It was built in the late 1200s, not long before Mesa Verde was abandoned by the Anasazi. The visitors' trail leads out of Step House on the east side.

Site 16 and Mug House

Nordenskiold, writing in 1893, said,

> North of Long House, still on the west side of Wetherill's Mesa, lie two extensive ruins. The first of them (16 in the map) is reached from the mesa above it by steps cut in the rock. Similar steps, once used by the cliff people, occur in several places among the ruins. It is evident that a lively intercourse existed between the inhabitants of the different cliff-dwellings. . . . Still farther north lies another large ruin, named *Mug House* from the quantity of pottery, especially mugs, which has been found there.

Site 16, the site Nordenskiold refers to, can be seen from an overlook west of the parking area. It is a two-level, Pueblo III cliff dwelling. The upper ledge was filled with masonry rooms. Nine are still standing. Several have collapsed. On the lower level several of the house blocks were multistory and extended from the base of the cave to the overhang above. Two kivas can be seen in the center. At the south end was a tower.

Mug House lies north of Site 16. It is not open to the public, although it has been stabilized and is in an excellent state of preservation. Arthur H. Rohn, one of the leading archaeologists who excavated and restored Mug House in 1960, wrote an excellent and detailed report on the work there, entitled *Mug House, Mesa Verde National Park, Colorado*. The book grew out of the Wetherill Mesa Archeological Project and was published by the National Park Service in 1971. In addition, Rohn wrote the section in Ferguson and Rohn, *Anasazi Ruins of the Southwest in Color*, entitled "Life in the Mug House Cliff Dwelling." Both are excellent and readable descriptions of the Pueblo III cliff dwellings and the Anasazi who lived there.

Badger House Community Mesa-Top Ruins

As part of the Wetherill Mesa Archeological Project, a group of mesa-top sites were excavated and connected by the Badger House Community trail. The trail begins near the Wetherill parking area.

At Step House, the Park Service has excavated several pithouses dating from the early A.D. 600s. The one with a roof has been restored to show how the pithouses were made: poles extended slantwise from the bench that encircles the interior to roof beams that were laid post-and-lintel fashion on four upright posts. A matting of small poles and branches was then laid over the slanting poles. Finally, the matting was covered with mud as plaster. The residents entered the pithouse by a ladder through the roof.

In the foreground of this photograph are the ruins of a kiva and room blocks from the Pueblo III occupation of Step House. Excavated pithouses are in the background. Here we see a cliff dwelling of the 1200s (Pueblo III period) built over dwellings of the early 600s (Basketmaker III period). The occupation was not constant, but the site shows that the culture continued for six hundred years—a span of time that, in length, equals the one that stretches from one hundred years before the European discovery of America to today. In the extreme background, you can see the remains of the stairway from which Step House got its name.

Basketmaker III Pithouse

The National Park Service guide to the Badger House Community indicates as Stop 1 an excavated Basketmaker III pithouse built around the middle of the A.D. 600s. This pithouse had two rooms. One of them was a large living area with a fire pit in the center, and wing walls to set off the main living space. Four poles supported the roof. The side walls were made of poles leaned from the banquette and against the rafters that rested on the four support poles. The roof and

This photograph shows Site 16, a neat little cliff dwelling that can be seen from an overlook at the end of a trail that leads from the Site 16 minitrain stop. The Site 16 pueblo was built in Pueblo III times in Rock Canyon between Long House and Mug House, on a cliff facing west. Note, on the left, the remains of a house block of six rooms, three lower ones and three upper ones. You can see the pole sockets for the ceilings of the lower rooms and floors of the upper rooms. On the ledge above the living quarters and kivas sits a string of storage rooms.

Mug House is a beautiful Pueblo III cliff dwelling that was occupied during the 1200s by some one hundred people. It was built facing west, in the cliffs off Rock Canyon. It is closed to visitors.

This photograph of a pithouse shows the living quarters of the Badger House Community. The residents of this pithouse were members of the Basketmaker group that, by the late A.D. 500s, became the first Anasazi to settle on Mesa Verde. This pithouse, like the others in which the Basketmaker people lived, had a roof and was partially underground.

walls were woven branches covered with mud as plaster. These pithouses had an opening in the roof to act as a chimney but not for getting in and out of the room. Instead there was another room, in the front of the living room and built in a similar fashion, that served as an entrance to the pithouse and as a storage area.

Pueblo I Masonry Rooms

The next stop on the trail is a site from Pueblo I times, which began about A.D. 750. At this site, the foundation of a pueblo has been excavated and covered by a modern roof. The pueblo consisted of rooms built in an L-shaped row. For a foundation, shallow excavations were made and stone slabs were inset along the inside edges. Walls of these early pueblo buildings sometimes consisted of jacal and sometimes of stone blocks. The rooms at this site were part of a complex that contained large pit structures.

Great Kiva

At one end of the excavated L-shaped foundation are a kin kiva and a great kiva. The great kiva was constructed about A.D. 860. Great kivas first appeared in Anasazi communities as early as Basketmaker III times and continued to be built right up to the time Mesa Verde was abandoned. Pueblo III great kivas can be seen at Long House and Fire Temple. Sun Temple may have served as a great kiva. A completely restored Anasazi great kiva can be visited at the Aztec ruin at Aztec, New Mexico.

Badger House Kiva-Tower Complex

The excavated ruins at this site show two occupations: the first around A.D. 1050, during Pueblo II times, and the second about 1258, during the Pueblo III period. The Pueblo II masonry is single-coursed, and the stones were chipped along the edges but otherwise left rough. The later, Pueblo III masonry, was placed in two parallel rows, and the space between the rows was filled with mud and small rocks. The walls were finished by pecking.

Part of the Pueblo III construction is a kin kiva that is connected to a tower by a tunnel. This forty-one-foot tunnel is the longest yet discovered in Mesa Verde, and was built by digging and covering a trench. Tunnels were not uncommon.

This pueblo was built near the end of peaceful times on the mesa. The timbers were removed when the villagers moved from the mesa and into the cliffs, where they lived until they abandoned Mesa Verde.

Anasazi kiva-tower complexes were built throughout the Northern San Juan region. Many other towers stood alone. Some of the towers may have been for observation, but most had to do with Anasazi religious practices.

The Badger House kiva is typically Mesa Verdean in style. It had a cribbed roof with the cribbing poles resting on the short masonry pilasters. The roof was level with the courtyard. The interior was reached by a ladder through a hole in the roof.

Two Raven House (Stockaded Village)

Two Raven House is a Pueblo II village occupied while the Anasazi were living on the mesa top. Akin to the Far View settlements, it shows Chacoan influence. The two excavated kivas there (one very small) were built within the room blocks. These kin kivas were covered by a plaza around which stood masonry residential rooms. There was a stockade around the northeast corner of the village. It consisted of erect poles interwoven with branches. Park Service literature suggests the stockade was designed as a windbreak or to keep turkeys in or out.

The Badger House Community demonstrates, in a compact area, the development of Anasazi architecture: it includes a Basketmaker III pithouse, a Pueblo I aboveground room-block-and-pithouse complex, a Pueblo II pueblo with kin kivas (Two Raven House), a great kiva, and Pueblo III aboveground room blocks with a kiva-tower complex (Badger House).

The photographs above and on page 71 show an excavated kiva, the base of a round stone tower, and room block foundations that represent several periods. A tunnel forty-one feet long connected the kiva with the tower. In the room block area, the older rooms were single walled. The walls of later rooms consisted of double rows of stones, and the space between the rows was filled with rubble. The oldest occupation of this site was in Pueblo II times, between A.D. 900 and 1100. The latest occupation, which occurred about 1258, during early Pueblo III times, accounts for the kiva and tower. The fact that the tunnel connects the kiva and tower indicates that the tower played a role in the kiva's ceremonial functions—and that it was not used as a lookout. Many such towers were built on Mesa Verde and in the Northern San Juan region. This site was one of the last aboveground pueblos at Mesa Verde.

MESA VERDE POTTERY

The late A.D. 500s were a watershed for the Mesa Verde Anasazi. Just as the sun was setting on the glory of ancient Rome, the dawn was breaking for the Anasazi.

For hundreds of years in Basketmaker II times, before 500, the Anasazi hunted with atlatls, carried water in gourds, and cooked in baskets. True, they were excellent basketmakers—that is how

they got their name. Their baskets were woven so tightly that they held water. Early Basketmakers cooked either on an open fire or in coals, or by dropping hot rocks into baskets filled with water and food.

In the late 500s, not instantly but over time, three startling changes occurred in the Anasazi way of life. First, the bow and arrow replaced the atlatl; second, the Anasazi began to grow corn, beans, and squash; and third, they began to make pottery. Pottery enabled people to adopt a way of cooking that hasn't changed that much—at least not until the invention of the microwave oven. The Anasazi learned to make utility vessels for cooking, water carrying, and storage, and all sorts of fine decorated pottery for dinnerware, ceremonies, and keepsakes.

The utility ware was gray, and the fine ware was painted white or red. Both white and gray pottery made at Mesa Verde from A.D. 550 to 1300. Norman T. Oppelt's book was *Earth, Water, and Fire: The Prehistoric Pottery of Mesa Verde,* is an excellent and readable treatment of the dating, making, and design of Mesa Verde pottery. Oppelt suggests that the Anasazi, like the modern Pueblo people, viewed everything in the world, both animate and inanimate, as interrelated. They believed that by making a pottery vessel, by mixing the clay of the earth with water and fire, they created something with its own spirit.

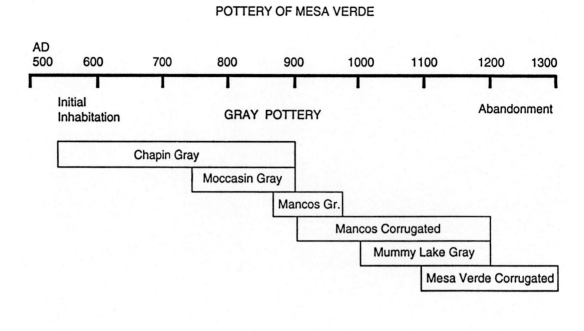

POTTERY OF MESA VERDE

Pottery Making

Pottery probably came to the Anasazi from Mexico through the Hohokam and Mogollon peoples of the Southwest. Among the Anasazi, it was made by women. Easily workable clay came from the shales of Mesa Verde. The clay was cleaned and some moisture added. A little *temper* (crushed stone) was then worked into the clay to keep it from cracking. The tempered clay was then rolled into coils. The vessel was shaped by winding finger-thick coils of tempered clay, one above the other. The coils were then bonded together by rubbing or scraping. Corrugated utility pots were bonded on the inside and finger crimped on the outside. For fine whiteware, the surfaces were smoothed and polished with a small stone and coated with *slip* (a mixture of fine clay and water) to make the pot white. Next, the pot was allowed to dry. This was done slowly, in the shade, to prevent cracking. A black, painted design was then added.

Archaeological Value of Pottery Sherds

The Anasazi had no system of writing. What is known about them comes from what they left behind: stone and wooden tools, baskets, weapons, fabrics, buildings, and, most important of all, broken pieces of pottery. Ancient cultures the world over are dated by the pottery sherds they left behind. Oppelt reports that there are more than twelve hundred types of pottery in the Southwest. Some fifteen types were made on Mesa Verde, or in nearby areas of the Northern San Juan region, between A.D. 550 and 1300. Nine traded pottery types from outside the region are common to Mesa Verde.

Pottery sherds are classified according to their type and where they were produced. For example, Mesa Verde Black-on-white pottery was made on Mesa Verde and at other sites in the Northern San Juan region.

POTTERY OF MESA VERDE

AD
500   600   700   800   900   1000   1100   1200   1300

Initial   Abandonment
Inhabitation

WHITE POTTERY

| Chapin Black-on-white |
| Piedra B/w | Cortez B/w |
| Mancos Black-on-white |
| McElmo Black-on-white |
| MV B/w |

Basketmaker III | Pueblo I | Pueblo II | Pueblo III

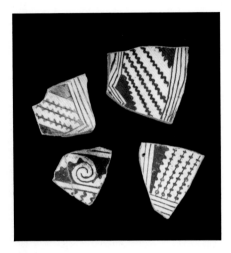

Cortez Black-on-white was made in the Mesa Verde region for about one hundred years, beginning around A.D. *900. These sherds are pieces of bowl rims.*

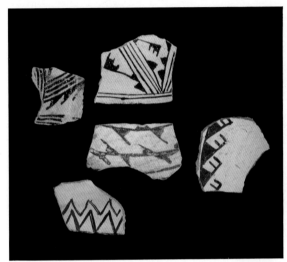

Piedra Black-on-white pottery was in use during Pueblo I times. These pieces are bowl and jar sherds.

McElmo Black-on-white was used from about 1025 until about 1250. These sherds are bowl rims.

Mancos Black-on-white was fired at Mesa Verde for nearly three hundred years, from the beginning of Pueblo II times to the middle of the Pueblo III period. Note the intricate, abstract designs on these sherds.

Mesa Verde Black-on-white is probably the best-known prehistoric pottery in the Four Corners region—and rightly so because of the beautiful decorations like the ones on these pots. Mesa Verde Black-on-white is associated with the cliff dwellings built at Mesa Verde during the last hundred years of Anasazi occupation. The sherds shown are bowl rims.

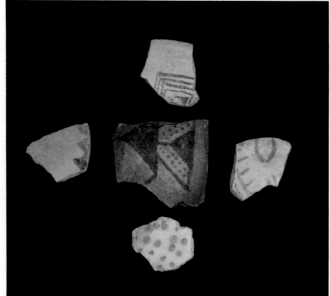

Chapin Black-on-white pottery covers the period at Mesa Verde during most of Basketmaker III and all of Pueblo I times. These five pieces are bowl rims.

San Juan Red ware, clockwise from upper right: Deadman Black-on-red bowl rim, Deadman Black-on-red pitcher sherd, Bluff Black-on-red bowl rim, and Abajo Red-on-orange bowl sherd.

In these three photographs, the Crow Canyon Archaeological Center and Clint Swink fire pottery using the methods employed by the Pueblo II and III Anasazi. The first photo shows the primary firing, the purpose of which is to (1) dry out the pit, (2) heat the sandstone slabs, which later will be used to support the pots in the fire, and (3) dry out the pottery vessels. The next photograph shows the setting process. The slabs are placed on the bed of coals to support the pottery vessels and to allow proper circulation of heat. The third photo shows the cover sherds that are placed over the vessels being fired. A fire is built on top of these sherds and allowed to burn down. It is then smothered with soil. The heat inside rises to fourteen hundred to fifteen hundred degrees Fahrenheit. After eighteen to twenty-four hours, the kiln can be opened and the fired pots removed.

Pottery experts can look at the trash dump of an Anasazi village, pueblo, or cliff dwelling and tell who lived there and when—give or take two or three generations. On Ruins Road, Deep Pithouse, Site 101, and Pithouse B are Chapin Gray–type sites, which means that they were occupied while Chapin Gray pottery was being made on Mesa Verde between A.D. 575 and 900.

Chapin Gray is also found on Wetherill Mesa, at Badger House Community and Step House. The strikingly beautiful Mesa Verde Black-on-white fine whiteware is found only in the Pueblo III cliff dwellings that were built during the 1200s. The number of sherds at a site indicates the number of people who lived there, and the layers of refuse pottery reveal the times of occupancy.

In more than seven hundred years at Mesa Verde, gray and white pottery changed in style only six times. Chapin Gray utility pottery and Chapin Black-on-white fine pottery were Mesa Verde standards for more than three hundred years—from A.D. 600 to 900. Fifteen generations! Why was this pottery made and designed the same way for so long? Anthropologists suggest that tradition was the key to maintaining order in a society where there were no chiefs and no elite, where everyone lived according to the established customs and traditions. Pottery design was one of these traditions. Other Anasazi had different pottery designs but clung to them with equal tenacity. Pottery was made in a number of different forms, such as cooking pots, water carriers, canteens, dippers, bowls, plates, mugs, seed jars, *ollas* (large, widemouthed vessels), pitchers, kiva jars, pipes, miniature sculptures, and effigies.

San Juan Red ware was, chronologically, the third pottery tradition of the Northern San Juan—after gray and white pottery. Norman Oppelt places redware firing dates between A.D. 700 and 1000. Most of this pottery was made in the Northern San Juan region west of Mesa Verde, but it is nevertheless considered to be "Mesa Verde" pottery. Red pottery gets its color from being fired in an oxidizing atmosphere with free oxygen, which allows the clay to oxidize and turn orange or red.

Abajo Red-on-orange is the earliest type of San Juan Red ware. The Anasazi made it between A.D. 700 and 850. Bluff Black-on-red dates from A.D. 750 to 900, and the latest type, Deadman Black-on-red, was made during Pueblo I and Pueblo II times, between A.D. 800 and 1000.

Clint Swink of Bayfield, Colorado, has developed a pottery-firing method that is closely akin to the method used by the ancient Anasazi. The pottery is fired in a trench kiln in four stages: primary firing, setting, secondary firing, and smothering. The initial stage, the primary firing, dries out the pottery and the sandstone slabs that later will be used to support the pots in the fire. After the primary firing, the sandstone slabs are placed on the coals from the primary fire and the pots are arranged on top of the slabs. Next the pots are covered with flat *sherds* (pieces of broken pottery).

When the pots are in place, a big fire is built over the kiln and allowed to burn down. This is the secondary firing. When the fire has burned down, the pit is covered with soil to smother the fire. The kiln remains covered for around twenty-four hours. The process is complete when the pots are removed from the kiln.

■

Chapter Two

✪ *Southwestern Colorado*

UTE MOUNTAIN TRIBAL PARK

Mesa Verde–Ute Tribal Park Anasazi

The Ute Mountain Tribal Park, a 125,000-acre tract of mesas and canyons, borders Mesa Verde National Park on three sides—east, south, and west. When the land of Mesa Verde National Park was set aside, the mapmakers who delineated its boundaries had never seen the region, so the park is cut out of Ute territory without regard to the topography of the land or the interrelationship of the ruins in the two parks. The Tribal Park is part of the Ute Mountain Ute Reservation. Tours are conducted by an approved Ute guide. Ute Mountain Ute Chief Jack House originated the idea of the park in 1967 and stabilization of portions of the spectacular Lion Canyon cliff dwellings began in 1971.

The Ute Tribal Park and Mesa Verde National Park are made up of a series of mesas cut from north to south by more than twenty deep canyons. Together, these smaller mesas form a single, rugged, high mesa that is shaped like a huge horseshoe and is bounded on three sides by cliffs. It is bounded on the north by an escarpment that rises nearly two thousand feet from the Montezuma Valley floor. The east side of the horseshoe is bounded by the Mancos River. The approach to Mesa Verde on U.S. 160 from the east silhouettes Point Lookout, the most northerly point of the mesa, from which a one-thousand-foot wall banded by white sandstone extends to the southeast. The west side of the mesa—from Cortez, Colorado, south—is only slightly less imposing. The mesa tips downward from eight thousand feet above sea level on the north to sixty-five hundred feet at the Mancos River on the south. The combined region of mesas and canyons is roughly seventeen miles from east to west and fifteen miles from north to south. All of the mesa's twenty canyons drain into the Mancos River. The canyons start at the Mancos Valley and extend north like fingers through Mesa Verde National Park.

The Mancos River flows southwest, rising on the western slopes of the La Plata Mountains north of Mancos, Colorado. It loops through the Ute Tribal Park and continues west to join the San Juan River at the Four Corners. Across the Mancos River Valley to the south, within the Ute Tribal Park, are additional canyons and mesas. On the north side of the Mancos, Navajo Canyon and its branches—Rock, Long, and Spruce Tree canyons—extend from the river to Mesa Verde's Wetherill Mesa and the national park headquarters. At the Navajo Canyon Overlook on Ruins Road, across from Echo House, you can see Navajo Canyon running south toward the Mancos. In Anasazi times, the canyon bottom was like a highway running from south to north. The Anasazi of Mesa Verde built a watchtower, now called Navajo Tower, overlooking the canyon, not far from what is now the national park headquarters. A bit farther up the Mancos Valley, Cliff Canyon runs north directly to Sun Temple. Mesa Verde was an integrated region easily reachable from the south.

A look at a map shows the Mancos joining the San Juan at the Four Corners, and the San Juan flowing across southern Utah, cutting through Comb Ridge, and rolling on to join the Colorado River in Glen Canyon. The San Juan and Mancos rivers together provided an easy route from Monument Valley to Mesa Verde. This entire region was Anasazi country and is filled with

LION CANYON RUINS
UTE MOUNTAIN TRIBAL PARK

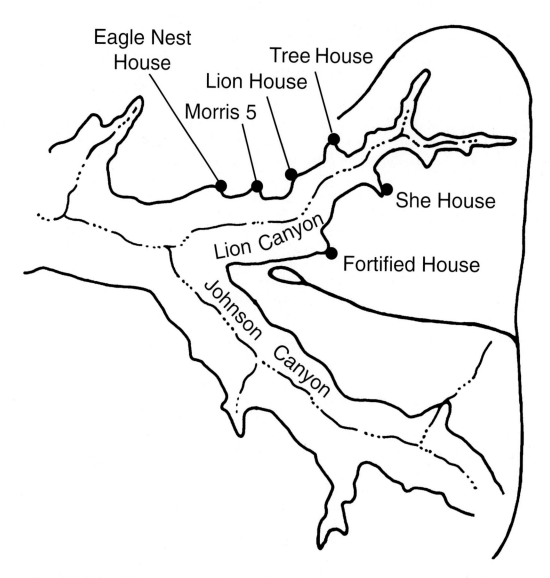

artifacts left behind by the Anasazi people who lived here off and on from Basketmaker through Pueblo III times. Mesa Verde and Ute Tribal Park lands were a single Anasazi homeland.

The Anasazi of the Lion Canyon pueblos may well have been a part of the Sun Temple–Fire Temple ceremonial community at the junction of Cliff and Fewkes canyons on Mesa Verde. The trip from Lion Canyon to Sun Temple consisted of a three-and-one-half-mile crossing of Lewis Mesa to the Mancos River and then a three-mile trip up the floor of Cliff Canyon. Many other ancient settlements in the Ute Tribal Park region could have participated in community activities at Sun Temple or on Wetherill Mesa. At Wetherill, there were great kivas at Long House and on the mesa above. Ceremonial complexes also existed at Kiva Point, at the southern end of Chapin Mesa.

She House is a small but very picturesque Pueblo III ruin. It is in a southern spur of Lion Canyon, east of Fortified House. The settlement was constructed on two levels. A fully dressed mummy of a woman was discovered here—thus the name She House.

The Ute Tribal Park region, including Johnson and Lion canyons, was first excavated by the Wetherills between 1888 and 1890. They named two of the cliff dwellings—She House and Fortified House. Professional work was first done here by Earl H. Morris in 1913. He is responsible for the names Eagle Nest House, Morris No. 5 House, Lion House, and Tree House.

Population estimates produced by the Paul R. Nickens survey done for the University of Colorado in the early 1970s suggest that the total population of Johnson Canyon sites was between 134 and 138. These figures were based on an estimated number of habitation rooms multiplied by an estimated number of persons per room. The report suggests, in round numbers, the following site totals: Lion House, 24 persons; Eagle Nest House, 10; Morris No. 5 House, 15; She House, 8; Fortified House, 16; and Tree House, 20.

Lion Canyon Cliff Dwellings

Lion Canyon branches off Johnson Canyon about four miles northeast of the Mancos River. A string of four of the most delightful cliff dwellings in the Southwest begins with Tree House at the head of a tributary of Lion Canyon. Down the trail from Tree House, along the canyon's north wall, are Lion House, Morris No. 5 House, and Eagle Nest House. These four Pueblo III cliff dwellings have recently been stabilized under the direction of Douglas Bowman as a result of the "Adopt a Ruin" financing program.

The pressure and unrest that began in early Pueblo III times affected the Ute Tribal Park Anasazi as it did the rest of the Northern San Juan region. The mesa tops had been occupied since the Pueblo I period. Along the road to Lion Canyon from U.S. 160, where it crests the mesa from Mancos Valley, there was a huge Pueblo I mesa-top settlement. This pueblo, known as Morris No. 33, had as many as one hundred sites per square mile and included a great kiva. On the mesa, next to Lion and Johnson canyons, the Anasazi farmed and lived on the flat lands. Then, about 1130, they began building—and moving into—the cliff dwellings. There were two main periods of construction in Lion Canyon—from 1130 to 1160 and from 1195 to 1230. The latest known construction occurred in 1241. The cliff dwellings of Lion Canyon were probably abandoned by the mid-1200s, a generation earlier than those of Mesa Verde.

The tour of the four Lion Canyon cliff dwellings is particularly interesting because the ruins appear much as they did when first seen by the Wetherills. The path to the sites is not paved, there are sherds on the ground, the ruins (although stabilized) have not been rebuilt, and there are ax- and awl-sharpening grooves in rocks at the sites.

The most interesting of the four sites is Eagle Nest House, the top level of which is almost intact. Wooden poles that protrude from the masonry walls once supported a balcony for access to the upper rooms. Exciting, too, is the "hands and knees" approach to the cliff dwelling from the top of a ladder. The whole ambiance is one of solitude—no cars and only a few people. With a little imagination, you can still feel the presence of the Ancient Ones who left here eight hundred years ago!

Across the canyon—and a good spot from which to take telescopic photographs of the Lion Canyon cliff dwellings—is Fortified House, which sits beneath the cliff rim. In Anasazi times, a catchment basin on the cliff above caught rainwater runoff. Nearby She House, built at the head of a fingerlike offshoot of Lion Canyon, is a series of tiny round-walled rooms on several levels. Other interesting ruins in the Ute Tribal Park are Bonal House, Two Story House, Sandal House, Casa Colorado, the Red Pottery Site, Hole-In-The-Rock, and Inaccessible House.

Visitors to these and other Ute Mountain Tribal Park ruins must be accompanied by a guide obtained at Ute Tribal Headquarters. Fine coverage of the Ute Tribal Park is provided by Jean Akens in *Ute Mountain Tribal Park: The Other Mesa Verde*, which gives site descriptions and discusses Ute Tribal Park history, regulations, flora, fauna, geology, hiking, and backpacking.

Mancos Valley Rock Art and Ruins

Douglas Bowman's research indicates that the Mancos Valley portion of the Ute Tribal Park was occupied in Archaic times. We know from the discovery of a sandal at Old Man Cave on Comb Wash, within the Northern San Juan region, that the Archaic people were in the region more than seven thousand years ago. Archaic rock art is common along the San Juan River. The Archaic people were probably not the ancestors of the Anasazi. But the Anasazi lived in the Mancos Valley after the Archaic people did, from A.D. 500 to Pueblo III times. The Mesa Verde Anasazi probably came down the canyons to the valley to farm and hunt. The valley is filled with towers, small sites, Basketmaker pithouses, and Pueblo III ruins.

The road into the Ute Tribal Park follows the Mancos River for about sixteen and one-half miles to the mouth of Johnson Canyon and then climbs onto the mesa, where it passes through the big Morris No. 33 Pueblo I site. The road then swings around the end of Johnson Canyon and back west to Lion Canyon.

Tree House is the first cliff dwelling you see when the trail dips into Lion Canyon. Tree House was built during Pueblo III times.

This is a view of Lion House from the west, showing the standing two-story room block and the standing wall in the center of the ruin. Desert varnish paints the cliff above.

This structure at Tree House contains rooms that resemble swallows' nests inasmuch as they were constructed in a crevice in the canyon wall. Note the traditional T-shaped doorway.

Morris No. 5 House was named by Earl H. Morris, who excavated the pueblos of Lion Canyon in the 1910s. This was the fifth cliff dwelling he excavated while working in Lion Canyon. The room blocks in this photograph show the multistory construction of the Anasazi cliff dwellings. Three levels are visible. The lower room has smoke-blackened walls, indicating its use as living quarters. Above that room is a second-story room with a doorway outlined at the top and bottom with stone lintels. The third-story room has very fine masonry similar to the Chacoan style, with small, carefully laid stones. Archaeologists assume that each family built its own group of rooms for living, sleeping, and storage. It would certainly appear here that the upper room was constructed by a different mason than was the lower room. The rooms in the front, starting with the smoke-blackened one, probably extended upward for another story to give access to the doorway in the smooth-finished top room. Morris No. 5 House is reached by a trail that runs along the cliff base of Lion Canyon from the Tree House ruin to Eagle Nest House. These ruins are Mesa Verde Pueblo III settlements and may be visited with a Ute guide.

About three miles up the valley from U.S. 160 is a wall on the high point of the mesa to the north. This lookout point would have allowed the Anasazi a view of the Mancos Valley from either direction. Another two miles up the canyon is the Red Pottery Site, a small, unexcavated ruin with a scattering of red sherds along with other pottery. This site was occupied from Basketmaker III to Pueblo III times, for a total of seven or eight hundred years. The redware for which the site is named came, in early times, from southeastern Utah as Bluff Black-on-red, or, later, from Kayenta as trade ware in the form of Tusayan Black-on-red. The Red Pottery Site was a canyon-bottom pueblo with thirty or forty rooms and two kivas. Some of the room blocks were two or possibly three stories high.

Eagle Nest House faces southwest, which makes it sunny in winter, when the sun moves to the south, and cool in summer, when the overhang produces shade under a high-angled sun. The protruding beams supported a balcony that gave access to the second-story rooms. The rooms were built under the overhang, against the back wall of the cave. The ladder to the right gives visitors access to the cliff dwelling. A very low passage allows the visitor to reach the ruins.

The Mancos and San Juan rivers were trade routes between the Northern San Juan and Kayenta Anasazi. In 1991 Douglas Bowman discovered evidence of an ancient Anasazi road beginning near the mouth of Mancos Canyon. Numerous ancient roads fanning out from Chaco Canyon have also been identified. Several of them have been found in the Northern San Juan region. The Northern San Juan Anasazi constructed roads, but they are more difficult to make out than are those in the dry flatlands of New Mexico. Ancient roads have been found at Comb Wash, Montezuma Creek, Cottonwood Canyon, Butler Wash, Sand Canyon, Wallace Ruin, and the Lowry-Pigg area.

Three miles up Mancos Canyon from Kiva Point you can see, on the south side of the river, the base of a masonry tower. There are dozens and dozens of tower remains from here to Comb Ridge. Some stand alone, others are part of a pueblo, and still others are connected to kivas. Some were watchtowers, and others were ceremonial centers.

Kiva Point Rock Art

At Kiva Point, at the base of Chapin Mesa, is a splendid display of Anasazi rock art. On the wall at Kiva Point are broad-shouldered figures carved by the Basketmakers sometime before the 700s. Among the stick figures, one couple with birdlike headdresses hold a ball between them. The figures with raised arms and spraddled legs are "lizard" figures from middle Pueblo times, around 1100. Note also the couple with chicken hands and feet drawn just above a mountain sheep.

These types of figures are found all along the San Juan River. The birdlike figures with a round body, long neck, small head, and bird legs may not represent birds. Sally Cole suggests they represent men who have erections and are wearing a headdress.

Kiva Point and Sand Island, which is on the San Juan River near Bluff, Utah, are places where visitors can easily reach panels that have a variety of ancient petroglyphs. At these sites are examples of rock art carved over hundreds of years. Sally J. Cole's *Legacy on Stone* contains an informative chapter on Anasazi rock art.

Besides the Anasazi petroglyphs, there are also splendid Ute pictographs in the Mancos Canyon. Examples include a painted, red Ute horseman on a high-headed pony with saddle, bridle, high-heeled boots, Spanish roweled spurs, and chaps and a poignant panel depicting a group of five Ute women.

Ute Tribal Park–Mesa Verde Anasazi Connection

From A.D. 800 to 1250, Pueblo I to late Pueblo III times, Kiva Point was the locale of several pueblos on two levels. The ruins of these pueblos remain unexcavated. On the lower level was a great kiva, a kiva-tower complex, and a number of masonry living quarters. A small Pueblo III cliff dwelling clings to the cliff. On Chapin Mesa above Kiva Point was a ceremonial center. It included three great kivas, multistory room blocks, and kin kivas. This group of buildings is only six miles south of the Sun Temple complex—no farther than Far View is from the Mesa Verde National Park headquarters on Chapin Mesa.

Ritual Killing

In the Mancos Valley are two sites of ritual killing. Across from Hole-In-The-Rock, along an ancient wall near the road, nine disarticulated skeletons were found. The bones had been cut open, and some had been burned. This could be interpreted as cannibalism, but it probably represents religious killing that was not necessarily related to cannibalism.

When the Mancos Canyon road was being constructed, another site was discovered. Here the remains of thirty-five killed people were found. The killings probably occurred in late Pueblo II or early Pueblo III times. The bones were all placed in a corner of a room. Douglas Bowman suggests hard times may have caused religious fervor that resulted in the killing of Anasazi by Anasazi and became one of the factors precipitating the final migrations.

ANASAZI HERITAGE CENTER AND MUSEUM

The Bureau of Land Management and the Bureau of Reclamation agreed in 1978 to build a cultural resource facility, the Anasazi Heritage Center, between the Dominguez and Escalante ruins. These two little pueblos are thought to have been, and probably were, visited in 1776 by the Franciscan priests Silvestre Velez de Escalante and Francisco Atanasio Dominguez. The center's sixty-room, 40,000-square-foot building houses a museum, offices, a storage facility, and laboratory space for archaeological materials from the Northern San Juan region. There are thousands of ancient sites in the area. The Dolores Archaeological Program, the Bureau of Land Management, the Crow Canyon Archaeological Center, and others have deposited Anasazi materials at the Heritage Center. One of the center's most spectacular treasures is the Chappell Collection of Anasazi artifacts.

The Anasazi Heritage Center was made possible largely by the construction of the McPhee Reservoir, which lies near the center. The reservoir dams the Dolores River and impounds forty-five hundred acres of water for irrigation and recreation. The Dolores Program was designed to make a thorough archaeological study of the land that would be covered by the lake.

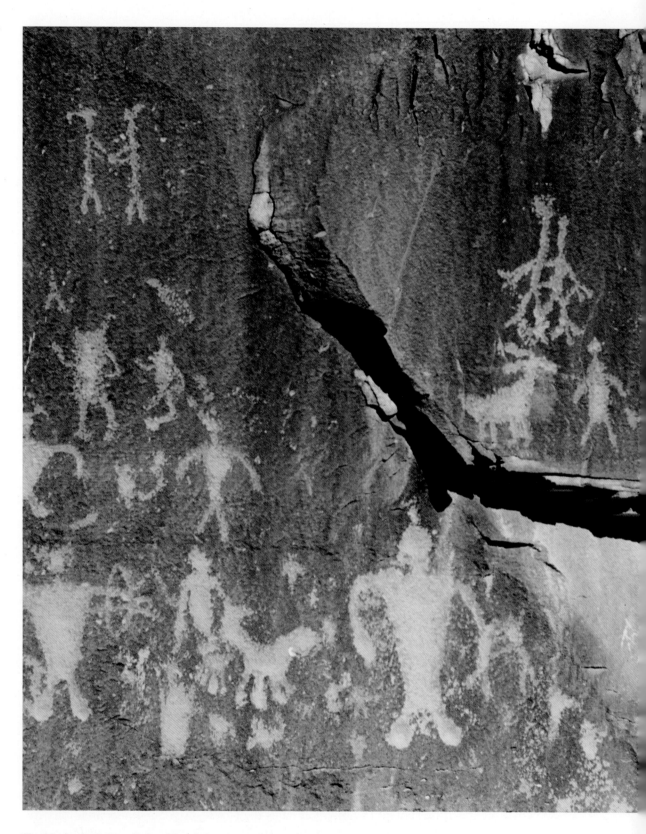

The big-bodied, broad-shouldered, long-armed figures in these two photographs were cut in the Kiva Point Rock Art Panel, at the base of Chapin Mesa, during late Basketmaker or early Pueblo times, probably during the A.D. 600s.

This is a view of the Anasazi Heritage Center complex (J-4) from the southwest. The center's main building, in the foreground, contains a museum. The tiny Dominguez Ruin occupies the green area bordered by the semicircular walkway that runs from the parking lot to the building. In the background is the McPhee Reservoir. On the low hill in front of the reservoir and to the left of the building is the Escalante Pueblo. The Heritage Center, which also includes a laboratory and storage facility for Anasazi artifacts, was an outgrowth of the Dolores Archaeological Program, which studied the Dolores River Valley before it was flooded to create the McPhee Reservoir. More than two hundred people under the direction of David A. Breternitz worked for five years, beginning in 1978, to make an archaeological survey of the region. The project gathered thousands of artifacts, which now constitute the Anasazi Heritage Center collection.

The program had the time, money, and personnel to do the most thorough archaeological study ever conducted in the Southwest. Pueblo I Anasazi villages were carefully dug and mapped, and pottery was collected that showed Anasazi development from A.D. 600 to 950. At the end of the project more than two million artifacts and documents were turned over to the Heritage Center.

A full-size reproduction of an Anasazi pithouse fills a portion of a large room in the Anasazi Heritage Center Museum. The museum staff have placed artifacts in the pithouse to show how the interior may have looked. The items displayed in the photograph are identified in the labeled drawing. They have been identified by Susan Thomas, curator of the museum.

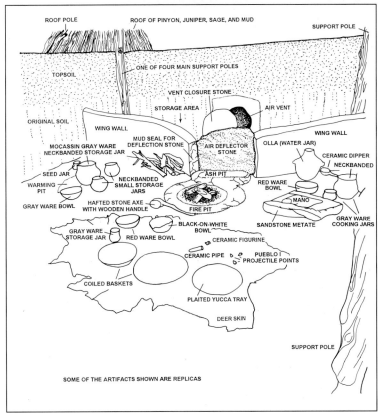

ROOF POLE ROOF OF PINYON, JUNIPER, SAGE, AND MUD SUPPORT POLE

TOPSOIL ONE OF FOUR MAIN SUPPORT POLES

VENT CLOSURE STONE

STORAGE AREA AIR VENT

ORIGINAL SOIL

WING WALL MUD SEAL FOR DEFLECTION STONE AIR DEFLECTOR STONE OLLA (WATER JAR) WING WALL

MOCASSIN GRAY WARE NECKBANDED STORAGE JAR CERAMIC DIPPER NECKBANDED

SEED JAR ASH PIT RED WARE BOWL

WARMING PIT NECKBANDED SMALL STORAGE JARS MANO

GRAY WARE BOWL HAFTED STONE AXE WITH WOODEN HANDLE FIRE PIT SANDSTONE METATE GRAY WARE COOKING JARS

BLACK-ON-WHITE BOWL

GRAY WARE STORAGE JAR RED WARE BOWL CERAMIC FIGURINE

CERAMIC PIPE PUEBLO I PROJECTILE POINTS

COILED BASKETS

PLAITED YUCCA TRAY

DEER SKIN

SUPPORT POLE

SOME OF THE ARTIFACTS SHOWN ARE REPLICAS

Copper bell from the Goodman Point region. This piece, from the Chappell Collection, was a trade item and possibly Mesoamerican in origin. It was found together with Kayenta Red pottery.

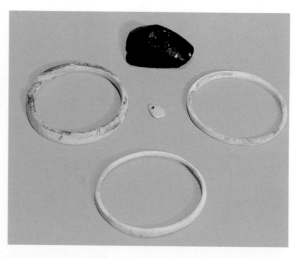

Five Pueblo I trade items from the Dolores River Valley, including three glycymeris shell bracelets and a jet fragment from McPhee Pueblo, a Pueblo I village. In the center is a turquoise pendant. These items date from the A.D. 700s.

Shell and turquoise beads from the Dominguez site. Some of the beads are in matrix and some are loose. The Anasazi acquired the turquoise and shells from New Mexico and the Pacific Coast by means of trade. The discovery of these beads at the Dominguez site indicates the presence there of an elite or high-status woman—one of the few indications of status among the Anasazi in the Northern San Juan region. Dominguez is an unusual site with Chacoan characteristics. It is complex for its small size and contains a grave that held a large amount of trade goods. The opulence of the burial's contents suggests the deceased may not have been a resident of the Northern San Juan, but rather a transient passing through when overtaken by death.

Collections data and site reports are cataloged in electronic databases at the center. Material is added regularly. The Heritage Center staff includes archaeologists, curators, and interpreters of Anasazi artifacts.

The museum at the Heritage Center contains a large first-floor gallery with Anasazi exhibits for visitors of all ages. The staff includes professionals and a large group of volunteers whose guidance makes a visit especially rewarding. In addition, the museum has a special exhibit gallery for temporary displays. A theater adjoining the main exhibit room is used for presentations relating to the museum's displays and for special programs. All of this is free!

There are two especially interesting and instructive permanent exhibits, each of which is worth a visit. The first is a full-size reconstructed and furnished Anasazi pithouse. Visitors to Mesa Verde can visualize life in the cliff dwellings by looking at Cliff Palace or Spruce Tree House, but the pithouse excavations on Ruins Road are far more difficult to comprehend. The well-done pithouse reconstruction at the Anasazi Heritage Center brings to life the way in which the Basketmaker

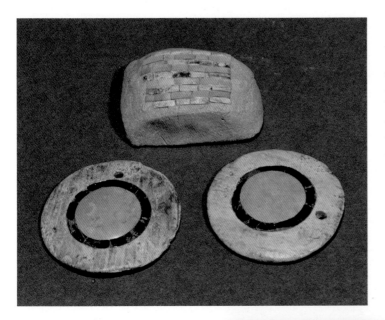

Three pendants. The bottom two consist of specular (gray) hematite, turquoise, and shell. The one on top was a mosaic of turquoise and shell and has been reconstructed in a clay platform. The reconstruction is based on how the item was found in the burial context. The matrix holding the mosaic had disintegrated.

A Chapin Gray seed jar and other artifacts. The corn cob with an inserted wooden stick or point is unusual. Possibly it is an awl or a punch-type tool. Below it is a bone flesher or scraper, and to the right of that is a knotted corn husk. In the foreground is a sampling of projectile points ranging in origin from A.D. 600 to 850. All of the items in this photograph were collected by the Dolores Program.

Twilled yucca sandal with fragments of cords. This item comes from the Pueblo I Singing Shelter, one of the few large shelters excavated by the Dolores Program. Many well-preserved woven items were recovered from this site. The cords around the edge of the sandal allowed a lacing across the top of the foot to hold the sandal in place.

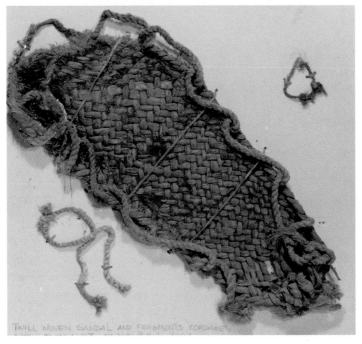

Chapin Gray, Moccasin Gray, and Cortez Black-on-white. The vessel on the left is a Chapin Gray seed jar. Such jars are typically rounded with a small opening. Note the two drilled holes near the top of the vessel. These holes were drilled in prehistoric times so that the pot could be tied together with cords or leather thongs where there was a crack. Holes were also drilled so that the pot could be hung by cords. For that, however, only one hole was drilled on each side. The large pot in the photo is Moccasin Gray, with neck banding common in early Pueblo I times. In Moccasin Gray vessels, only the neck was banded. The bottom of the pot is plain gray ware, one of the earlier utilitarian wares that predated later corrugated cooking pots. The small fragment in front of the large pot is Pueblo II Cortez Black-on-white. It has a highly polished white undercoat and a sectionalized design of black markings. Each section is distinctive. The two small bowls on the right are Chapin Gray. The smaller one is a miniature jar and the larger one a seed jar. The reason for the miniaturization is not known. Perhaps miniatures were made for children or for use with small objects—or as models for larger pots.

people lived. Pottery vessels, corn-grinding tools, baskets, a stone ax, and an animal skin are displayed in ways that show how they may have been placed and used by the ancient Anasazi. The exhibit makes Anasazi architecture understandable as well. The walls, roof, support poles, fire pit, draft-control stone, and wing walls are all in place. The center's collections include beautiful turquoise and shell beads, two shell pendants with turquoise centers, a startlingly delicate frog with turquoise bands and eyes, and a turquoise pendant.

ESCALANTE AND DOMINGUEZ PUEBLOS

Escalante Pueblo

The Escalante Pueblo sits on a hill overlooking the McPhee Reservoir to the northeast and the Anasazi Heritage Center to the south. The Dominguez Ruin lies next to the main building of the Heritage Center. The Escalante and Dominguez ruins bear the names of two Franciscan priests, Silvestre Velez de Escalante and Francisco Atanasio Dominguez, who passed this way in 1776 looking for a passage from New Mexico to California. They didn't succeed, but Escalante mentioned in his journal that there was a pueblo ruin here similar to those they had seen in New Mexico. It is assumed he may have been referring to the Escalante ruin. Jesse Walter Fewkes gave the pueblo the name Escalante. The Spanish exploration party stayed in the Dolores River Valley and

Ladles and other vessels. In this photo, five ladles are displayed with a mug and, to the right of the mug, a saltshakerlike vessel whose use is unknown. Several of the ladles are missing part, or all, of their handles. The ladle on the far right, without a handle, closely resembles the Mesa Verde Black-on-white style, having bands on the top and bottom of the painted design. The other ladles are Mancos Black-on-white, with a painted design of pointed shapes that extend downward from the bowl rims. The bowl of the ladle on the left was made before the handle was applied. The two ladle handles visible in the photo were incorporated into the whole vessel. The handles were usually hollow—see the ladle directly in front of the mug. Sometimes, clay beads were placed inside the handle to make the ladle rattle.

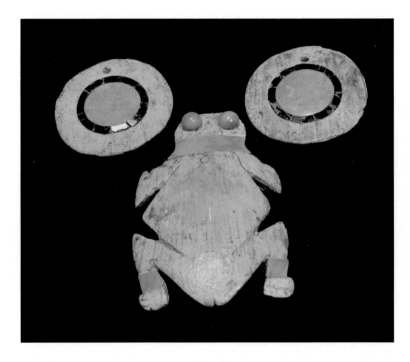

Items from the Dominguez site. The two circular objects consist of shell, hematite, and a turquoise center. The hole at the top of each of them indicates that they probably were used as earrings or pendants. The frog, also a pendant, is a most unique item. It has turquoise bands and turquoise eyes, and there is an abalone surface on the bottom side. When the frog was found, it was fairly intact, but it has been reconstructed. The two circular objects also have been reconstructed. These are trade items. None of the material is local.

An assortment of pottery styles. These items include two Mesa Verde Corrugated vessels, rear left and rear right. The rim of the larger one is very wide. The surface of the smaller one shows the use of indented coils. On the larger vessel, the coils have been smoothed. The pitcher between the two corrugated vessels is Mancos Black-on-white, from Pueblo II times, as is the tall canteen in front of it. The two birdlike effigy vessels on the right are similar, except that one has a handle and the other does not. The miniature ladle, front right, is Mancos Black-on-white. The small jar to the left of the ladle is early painted ware, probably Mancos Black-on-white.

A pendant from the Dominguez site shows the excellent craftsmanship of Anasazi jewelry. This piece has a turquoise outline and a center of hematite. The parts were glued together with pitch. The hole drilled in the top indicates that the piece was worn as a pendant.

didn't climb to the top of Mesa Verde. Otherwise, the Mesa Verde cliff dwellings would have become known to the modern world about one hundred years sooner.

The Escalante Pueblo appears much smaller than it actually was because only seven of twenty-five rooms have been excavated. The pueblo design shows Chacoan influence. The rooms are taller than Mesa Verdean rooms and their walls consist of *core-veneer masonry*—that is, double-coursed masonry with a veneer of tablet-size stones. The excavated kiva also has Chacoan attributes—it is deep, with low masonry pilasters and a subfloor, Chacoanlike ventilator. In recent years, it has become more evident that the people of Chaco Canyon had strong ties to and a heavy influence on the Anasazi of the Northern San Juan region from 900 to 1150. At Escalante, the masonry is blocky like that of Mesa Verde, not done in the refined Chacoan way, but the walls are core-veneer like those of Chaco Canyon.

Other evidence of Chacoan penetration appears in the Wallace Ruin to the south of Escalante and in the Lowry Pueblo to the northwest. Escalante was probably part of a much larger hillside community that also included the Dominguez Ruin. Escalante is easily reached by a paved footpath that begins near the Heritage Center building.

Dominguez Ruin

There is not much to see at the Dominguez Ruin, only the foundations of three rooms and a kiva. The excavation of one of the rooms of this little pueblo produced a cache of turquoise beads and several pendants, including a tiny frog pendant with turquoise eyes.

Many small villages in the Montezuma Valley during Pueblo II and III times were similar to Dominguez. The archaeologists speak of a "Mesa Verdean" style of architecture, pottery, lifestyle, and so on in the Northern San Juan region, but the people who lived here were local folks, not Mesa Verdeans. Their architecture and masonry were slightly different from those found on Mesa Verde.

McELMO CREEK DRAINAGE SITES

From the Park Point Overlook on the Mesa Verde National Park entrance road, a valley once occupied by the Northern San Juan Anasazi can be seen extending to the Abajo Mountains sixty miles to the northwest. The view is seldom clear, because of the smog that rolls up the valley from the Four Corners Power Plant at Farmington, New Mexico. Sleeping Ute Mountain lies to the west and the La Plata Mountains to the east. To the north, the recently constructed McPhee Reservoir, which dams the Dolores River, can be seen across the Montezuma Valley. Beyond that, on the northern horizon, are Lone Cone, Mount Wilson (a 14,250-foot peak), and the Dolores Peaks.

The sweep of the valley appears flat. In earlier times it was called the Great Sage Plain because of its apparent flatness. But in fact, the valley is cut by a dozen canyons that run from northeast to southwest. The valley encompasses some twenty-five hundred square miles and extends all the way to Comb Ridge in southeastern Utah. The Anasazi of the Northern San Juan lived in the valley from early Basketmaker times in 1500 B.C. to shortly after A.D. 1280.

On the mesas between the canyons is rich farmland, red-soiled bean fields that were as productive for the Anasazi as they are for farmers today. In the canyons are creeks, springs, and seeps. Because the farmland was much more productive than the thin soil of Mesa Verde, it supported many more people. Just how many, however, is the subject of ongoing debate. Estimates of the ancient population are based on formulas keyed to the number and size of ancient habitation rooms (and the proportion of rooms to kivas) and to the population density of modern pueblos.

The Crow Canyon Center's research indicates that during late Pueblo III times (1225–1300), there were four big Anasazi towns in the valley: Moqui Springs and Yucca House in the south, and Sand Canyon and Goodman Point in the north (north of McElmo Creek). In addition, there were about two dozen smaller sites, such as Castle Rock, Cannonball, Yellow Jacket, the Hovenweep

This is an aerial view of the Escalante ruin (J-4), which caps the hill behind the Anasazi Heritage Center. The ruin overlooks the Dolores River Valley and the McPhee Reservoir. The ruin can be reached by a surfaced trail that begins at the Heritage Center parking lot. This pueblo was probably seen by, and has been named for, Silvestre Velez de Escalante, a Spanish friar who passed this way in 1776 while looking for a passage to California. This photograph was taken in 1992. The observation platform seen here has been removed because it was not accessible to the disabled.

The Escalante Pueblo was part of a larger hillside community. Its interior kiva and the overall design indicate the Chaco Canyon influence that was felt throughout the Montezuma Valley during Pueblo II times. The tablet-shaped stones used as veneer on the walls and on the inside of the kiva are Chacoan in style. Otherwise, the style of the masonry is Mesa Verdean. In the background is the sage plain of the Montezuma Valley.

The enclosed kiva in the center of the Escalante ruin displays the Chacoan features of low banquettes, a subfloor vault, and eight low masonry pilasters. The Escalante ruin overlooks the McPhee Reservoir.

group, and Coal Bed. Some estimates suggest the region was home to thirty thousand or more people. By comparison, around three thousand people lived on Mesa Verde. Bruce Bradley of the Crow Canyon Center, however, has concluded that the number of Anasazi in the valley at any one time during the 1200s would probably not have exceeded fifteen thousand. His estimate is the result of the center's excavations, which have revealed that Sand Canyon Pueblo was viable for only forty or fifty years. That is a short period compared with the two hundred years (1100–1300) of the Pueblo III period, so it cannot be assumed that all or most of the Pueblo III pueblos were occupied at the same time. Further, Sand Canyon was never fully occupied—families would abandon living quarters and build another group of rooms up the canyon. Thus, a count of habitation rooms at the ruins of any one pueblo, or a count of all the room foundations in the valley, cannot be relied upon to give an accurate estimate of the ancient population at any given time.

Between this Bureau of Land Management sign and the Anasazi Heritage Center building in the background, a row of three rooms has been excavated and named for Friar Francisco Atanasio Dominguez, who accompanied Escalante in the latter's search for a way to get from New Mexico to California. This ruin was part of a larger community that included the Escalante Pueblo. Turquoise jewelry and other artifacts were obtained from the Dominguez site.

Castle Rock Pueblo

The Crow Canyon Archaeological Center has for many years been on the cutting edge of Anasazi research. The center is located northwest of Cortez, Colorado, on land once occupied by the Anasazi. The Crow Canyon program combines research and education, including hands-on excavation by students. Detailed excavations have been conducted at Castle Rock, Sand Canyon, and Duck Foot. Crow Canyon's archaeologists have played a central role in recent contributions to our knowledge of the Northern San Juan Anasazi.

In the early 1990s, the Crow Canyon Center conducted a dig at Castle Rock Pueblo, a late Pueblo III village on McElmo Creek. Castle Rock rises on the north side of the road that runs between Cortez, Colorado, and Aneth, Utah. Tree-ring dates indicate that the village at Castle Rock was begun during the mid-1250s and was completed during the 1260s. There was very little construction during the 1270s. The discovery here of Mesa Verde Black-on-white and Mesa Verde Corrugated pottery, two 1200s styles, fits nicely with the tree-ring dates. Abandonment came by 1280, after an occupation of not more than thirty years.

Ricky Lightfoot suggests that the 1200s were a time when the Anasazi of the McElmo drainage and Hovenweep began to gather together and build pueblos that could be defended. Sand Canyon, Mud Springs, Cannonball, and the Hovenweep sites all contain evidence of this *aggregation* (coming together) of the Anasazi people. The cliff dwellings of Mesa Verde, Comb Ridge, Butler Wash, Little Westwater, Big Westwater, and Cedar Mesa also offer evidence that the 1200s were troubled times for the Anasazi of the Northern San Juan region.

Kenneth L. Peterson, a member of the Dolores Program, concluded there was a twenty-five-year drought in the region during the 1200s. The tree rings show the drought to have been most severe in 1285. The weather in the 1200s also began to turn cooler. By 1300 the Southwest entered what Peterson calls a "Little Ice Age." No climate records were kept in the Americas at that time, but in Europe the records show a period of cold weather that continued from 1300 to 1800. In the Montezuma Valley, the combination of cold weather and drought sharply curtailed the corn crop, which was the main staple of the Anasazi diet. Corn requires at least 110 frost-free days and fourteen inches of rain. The combination of insufficient frost-free days and lack of rain made for very tough times for the Anasazi in the 1200s. This contrasts with the good times of the Pueblo II period, when the weather was mild and there was a long corn-growing season with plenty of rain.

Recent work at Castle Rock shows how troubled the times were. Skeletons found there indicate that there was a battle in which at least thirty-nine people were killed. The total population probably did not exceed seventy-five to one hundred. Archaeologists Ricky Lightfoot and Kristin

This is a view of Castle Rock (G-6), the small butte in the foreground, from the northeast. It stands in McElmo Canyon, between the Ismay Trading Post and Cortez, Colorado, on the McElmo Canyon road. Built in a defensive posture, the small pueblo at Castle Rock was occupied between the 1260s and the 1280s, during the troubled Pueblo III times. The pueblo was built against the base of the butte with kivas in the talus slope below. The pueblo had fifty to seventy-five rooms and at least thirteen kivas.

Kuckelman conclude there must have been a final battle—a massacre. The Anasazi of Castle Rock were aware of the danger. The pueblo at Castle Rock was built with many of the room blocks backed against the cliff sides. Rock art carved there shows two figures back-to-back with bows and arrows and shields and a third with a shield. These images indicate the presence of warfare.

The aggression probably began in the early 1200s, resulting in the construction of villages in the canyon heads, with defensive walls and towers. The Pueblo III villages of the Northern San Juan region from Mesa Verde west to Cedar Mesa show by their planning and construction that by the mid-1200s their residents had to defend and protect their water supply. Bruce Bradley also mentions additional factors that contributed to the change in the Anasazi way of life during the mid-1250s, factors that ultimately helped lead to the migrations out of the region: drought, colder weather, and too many people to feed. Bradley suggests people began to look back, through stories and ceremonies, on the better times of the Pueblo II period. They turned to new deities because the old ones were failing them. Perhaps the priests told them it was time to move on.

Migration is not a novel reaction to change. The New World, from Alaska to Cape Horn, has been populated by people who migrated here from Asia and Europe. The Anasazi and their forebears moved in and out of the Four Corners region for eight thousand years. A sandal at Old Man Cave has been carbon-dated at 6470 B.C., showing Archaic occupation of southeastern Utah by that early date. The Archaic occupation lasted about seventeen hundred years. Four thousand years later the cave was reoccupied by the early Anasazi. The Navajos and Utes moved into the region a few generations after the Anasazi moved out. These are just some of the examples of the movement of peoples in the Southwest over the millennia.

Sand Canyon Pueblo

Under the direction of Bruce Bradley, the Sand Canyon Project has been an ongoing Crow Canyon Center undertaking since the early 1980s. Sand Canyon Pueblo was a big, walled, canyon-head settlement with some 400 rooms, 14 towers, more than 100 kin kivas, and, for ceremonies, a great kiva. Each year, a segment of the pueblo has been excavated, studied, and documented, then *backfilled* (re-covered) at the end of the excavation season to protect the ancient walls. The Crow Canyon Center's detailed examination of Sand Canyon has shed new light on the final one hundred years of the Anasazi occupation of the Four Corners region. An examination of household room blocks has revealed that at Sand Canyon each block was occupied for only about twenty years. Apparently, when children became adults, they built new households and on the death of the parents, or sooner, the old room blocks were abandoned. This revelation changed the earlier concept that population could be estimated by counting living spaces. As a result, Bradley now believes that the entire population of the Northern San Juan region outside Mesa Verde would not at any one time have exceeded fifteen thousand. This sharply reduces the original estimates, which ran from thirty thousand to fifty thousand. The Mesa Verde estimate for any given time during Pueblo III totals about two thousand to three thousand people.

Sand Canyon Pueblo, like Castle Rock Pueblo, was short-lived. After its founding in the mid-1200s, it probably lasted only forty or fifty years. Tree-ring samples indicate construction from the 1240s through the 1260s, with the last roof beams being installed in the late 1270s. Like the Cannonball and Hovenweep settlements, the Sand Canyon village was built surrounding a canyon head to protect the water source. The Sand Canyon village had a companion pueblo, Goodman Point, four miles to the east.

The influence of the Chaco Canyon culture on the Northern San Juan region is now believed to have been very significant during Pueblo II times. The Wallace Ruin, which is not far from the entrance to Mesa Verde National Park, was a Chacoan outlier built and occupied by Chacoans between 1045 and 1125. Chacoan influence also appears at the Escalante, Dominguez, and Lowry sites, across the Montezuma Valley from Sand Canyon. Bruce Bradley suggests that in the Northern San Juan region, much of the Chaco lore of the 1100s was carried over into the 1200s by myths and ceremonies. When times got tough in the mid-1200s, there was nostalgia for those good old days of a century before. The Pueblo III culture began to fall apart about 1250.

Sand Canyon had a violent end. The skeletons there show that people were killed by blows to the head. Kivas were burned as if Sand Canyon's Anasazi enemies had decided on a ritual killing of the buildings of the settlement. The burning of Sand Canyon Pueblo may have occurred just before the beginning of the Anasazi exodus to the San Juan region of New Mexico. There still is no evidence of attacks by alien peoples from the outside. The natural conclusion is that the Anasazi were destroying themselves.

Cannonball Pueblo

The Cannonball ruin, a Pueblo III canyon-head settlement, sits on the northwest edge of Cannonball Mesa between Yellow Jacket and McElmo creeks. Its excavation, which ended in 1908, is part of the lore of the Southwest. As Jack Smith points out, "We had absolutely no dates at this point [the 1890s], the people speculated that these [Anasazi] ruins were a few hundred to tens of thousands of years old. There was speculation about [a] lost race, and the attribution of these ruins to just about every foreign group in the world, from the Phoenicians to the Egyptians."

This painting of the Sand Canyon Pueblo (H-5) by Glenn Felch reveals how the buildings of canyon-head settlements were arranged. Cannonball and the Hovenweep pueblos Square Tower, Holly, Horseshoe, Hackberry, and Cajon all resembled Sand Canyon in that their buildings were clustered on cliffs and slopes near a spring at the head of a canyon. The Crow Canyon Archaeological Center has excavated portions of Sand Canyon for a number of years. Its work has shown that the buildings of the pueblo were not all occupied at the same time. There were never as many people living there at one time as the number of rooms would seem to indicate. Some of the room blocks were abandoned even while the pueblo was still occupied. The pueblo was active only about forty years—two generations in those times—before it was abandoned entirely. The Crow Canyon Center is continuing to investigate other late-thirteenth-century settlements in the McElmo drainage.

Two Harvard archaeology students, Silvanus Morley and Alfred Kidder, were assigned to evaluate the region, including Cannonball Mesa. Both later became stars as archaeologists, Morley particularly. He became the foremost authority of his time on the Maya of Central America.

Morley's report, "The Excavation of the Cannonball Ruins in Southwestern Colorado," was published in 1908. Morley says this of southwestern Colorado:

> The San Juan river and the canyons which its tributaries have cut for themselves in this part of the Great American Plateau offered a more suitable environment for the development of a primitive culture than for the support of our own race, of which a few stragglers only have been able to win a doubtful foothold in the arid canyons and on the barren mesas in which this region abounds. On every side, sometimes a two or three days' ride from known water, one encounters the shapeless piles of fallen masonry overgrown with sage, cactus, and piñon, which so eloquently testify to the former density of the population.

Morley recognized the defensive style of the canyon-head pueblos, saying of Cannonball,

> This group is composed of two pueblos on the opposite rims of the canyon from each other, and a square tower built upon a detached rock in the bed. The two pueblos are built upon the very edges of the mesa. The canyon wall below them drops twenty feet or more sheer. This huddling close to the rim insured impregnability from any attack that might have been directed against the settlement from enemies in the canyon itself, while the watchtower was so placed as to give ample warning of invasion from that side and thus afforded an additional element for safety. It was from the mesa side—the backyards of their houses so to speak—that danger from without was chiefly to be apprehended; and the manner in which this difficulty was overcome illustrates well the architectural adaptability of this people. They built no first-floor outside doorways in walls facing upon the mesa, a practice that holds true not only for the two pueblos in the Cannonball group, but also for all the more important ruins of the McElmo area.

Morley could not have known Cannonball was a Pueblo III site. From his report and the character of the settlement, we now know that it was built, occupied, and abandoned during the mid- to late 1200s. The Cannonball site is similar to Sand Canyon and the Hovenweep canyon-head villages, and the pottery Morley found at Cannonball was Mesa Verde Black-on-white. This pottery was a late bloomer for the Anasazi. It is amazing, however, how accurate Morley was nearly one hundred years ago. He recognized so many of the Anasazi cultural characteristics: (1) that the pottery-making method was the same in all the villages, but the designs varied from village to village; (2) that the pueblo's construction was defensive in nature; (3) that the pueblo was not pre-planned but was expanded from time to time (Morley assumed that the pueblo grew because of increased population, and in this regard he may have been in error because we now know that in Sand Canyon, rooms were abandoned as new ones were constructed); (4) that there was violence; (5) that the kivas were kin or family kivas; (6) that the tower inside the pueblo was ceremonial and the one standing outside was defensive; (7) that the main foods were corn and squash (and that the Anasazi's teeth suffered from the corn diet and the grinding methods); (8) that, as farmers, the Anasazi used water management; (9) that they were not a warlike people, because of the absence of spear or arrow points; (10) that the skulls were flattened; and (11) that the Anasazi were only a little more than five feet tall.

Perhaps his most spectacular deduction was his evaluation of the significance of the kiva to Anasazi society. Of this he said, "The importance of the kiva and the part it played in the life of the aboriginal inhabitants . . . cannot be overestimated." And further: "These are the rooms

Cannonball Pueblo (G-6), a canyon-head pueblo, was in ancient times part of the Hovenweep group of settlements. To reach it, you travel twenty and four-tenths miles west on the McElmo Canyon road, then turn right and go one and one-half miles north to a left fork in the trail. The left fork climbs west about one-fourth of a mile to Cannonball Mesa, where the historic Wood Road—a former wagon trail to Bluff, Utah—runs across the top of the mesa for two miles. After traveling the two miles on Wood Road, another left fork leads northwest to the edge of the mesa and the Cannonball ruin. The elevation at the ruin is about fifty-three hundred feet above sea level. The excavated ruin is now surrounded by a chain-link fence, through which visitors may pass. Cannonball sits in the shadow of Sleeping Ute Mountain.

These walls stand on the caprock at the Cannonball site. The spring that supported the pueblo seeps from beneath the cliff overhang between the clusters of buildings on each side of the canyon head.

where preparations for the dances are made, where councils are held, and where the ceremonies of the pueblo take place—where, in short, the religious life of the group centers, and from which emanates the influence that regulates all the affairs of the daily life as well as defines man's duties and obligations to his Makers."

YELLOW JACKET SITE

Frederick Lange, Joe Ben Wheat, and others, in their book *Yellow Jacket: A Four Corners Anasazi Ceremonial Center*, demonstrate, in a readable way, that Yellow Jacket was an important Pueblo I and Pueblo II center. It was a religious, trade, and food distribution center with an importance akin to that of Mesa Verde and Chaco Canyon. But it has not been excavated; it has no standing walls or restored kivas. By careful comparison of the aerial photograph and the map you can make out some of the features of the one-half-mile-long Yellow Jacket site.

The green mesa can be seen to the west from U.S. 666, where that highway crosses Yellow Jacket Creek south of Pleasant View, Colorado. The site contained a great kiva at the north end, 5 big kivas, and between 125 and 165 smaller kivas. Because Yellow Jacket has never been excavated, kiva counts are difficult. But a number of multistory-building mounds, several towers, shrines, and a reservoir are visible although covered with brush. The site is on private property.

When a site is called a "ceremonial center," it means people from elsewhere came together there for ceremonial purposes—to supplicate rain, for instance, in this semiarid region that is always short of moisture. Sun Temple at Mesa Verde enjoyed a similar status. The modern puebloans of New Mexico and Arizona have ceremonies on a regular basis. Because they are in part the descendants of the Anasazi, it is fairly safe to assume that ceremonies were passed down to them from their ancestors.

The Yellow Jacket site may have included outdoor markets similar to those found in both prehistoric and historic times in Mexico and Central and South America, although this is disputed by some archaeologists because there is no hard evidence of the existence of markets at Yellow Jacket. Pottery was definitely a trade item in the Northern San Juan region, however.

Kayenta pottery sherds are found all over the region. Other trade items included obsidian, turquoise, agates, beads, petrified wood, red shale for pendants, and seashells. At Chaco Canyon there is evidence that live scarlet macaws were brought all the way from southern Mexico!

Joe Ben Wheat suggests, too, that food may have been stored at Yellow Jacket for distribution to outlying areas in times of shortage. It has been suggested that this was also one of the functions Chaco Canyon settlements served for the Chaco outliers.

Research indicates that the Yellow Jacket region was occupied from about A.D. 500 to 700, during Basketmaker III times, but was strangely vacant during the Pueblo I period and was not reoccupied until Pueblo II and III. Pueblo II is the period when Chaco exerted the greatest influence on the Northern San Juan region. Evidence of the connection between the two regions is seen clearly at Wallace Ruin. Also, at Lowry there is a *great house* (center for ceremonial administration) built in the Chacoan style, and at Far View on Mesa Verde the architecture, with its big

Yellow Jacket Pueblo (H-4) once stood on the promontory in the center of this photograph, a piece of land that is nearly surrounded by canyons. The ruins lie in the midst of heavy vegetation. A close look at the photograph, which was taken from the northwest, reveals open spots in the vegetation where some of the ruins lie. Arthur H. Rohn, who prepared the map of the Yellow Jacket site, notes that Yellow Jacket was surrounded by numerous small settlements and that it probably served as a ceremonial and community center for the region. Rohn calculates that Yellow Jacket Pueblo, at its peak, had a total of around twenty-seven hundred people. Joe Ben Wheat suggests Yellow Jacket was not a residential pueblo, because there are so many kivas in proportion to the number of room blocks. Wheat reasons that the kivas were not family or kin kivas built and used by the residents as they ordinarily would have been in Anasazi pueblos, but rather ceremonial and ritual kivas used by Anasazi who lived outside Yellow Jacket, in the surrounding region. Wheat's concept substantially reduces the likely number of residents.

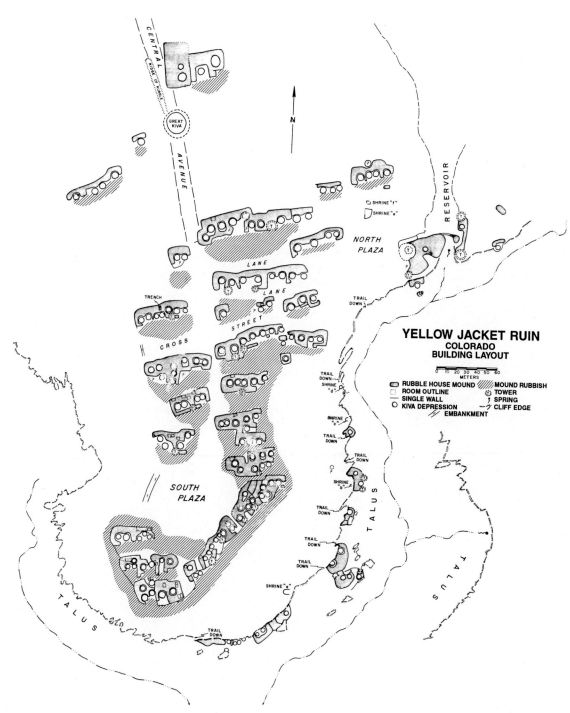

YELLOW JACKET RUIN
COLORADO
BUILDING LAYOUT

0 10 20 30 40 50 60
METERS

▨ RUBBLE HOUSE MOUND ▨ MOUND RUBBISH
▢ ROOM OUTLINE ✳ TOWER
— SINGLE WALL 🌀 SPRING
○ KIVA DEPRESSION — CLIFF EDGE
▨ EMBANKMENT

This map, prepared by Arthur H. Rohn, displays in detail the arrangement of the unexcavated ruins that lie on the promontory in the photograph of the site. A great kiva stands at the north end of the mesa, next to a large room block. Notice that within the room block is a clearly defined kiva depression. Locate these landmarks on the left side of the photograph (page 105). From this starting point you can follow the ruin mounds from the great kiva at the north end all the way to the cliff at the south end of the promontory, which appears near the top of the photo. The building mounds appear in sequence, almost like a procession, from north to south. At the tip of the mesa, middle right in the photo and lower left on the map, you can make out a row of kiva depressions within two big room blocks. Two vacant areas, one at the south end and the other at the northeast end of the promontory, are assumed to have been plazas. The vacant strips between the rows of room blocks may have been streets. In the northeastern part of the promontory, at the edge of the canyon, was a reservoir.

rooms and built-in kivas, looks Chacoan. Wheat, however, dismisses the suggestion that Yellow Jacket was a Chacoan outlier, pointing out that there is very little Chacoan pottery to be found there—lots more Kayenta pottery than Chacoan. He does suggest that Yellow Jacket may have functioned as a great house, much as Pueblo Bonito did at Chaco.

There is disagreement among archaeologists as to the function of Yellow Jacket. Was it a residential pueblo, or was it occupied by only a few people engaged in ceremonial and ritual activities? Yellow Jacket was the largest settlement in the region and was surrounded by some eight villages. Arthur H. Rohn calculates that the pueblo housed as many as twenty-seven hundred people. The settlement contained 41 separate buildings, at least 2 and possibly 4 plazas, and 125 to 165 kin kivas. Near the pueblo were eight villages, each of which could house between 200 and 250 residents. If you include the eight villages, Yellow Jacket was a very large settlement.

Joe Ben Wheat, however, views Yellow Jacket in an entirely different context. He believes it was a ceremonial center for ritual activities and that it supported relatively few people.

LOWRY AND PIGG RUINS

The Lowry and Pigg ruins sit side by side at the end of a road, nine miles west of Pleasant View, Colorado. Both ruins were part of a single, large Anasazi complex in Pueblo II times. Lowry, located on Bureau of Land Management land, is partially excavated and stabilized. Paul S. Martin excavated a small part of the Lowry settlement in the 1930s for the Field Museum of Natural History in Chicago. Fort Lewis College, W. James Judge, Arthur H. Rohn of Wichita State University, and others have contributed to the mapping of Pigg ruin, which is on private land.

The aerial photograph shows, on the left, a room block excavated at the Lowry site by Martin. He counted thirty-seven ground-floor rooms. The pueblo had more than one story. Some of the buildings were three stories high. All told, this portion of the Lowry-Pigg ancient town probably had between sixty-five and eighty rooms. Tree-ring data indicate the earliest rooms were built about A.D. 1090. The most extensive building was done between 1103 and 1120—late in the Pueblo II period. The size of the rooms and the style of some of the masonry indicate a marked Chacoan influence. This is just about the right time for the Chacoans to have been in the Mesa Verde region. *The Chaco Phenomenon* is the name given to the Anasazi culture that was centered on Chaco Canyon and flourished between A.D. 920 and 1120. There is much evidence of the spread of the Chaco Phenomenon into the Montezuma Valley and southeastern Utah in the 1000s and early 1100s. The style and masonry of the great kiva at the site also display Chacoan characteristics.

Note the masonry surrounding the door of the room block's interior kiva. Walls like the one surrounding this door, with carefully fitted, tablet-size masonry blocks, are one of the hallmarks of Chaco Canyon construction. Another Chacoan characteristic is the construction of rooms two or three times the size of Mesa Verdean rooms. Lowry contains Chacoan-size rooms and carefully laid walls, but much of the masonry and the later construction reflect the Mesa Verdean style. Mesa Verdean masonry is characterized by large loaf-shaped stones that are held together with mortar, chinked with small stones, and less evenly laid than are Chacoan stones.

Only a very small portion of this site has been excavated. Sage and scrub cover the collapsed walls of the other buildings of the pueblo. Lowry is considered a Northern San Juan great house because of the Chacoan influence, the size of the rooms, and the interior kivas.

Rohn's map indicates that the Lowry-Pigg settlement originally covered nearly a square mile. Rohn's research indicates that twenty-four groups of buildings made up the ancient town, which contained more than one hundred residential units and an equal number of kin kivas. If all of the settlement's twelve hundred rooms were occupied at the same time, they could have housed fifteen hundred to eighteen hundred people. As we have seen, however, the Crow Canyon Center's research at Sand Canyon indicates that counting rooms and kivas does

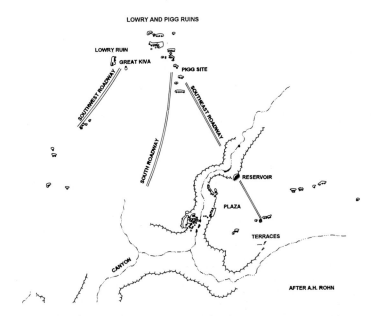

This map of the Lowry and Pigg region, prepared by Arthur H. Rohn, gives an indication of the size of an Anasazi town during Pueblo II and Pueblo III times. The ancient road segments extend south from the great kiva at Lowry and the two large kivas at Pigg.

These excavated portions of the Lowry-Pigg ruins (G-3) represent only a small portion of an Anasazi town that was occupied from the late 1000s until it was abandoned sometime before 1300. In this photograph, which was taken from the south, the excavated area on the left is Lowry Pueblo and the one on the right is a great kiva. Across the two-track road to the right was the Pigg settlement. The great kiva served as a ceremonial center for the surrounding town and smaller settlements. The pueblo and great kiva sit more or less in the middle of a pile of rubble that is all that remains of a number of masonry buildings constructed by the Anasazi. In the photo, rubble is indicated by the scrubby, short vegetation. Beneath the covered portion of the pueblo is an interior kiva that is open to visitors.

This is a view of the excavated Lowry Pueblo from the northeast. The large two-story portion shown in the photograph houses the pueblo's interior kiva. Rooms were backed against the big interior wall all around the pueblo. They were roofed and allowed access from the outside. The principal parts of the room block were connected to the kiva, and the central part of the pueblo may have been three stories high. Paul S. Martin, who excavated the site between 1930 and 1934, estimated that with the second- and third-story rooms built and occupied, the excavated portion of the pueblo would have contained sixty-five to eighty rooms plus eight kivas.

This great kiva at the Lowry site was central to the Lowry-Pigg settlement. The kiva's roof was supported by four columns that rose from masonry boxes. One of the boxes is visible as a square hole near the center of this photograph. The kiva was forty-five feet in diameter at floor level. A bench surrounded most of the wall. On the north side, which is on the right in this photo, was an anteroom with an entry stairway that led down to the floor.

Evidence of the Chaco Canyon Anasazi influence in the Montezuma Valley during Pueblo II times (A.D. 900 to about 1100) can be seen in the fine masonry of this wall and its doorway, which leads to the interior kiva of the Lowry Pueblo. These carefully laid, tablet-size masonry slabs are one of the hallmarks of Chacoan culture and are easily distinguished from the loaf-shaped building stones characteristic of the Mesa Verde Anasazi buildings.

The large kiva above housed in the Lowry room block is unusual because of the triple horizontal rails along its walls and the mural painting at its base. The photograph below, taken in 1981, shows a stair-step design similar to that found on Anasazi pottery. Salvaged portions of this mural are now in the Anasazi Heritage Center at Dolores, Colorado.

not necessarily indicate the number of people living in the pueblo at any one time. At Sand Canyon, some rooms were abandoned after others were built.

W. James Judge of Fort Lewis College has identified an unexcavated great house at the north end of the plaza between the Pigg and Lowry ruins.

■

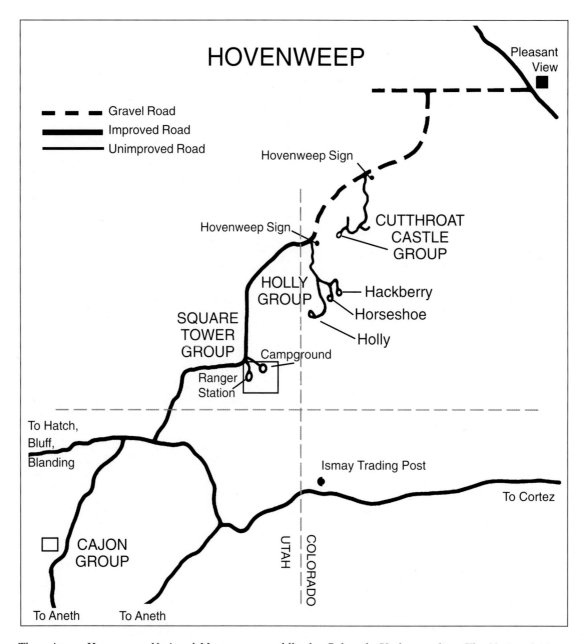

HOVENWEEP

Gravel Road
Improved Road
Unimproved Road

Pleasant View

Hovenweep Sign

Hovenweep Sign

CUTTHROAT CASTLE GROUP

HOLLY GROUP

Hackberry

Horseshoe

Holly

SQUARE TOWER GROUP

Campground

Ranger Station

To Hatch, Bluff, Blanding

Ismay Trading Post

To Cortez

CAJON GROUP

UTAH

COLORADO

To Aneth   To Aneth

The ruins at Hovenweep National Monument straddle the Colorado-Utah state line. The National Monument headquarters, which sit beside the Square Tower ruins, are reachable by gravel road from Pleasant View, Colorado, or by paved road from Blanding, Utah, by way of the Hatch Trading Post. Hovenweep is administered by Mesa Verde National Park.

Chapter Three
✪ *Hovenweep*

Hovenweep National Monument was established in 1923 and is administered by Mesa Verde National Park. The monument includes the Square Tower ruins and a ranger station, and four groups of outlying canyon-head ruins—Holly, Horseshoe, Hackberry, and Cajon—and the Cutthroat ruin, which the Anasazi built along a wash. The ruins all date from Pueblo III times and were built on the Cajon Mesa, which extends from Pleasant View, Colorado, to the San Juan River. The mesa becomes more arid from east to west, going from the piñon-juniper country at Pleasant View to the desert country bordering the San Juan. This is a wild, beautiful area, where service stations and fast-food stops are a long way apart! William H. Jackson, during his explorations in 1874, named the region Hovenweep, a Ute word meaning *deserted valley*.

Lowry Pueblo can be seen en route to Hovenweep with a slight detour. Visit Lowry by taking the west road from Pleasant View. To reach Hovenweep from Lowry, backtrack toward Pleasant View and take the first gravel road south. It joins the Hovenweep road, which is gravel most of the way to the national monument.

The gravel road to Hovenweep can also be reached from U.S. 666 at Pleasant View. There is a sign that reads HOVENWEEP NATIONAL MONUMENT 25 MILES ROUGH ROAD. Most of the road has been recently graveled and winds southwest across flat land that lies between canyons. Sleeping Ute Mountain is visible to the south. The road passes through newly irrigated fields of alfalfa and beans.

At the seven-mile turn, you can see the Carrizo Mountains to the south and Comb Ridge, which looks like a white wall, directly to the west. There is an abundance of rabbit brush on the roadside. Further on, the deep Cross Canyon bounds the north side of the road. The gravel ends after sixteen miles, and the road is then rough for about five miles until you reach the Utah state line, where a surfaced road begins.

Cutthroat, Horseshoe, Hackberry, and Holly are all in Colorado. The dirt roads into these ruins are not bad in dry weather, but they are much more difficult when wet. It is wise to contact the Hovenweep National Monument Headquarters before driving in. Cutthroat is the most easterly Hovenweep ruin. Seventeen and one-half miles from U.S. 666 is a sign that reads HOVENWEEP. Here a dirt road to the left wanders through the brush for about two miles down to Cutthroat. This ruin is a beautiful collection of Anasazi buildings straddling a wash in the piñon and juniper trees.

The entrance road to Holly, Horseshoe, and Hackberry is marked by a HOVENWEEP sign on the south side of the main road. After you turn onto this entrance road, a dirt road to Holly and Horseshoe splits off to the right (southwest) one-half mile from the main road. The road to the left (east) goes to Horseshoe and Hackberry. You will pass a sign saying HACKBERRY UNIT 126 ACRES.

The road to the right continues southwest for about another mile and a half to the Holly ruin. Across the state line in Utah, west of the Holly, Horseshoe, and Hackberry ruins, are the national monument parking lot, ranger station, and campground. Here are located the Square Tower ruins, a magnificent group of ruins scattered along the canyon rim and walls. A hiking trail goes through canyons from the Square Tower Group to the Holly, Horseshoe, and Hackberry ruins. In the summer take plenty of water and insect protection. Sometimes the no-see-ums are out in force!

Cajon is the southernmost of the Hovenweep ruins. A good gravel road to the site leaves the Hatch-Ismay-Cortez road four-tenths of a mile west of a sign for the Hovenweep National Monument. Follow this road—the Aneth road—southwest for two and seven-tenths miles. On your right (west), note a battery of oil tanks. Take the dirt road to the right just beyond these tanks. There is no sign here, but the ruin is only a few hundred yards off the highway. If you are still on the main road when it starts going downhill off the mesa, you have gone too far.

SQUARE TOWER GROUP

The Square Tower Group (F-5) was built by the Anasazi around the apex of Little Ruin Canyon. The name Square Tower comes from the square tower seen in the foreground of this photograph. East of the tower, on the rim of the canyon, stand the ruins of Hovenweep Castle. When the Square Tower Group was occupied in the 1200s, the part of the castle that is still standing was at the top of a housing block whose base lay below the canyon rim. Beneath the rim to the left of the square tower was a spring that furnished water to the community.

The Square Tower Group is a canyon-head settlement that was constructed in the late 1200s, perhaps as late as the 1270s. No more than one hundred residents lived here at any one time. Central to the village was the spring at the head of the left fork of the canyon, which is known as Little Ruin Canyon. The residents of Hovenweep cultivated the mesas between the canyons and built their homes and kin kivas along the rims, bottoms, and sides of the canyons.

The late 1200s were unsettled times all over the Northern San Juan region. During those years, the Anasazi moved their villages off the mesas. At Mesa Verde they moved into the cliffs. At Hovenweep they moved into the canyons. As Kenneth L. Peterson has noted, the turbulence of these times was exacerbated by a combination of drought and a cooling of the climate. The tree rings indicate that during the dry time of the 1200s, especially during the 1280s, an entire year's crop could be lost. Moreover, after years of cultivation, land loses its productivity, and crop yields are smaller. The Anasazi were probably fighting among themselves over the productive land.

Located near the center of Little Ruin Canyon, Square Tower gives its name to the group of Hovenweep ruins to which it belongs. Built down in the canyon, it was not a lookout tower. Instead, it was built adjacent to the canyon's spring, probably to demonstrate the Anasazi's appreciation of the water source.

The towers and D-shaped buildings of Hovenweep are evidence of the unsettled times. One of these structures, Square Tower, sits on a boulder in the bottom of the canyon. Its location doesn't seem to indicate that it was used for defense, so it was probably a ceremonial structure. On the canyon rims opposite Square Tower, the Anasazi built D-shaped buildings—Hovenweep House on the west and Hovenweep Castle on the east. These buildings seem to have served no utilitarian purpose. They were not used for living, storage, or defense.

And yet they were very carefully and laboriously constructed. Each stone had to be found, brought to the site, carefully shaped by hand, and precisely fitted into the walls of the buildings. Thousands of them were required for the pueblo and its buildings. Hovenweep was abandoned in the late 1200s, leaving but a few years for the building and occupation of the site. The same individuals who built these ceremonial structures—mainly the Anasazi men—had to do the farming, harvesting, toolmaking, hunting, and the construction and maintenance of living quarters; and all the other activities of daily life that were required of them. The women always had full-time obligations to grind corn, cook, care for the children, and make pottery and clothing.

The Anasazi men probably made this extra effort in an attempt to supplicate, pay tribute to, appease, or request guidance from the deities they believed in. An eight-hundred-year-old Anasazi culture was dying, and something had to be done. Bruce Bradley suggests that the late 1200s may have been a time of loss of faith in old deities and embracing of new ones because drought was more frequent, the weather had become colder, and there was outside harassment.

At Square Tower the construction of ceremonial buildings near the pueblo's water source, the canyon-head spring, probably demonstrates the people's concern for the continuation of the flow of water. On the canyon rim above the spring, the Anasazi constructed a dam to hold the runoff rainwater in a small reservoir. This impounded water soaked through the sandstone and increased the amount of water flowing from the spring below.

Hovenweep Castle, which stands on the east rim of the canyon's left fork, is the only remaining portion of a much larger pueblo. Originally, the D-shaped tower that makes up part of the castle was two-and-a-half or three stories high. The upper stories have collapsed, leaving the debris on the floor below. Living quarters were built adjoining the tower on the canyon rim and on the canyon sides below. The stones that litter the canyon are the remains of the old room blocks. One kin kiva was built on the upper level, next to the castle, and there were six additional kivas on the slopes below.

The castle was stabilized in 1986 and 1987. It stands on a double-coursed masonry foundation. The D-shaped tower, which is about eleven and one-half feet wide on the inside, and a rectangular room that measures ten feet by five feet on the inside, make up the west end of the castle. Three rooms with interiors that measure approximately six feet by six feet are connected to the tower and extend down the canyon rim.

The walls of the tower contain small openings through which the sun casts beams across the room inside. Ray A. Williamson, an astronomer, in his book *The Living Sky*, demonstrates that these shafts of sunlight mark all four major annual solar events: the summer and winter solstices and the spring and fall equinoxes. The four days on which these events occurred were important Anasazi ritual days. Williamson has determined that the equinox beams strike between an inner doorway and an outer one, and the solstice shafts hit the east corner of a doorway. At the Holly site, during a few days before and after the summer solstice, a shaft of sunlight crosses the center of a target ring incised on a canyon wall.

A portion of Hovenweep House, a D-shaped structure sitting on the canyon rim across from Hovenweep Castle, still stands. A pueblo once surrounded Hovenweep House. The aerial photograph shows the scattered dressed stones that once formed the walls of the pueblo's residential rooms. The extent of the rubble shows that the pueblo was built around the rim of the canyon head. Note that Hovenweep House had a symmetrically curved wall made of dressed, loaf-shaped stones that were carefully fitted into place and held together with adobe. In some places, small stones were inserted to ensure a smooth outer surface.

Hovenweep Castle consists of the ruins of a group of buildings originally built above and below the rimrock. Room blocks were built against these standing walls. The structure to the left (north) is D-shaped— a feature of Anasazi ceremonial architecture that appears in several of the Hovenweep ruins. Below this building were residential room blocks several stories high. Today all that remains of the room blocks is a pile of rubble. The buildings you see here were occupied late in Pueblo III times, during the 1270s, only a few years before the region was abandoned.

This photograph shows the rounded walls of Hovenweep House, which sits on the west side of the head of Little Ruin Canyon, across from Hovenweep Castle. The castle can be seen in the background of the photo. Hovenweep House was the center of the Hovenweep Square Tower complex, which was located at the head of the canyon.

In all, there were three pueblos at the canyon head. One stood around and below the castle, another surrounded Hovenweep House, and the third stood in the canyon below the canyon-head rimrock. A few walls still remain beneath the overhang of the canyon head. Arthur H. Rohn estimates that a total of one hundred people may have been living in the three pueblos during the late 1200s.

TOWER POINT RUINS

The National Park Service has laid out walking trails to enable visitors to see the Square Tower Group of ruins at the head of Little Ruin Canyon as well as the ruins farther down the canyon. A trail known as the Tower Point Loop follows the rims between the two forks of the canyon. This trail begins at the ranger station and, at Hovenweep Castle, overlooks Square Tower and

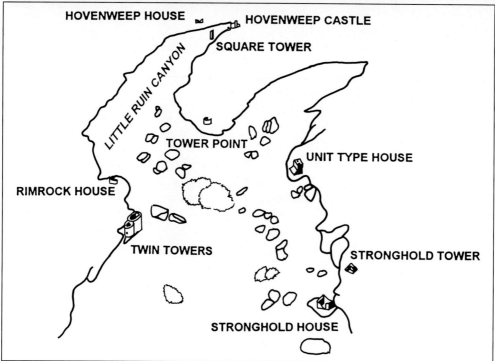

Here is an aerial photograph of Little Ruin Canyon and a drawing that shows the location of the ruins there. The left fork of the canyon is the site of Hovenweep Castle, Square Tower, and Hovenweep House. The spring is also located in the left fork. The Square Tower settlement was constructed around this canyon head. Other Hovenweep pueblos were built around the heads of other canyons. In the photograph, the monument headquarters appear as the white strip of buildings in the middle of the background. In the middle of the foreground can be seen Stronghold House on the right side of the canyon and Twin Towers and Rimrock House on the left side.

Stronghold Tower was originally constructed, in part, on logs crossing the crevice between a cliff and the boulder that supports Stronghold House. When the support timbers collapsed with age, part of the tower fell with them, leaving only this portion of what originally was an oval structure. Note Twin Towers and Rimrock House in the left background, on the other side of the canyon.

This is a view of Twin Towers with Sleeping Ute Mountain on the horizon in the background. Each of the towers was constructed on the surface of a boulder. These firm foundations have kept the buildings stable for nearly eight hundred years. The towers were residential units that together contained a total of some sixteen rooms. Note that the towers' bases were built to follow the shapes of the foundation boulders.

Tower Point Tower, above, was erected at the spot where Little Ruin Canyon divides into the left and right forks. The tower likely served as a lookout. Note Ute Mountain in the background.

Stronghold House, which now sits in isolation on the top of a huge boulder, was originally the top story of multistory room blocks built up from the canyon floor.

Hovenweep House. At the end of the mesa between the canyon's two forks stands Tower Point Tower. From this point you can see the ruins of the Square Tower Group up the left fork of the canyon, to the northwest, and directly down canyon to the southeast you can see what remains of three ancient pueblos, with Sleeping Ute Mountain in the far background. Looking down canyon from Tower Point Tower, you can see, on the canyon's west side, Round Tower, Rimrock House, Eroded Boulder House, and the beautifully symmetrical Twin Towers. Looking down canyon on the east side, you can see, on the canyon rim, Unit Type House, Stronghold Tower, and Stronghold House.

Tower Point Tower has all the attributes of a lookout tower. Built on a high flat ledge that overlooks the pueblos up and down the canyon, it would seem to have been part of a defensive system—particularly if the entire canyon-head settlement was designed for defense. Towers, however, were very common in the Northern San Juan region. Nearly every pueblo had one or more.

On the slope below Tower Point Tower, the Anasazi built Round Tower and, next to it, a kiva. This Pueblo III kiva-tower arrangement, like that at Far View on Mesa Verde, probably served a ceremonial function. The tower is almost perfectly round, is two stories high, and has no entry door at ground level. There are other kiva depressions close by, indicating a pueblo was built on the slope next to Round Tower. Just below Tower Point Tower, in the left fork of Little Ruin Canyon, are the remnants of a structure built on top of a flat boulder.

From Round Tower, where the canyon divides, all the way to Eroded Boulder House and Twin Towers, the canyon bottom and sides are filled with sage-covered rubble from collapsed pueblo room blocks. Eleven or more kin kiva depressions scattered through the rubble indicate that this was a large settlement. Rock art depicting a spiral and a T-shaped doorway with a bird perched on top can be seen on the cliff face at Tower Point. On the west canyon rim to the south are Rimrock House and Twin Towers. Both were residential sites. Note that each of the Twin Towers conforms to the shape of the boulder at its base, with the circular walls rising from a relatively flat rock foundation. These two towers served as two-story apartmentlike houses that together had a total of sixteen rooms.

Across the canyon from Twin Towers, a large pueblo built against the sides of the canyon extended from Stronghold House to Unit Type House. Stronghold House looks like a fort built on top of a cracked boulder. Near it, on the canyon rim, stands Stronghold Tower. These two structures are all that remains of pueblo room blocks that extended along the sides of the canyon. Originally there was a log bridge between Stronghold Tower and the boulder on which Stronghold House sits. When the log support rotted away, much of the tower fell into the crevice. Hand- and toeholds in the boulder below Stronghold House provided access to the two room blocks on the boulder top. Access in ancient times was probably also available by ladder from the roof of the now collapsed rooms below.

Up canyon from Stronghold House stand the ruins of Unit Type House, a different kind of Anasazi building. Unit Type House has seven first-floor rooms that together form a rectangle, and, on one side, a kiva enclosed by the rooms. The name *unit type house* was first used for this type of structure around 1900 by Southwest archaeologist T. Mitchell Prudden. The term *unit type* is used to describe any pueblo unit with storage and living rooms on the north, a kiva or pithouse in a plaza on the south, and a trash dump farther south. This sort of construction dates from the A.D. 700s and later.

Ray Williamson found evidence at Unit Type House, as he did at Hovenweep Castle, of the marking of the solstices and equinoxes by shafts of sunlight. Three openings in the east wall of the southeast room directed shafts of light from the rising sun to specific points in the building.

HOLLY PUEBLO

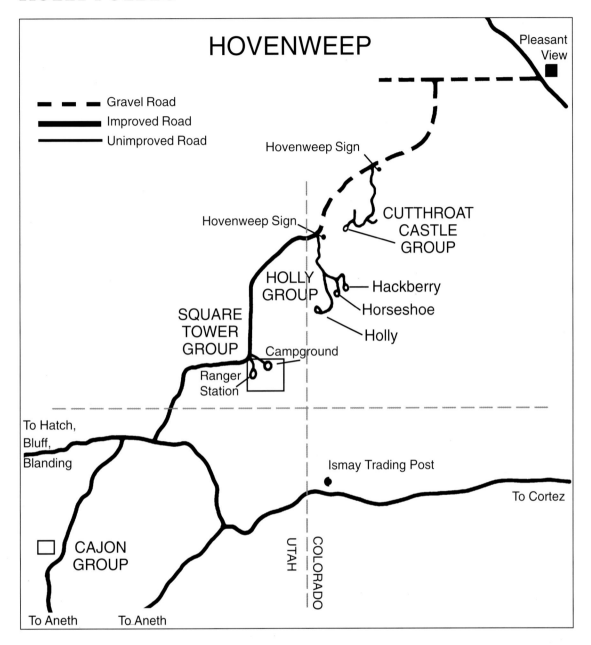

The Holly ruin's most spectacular attraction, one that happens only once a year, is its summer solstice Sun Dagger. Beneath a huge gamma-shaped (inverted L-shaped) cliff overhang is a cliff face upon which the Anasazi inscribed two spirals and a set of concentric circles. These three designs, located a few feet overhead, are aligned from east to west just below the overhanging rock. The spiral on the east end of the wall is intact, the middle spiral is partially eroded away, and the targetlike set of circles on the west end is still in perfect condition.

For several days before and a few days after about June 21 each year, all sorts of solar aficionados gather at sunrise to watch the sun dagger phenomenon. People sit on the scattered boulders at both ends of the little canyon and wait. The desert air is fresh and clean. Cameras are focused. There is some hushed chanting. The sun is up but has not yet reached the canyon.

Holly Pueblo

About one hundred yards southwest of Great House, the canyon wall curves to the west. There beneath the cliff, on the face of a boulder, the Anasazi carved two spirals and a set of concentric circles. Each year, the three figures are bisected by a line of sunlight, called the Sun Dagger, in early morning from a few days before until a few days after the summer solstice, which falls on about June 21. These three photographs show the Sun Dagger's course across the face of the cliff. In the photos, east is to the left and west to the right. The line of light comes from each side simultaneously. The first photograph was taken at 6:49 A.M. (top), the second at thirty seconds past 6:50 A.M. (middle), and the third at 6:52 A.M. (bottom).

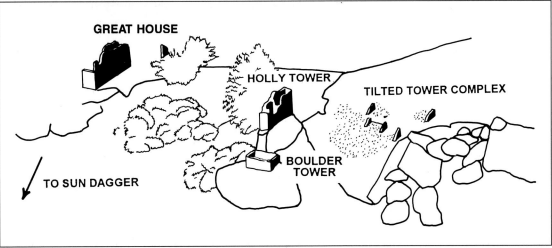

Holly (G-5) is a Pueblo III canyon-head village built around a spring. It resembles a number of other villages in the canyons of southeastern Utah and southwestern Colorado. The aerial photograph shows the ruins clustered around a point where a wash pours into the canyon below. Water in ancient times seeped from a spring below the overhanging rimrock. Visible in the photo are, from left to right, Great House, Curved Wall House, Holly Tower, Boulder Tower, and Tilted Tower. Holly village housed about 120 to 150 people.

At about 6:48 A.M. there is a sudden hush, then gasps of surprise and delight. A line, or "dagger," of sunlight on the cliff face begins to make its way toward the first spiral. Within a minute it moves rapidly from east to west. Then almost miraculously, another dagger of light approaches the three designs from the west side and crosses almost the exact center of the targetlike figure. By 6:53 the two daggers meet in the center of the cliff, passing through all three of the figures. More chanting. The ancient Anasazi have reached across the centuries and touched us! They knew and we know that the sun has stopped its march to the north. This is the summer solstice!

Holly was another of the Pueblo III canyon-head pueblos, built in the 1200s, that make up the Hovenweep group. The ruin may be reached by traveling just a bit less than two miles down a dirt trail from the main road or by taking a four-mile hiking trail from the Square Tower ruins. The pueblo's masonry rooms were built on the canyon slopes, beginning where the visitors' trail enters the ruin and extending around the canyon head and past Great House on the west canyon rim. There were some twelve or thirteen kin kivas in front of the residential structures. Probably more than 100 people lived here.

The original spring under the canyon rim just to the north of Holly Tower dried up long ago. Probably a portion of the cliff above collapsed and stifled the flow. Above the spring, the Holly Anasazi built a dam to hold rainwater so that it would seep down through sandstone and come out in the spring below. The Park Service reports that pollen samples taken here show that besides the Anasazi staples of corn and beans, beeweed seeds and greens were also eaten. Beeweed was also grown for making black dye for pottery painting. Evidence of wolfberry was also found. Its red berries are eaten by modern Hopi and Pueblo peoples.

The first great flat slab of sandstone along the visitors' trail split in ancient times and thus divides the masonry building the Anasazi had built there. Most of the walls have collapsed, spilling building stones on the boulder base and down into the canyon. The portion built on the now leaning boulder is called Tilted Tower. In the aerial photograph on page 123 you can see the enormous pile of shaped masonry stones around the remaining walls of Tilted Tower.

The graceful two-story, two-room rectangular building standing on a boulder near the apex of the canyon is called both Holly Tower and Boulder House. The Anasazi cut hand- and toeholds into the base boulder to reach the doorway. The Park Service reports that several projectile points, a scraper, turkey bones, and a fire pit were found inside the building. These findings indicate the building was used, at least in part, as a residence. The function of Boulder Tower, the small structure perched on a turtlebacklike boulder near Holly Tower and across from Tilted Tower, is unknown.

The huge triangular boulder upon which the masonry rooms in the far background of this photo were originally built has gradually tilted, opening a large crevice in the rock. The masonry walls, once upright, have tilted with the boulder. They are the remains of what has become known as Tilted Tower. Other ruined walls and piles of masonry indicate that, in the 1200s, the buildings of Holly Pueblo covered the cliffs around the canyon.

On the west rim of the canyon, the walls of two buildings still stand. These buildings are Great House (not a Chacoan great house) and Curved Wall Tower. The tower is unusual because its curved outer wall surrounds a square-walled inner building that could be reached from below through a crack in the canyon rim. Boulder House has been stabilized by the Park Service.

Great House was used as living quarters. A fire pit, plastered floor, stone tools, and pottery were found there. Also recovered was a jar of sacred animal and bird bones. Both Great House and Holly Tower were carefully built using pecked stones to make walls two or three courses thick.

HORSESHOE PUEBLO

Holly, Horseshoe, and Hackberry were all built in Pueblo III times at the head of small canyons that run southwest into Yellow Jacket Canyon and McElmo Creek. All belong to the Hovenweep group of villages. To reach any of these sites, you turn off the main road about one-half mile east of the Utah-Colorado state line, where a sign says HOVENWEEP. After you make the turn, the road to Horseshoe and Hackberry branches off to the left one-half mile south of the main road. This unimproved road to the two sites has some crankcase-bending, partially buried boulders as well as ruts and pools after rains, but it is passable by most vehicles with careful driving.

The D-shaped building known as Horseshoe House is the most interesting building at Horseshoe Pueblo. Horseshoe House was built facing the canyon overhang above an active spring. The standing double row of walls that can be seen in the aerial photograph was divided into three good-sized rooms, one on the east, one on the west, and one in the middle. There is no entrance to these rooms from ground level. In ancient times the building was taller, and the rooms were entered by ladders that led up to the second story. There were four small openings or peepholes in the outside wall of the center room, one in the wall of the east room, and one in the wall of the west room. Inside the open end of the horseshoe, partially encircled by the three outside rooms, was a circular room that may have been a kiva. This is a logical place for a kiva, but there is little evidence to support the notion that that is what the room was.

The Anasazi built a reservoir dam just to the west of Horseshoe House to stimulate the spring. Remnants of the old dam can be seen in the aerial photograph. In the canyon below Horseshoe House were several kivas and residential rooms. On the west side of the canyon stands a round tower. It was ideally located as a watchtower. Under the canyon rim is a small cliff dwelling, a kiva, and, on the wall, some ancient handprints.

The Horseshoe ruins indicate that the village there was not large. However, the structures at the site, particularly Horseshoe House, reflect the cooperative effort achieved by the people who did live there.

HACKBERRY PUEBLO

Although there is little to see here now, in its Pueblo III heyday Hackberry was a thriving village of as many as 250 to 300 people. Two strong springs ran from under the canyon rim. Room blocks and kivas were spread along the sides of the canyon both above and below the rim. The walls of room blocks on the west rim are still standing.

Beneath the canyon rim, next to the springs, were twelve residential rooms. Some handprints are still visible on the walls.

CUTTHROAT PUEBLO

Although Cutthroat was built during Pueblo III times and is contemporary with the other Hovenweep ruins, it differs in its settlement pattern. It was built astraddle a wash rather than at a canyon head. It is, however, similar to the Twin Towers–Rimrock House–Stronghold House group in Little Ruin Canyon. The wash at Cutthroat is still active with springs, as the vegetation along it shows. Most of Cutthroat's structures were built in the mid-1200s.

Reconstructed Three Kiva Pueblo, Montezuma Creek Canyon.

The dirt road into Cutthroat leaves the main road about eight miles northeast of the Hovenweep ranger station, next to a sign that reads HOVENWEEP. The road in, about two miles long, is usually rough and full of rocks and potholes. It's worth the drive, however, because at Cutthroat are a number of standing structures, six of which can be seen in the aerial photograph on page 130. Hovenweep National Monument's *Guide to Outlying Ruins* points out that the dirt road leads to a parking area and trailhead, and says further, "The trail register is 1/4 mile down the trail, across the cleared area. The ruins are another 1/2 mile. The ruins cannot be seen until you are almost among them." You can, however, drive down this last three-quarters of a mile to the ruins with an off-road vehicle.

The vegetation here is of the piñon-juniper variety. The site sits at a higher elevation than does the more arid region of Square Tower, Holly, and Cajon. Ian Thompson, in his *Towers of Hovenweep,* discusses the topography and vegetation of the Cajon Mesa from Pleasant View to Aneth, the region in which the Hovenweep ruins are located. He describes how the Cajon Mesa

The rooms built around the circular center room of Horseshoe House had no entrance at ground level, either from the inside or from the outside. Access was by ladders that led up to second-floor portals. A number of peepholes were set in the outside wall on the ground floor. The circular center room may have been a kiva, but no evidence other than the room's location supports that conclusion. West of Horseshoe House, the Anasazi built a dam to check the runoff water so it could soak through the sandstone and increase the flow of the spring below.

Horseshoe House, a D-shaped building at the Horse-shoe ruin (G-5), was built in the Pueblo III architectural style. Sun Temple at Mesa Verde is similar. In Horseshoe House, a circular center room is almost surrounded by a curved outside wall. Rooms were built between the center room and the outside wall. The front portion of the building is no longer standing.

About one-half mile northeast of Horseshoe is Hackberry (G-4), another canyon-head Pueblo III ruin. When occupied, it was a large village with 250 to 300 inhabitants. East Rim House, shown here, is all that remains of the structures that once stood on the east rim of the canyon. Arthur H. Rohn has identified three and possibly five kivas below East Rim House and one on the rim just to the north. On the other side of the canyon are six kiva depressions.

If from Holly you look to the southeast between Curved Wall Tower, left, and Great House, right, you can see Sleeping Ute Mountain on the horizon. Sleeping Ute Mountain is sacred to the Utes and Navajos, and we assume that it was sacred to the Anasazi as well. Curved Wall Tower consisted of a curved outside wall and a square interior building. Great House has the tallest standing walls of all the Hovenweep ruins.

This is a view of the Cutthroat site from the ground. From left to right are Northwest Tower, Cutthroat Castle, Stub Tower, and Round Tower. These buildings were surrounded by fourteen kivas. Nine kiva depressions lie on the northwest side of the wash and five on the southeast side near the round tower. Arthur H. Rohn estimates the village may have housed as many as 150 to 200 people.

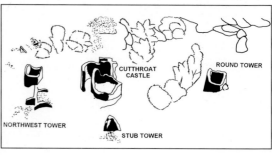

Cutthroat (G-4) was constructed by the Anasazi in the piñon-juniper region of the Cajon Mesa, at a higher elevation than the more arid sage land of Square Tower, Holly, and Horseshoe. The entire area covered by the photograph was once a pueblo, constructed, for the most part, in the mid-1200s. Only a few standing walls remain. The structures visible in the photo, from left to right, are Northwest Tower, Cutthroat Castle and Stub Tower, and Round Tower. Water came from the tree-lined wash that can be seen in the photograph. The photo was taken from the south.

Cutthroat Castle's architecture follows the "horseshoe" design so common in the Hovenweep settlements. Poised on a flat rock, the building extends over the cliff rim. Access to the lower-level rooms was through a crack in the base rock. A kiva was built inside a masonry circle. Its roof was supported by pilasters. The kiva's accoutrements—bench, fire pit, and deflector stone—were built in the Mesa Verdean style. These two photographs show the castle from two different angles.

This two-story tower, called Round Tower, was built across the wash from Cutthroat Castle. The tower was constructed with pecked sandstone. Each stone was fitted into the round walls and held in place with mud mortar.

slopes downward from Cutthroat to Cajon and becomes more arid as it nears the San Juan River. As it becomes drier, the vegetation changes from piñon-juniper at Cutthroat (the same type found at Mesa Verde) to desertlike sage and shrub at Cajon.

The wash at Cutthroat curves around the central group of structures, the largest of which is Cutthroat Castle. In ancient times the stream was dammed to make a reservoir. The remains of several terraces lie along the banks of the stream.

Cutthroat Castle was a three-story, D-shaped structure similar to Horseshoe House. Its base is a huge sandstone slab. A tunnel leads through a crack in the slab, providing a passageway up from the lower-level room. On the upper level, a central kiva was surrounded by a circular wall that was inset into a second circular wall. A two-story building was attached to the north side of the castle.

Flanking the castle on the east and west are two round towers known as Northwest Tower and Round Tower. The Hovenweep guide pamphlet points out that the towers were used as habitation, as granaries, or for some religious purpose, but that their general appearance is far more suggestive of forts or defensive units. The consensus on the purpose of Pueblo III Anasazi towers has recently begun to swing from "ceremonial" to "defensive" as archaeologists discover more and more evidence of unrest, warfare, and killing during late Pueblo times.

Cutthroat was a sizable settlement, having some 150 to 200 people. The principal part of the settlement surrounded Cutthroat Castle on the northwest side of the wash and included residential structures and at least nine kin kivas. Across the wash to the southeast were four or five kivas built next to Round Tower. The unusually large number of kivas suggests that Cutthroat may have functioned as a ceremonial center for the surrounding Hovenweep pueblos.

CAJON PUEBLO

Cajon, the southernmost Hovenweep ruin, became part of the national monument in 1923. It is surrounded by the Navajo Indian Reservation. The State of Utah has surfaced the road into the Hovenweep National Monument headquarters and ranger station. Utah 262 is surfaced from U.S. 191 south of Blanding, past the Hatch Trading Post, and all the way to the monument headquarters, except for a short gravel stretch east of Hatch. About one-half mile west of the Hovenweep headquarters entrance road that branches off the Hatch-Ismay-Cortez road, a good gravel road leads off southwest to Aneth. A bit more than two and one-half miles along this road, a dirt track to the west leads to Cajon. A battery of oil tanks stands just north of the ruin. If you follow the Aneth road off the mesa, you have missed Cajon.

Most of the construction of this small Pueblo III canyon-head village took place during the 1200s. Like all canyon-head pueblos, it surrounded a spring—in this case, more than one—coming from the cliff beneath the canyon rim. And as did the Anasazi at the other canyon-head pueblos, those at Cajon built a catch dam to feed the water source. At Cajon, this dam stood about one hundred yards up the mesa.

Today, almost all of the buildings on the east rim of the canyon, and the kivas below the rim, are just a pile of rubble. Beneath the east rim, however, are interesting pictographs on the room wall of a small cliff dwelling. Some are similar to Mesa Verde pottery decoration, with interlocking key-shaped frets. One pictograph is a four-legged animal with a birdlike body.

The most spectacular building at Cajon is a round tower fitted on the contours of a huge boulder. Known as Round Boulder Tower, it originally stood two stories high and had a room in the boulder at its base. Although many Anasazi towers are now thought to have been part of defense systems, this one was built down in the canyon, much lower than the two buildings on the west rim above. It may have been built as a tribute to the spring. A look around tells you that this is dry country, almost desert. Yet the Anasazi survived here, for a few generations at least, depending upon dryland farming. Why did the Cajon Anasazi choose to live on this dry mesa instead of along the banks of the San Juan River, about four miles away? Defense seems a logical explanation.

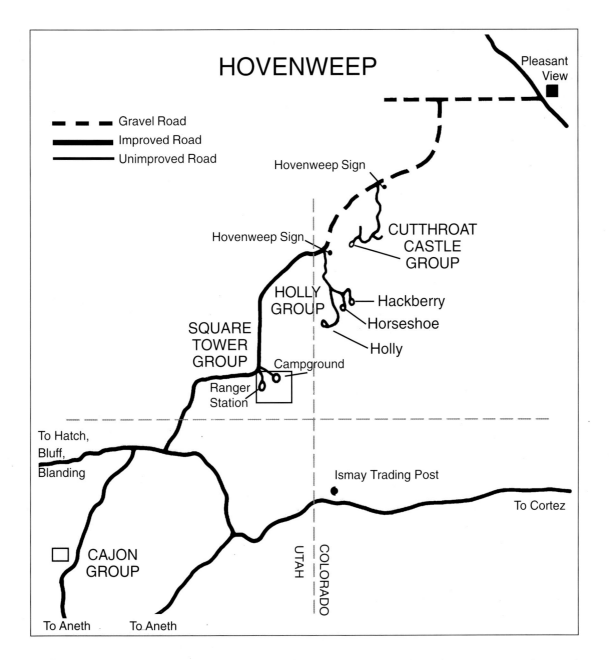

The two-story buildings on the west rim of Cajon Canyon are Observation Tower, to the north, next to the canyon head, and Great House, just above Round Tower. Two kin kivas lay on the slope below Great House.

Ray A. Williamson, in his book *The Living Sky*, notes that the south wall of Observation Tower is built along an imaginary line that points exactly to the places on the horizon where the sun rises and sets on the spring and fall equinoxes. He suggests that Great House and Observation Tower "operate with respect to each other as a giant yearly sundial, marking the seasons for all to see." In September, on the evenings after the fall equinox, Great House casts a shadow on the tower that grows day by day until the winter solstice in December and then recedes until the spring equinox in March. Modern Pueblo dwellers coordinate their ceremonies with the movements of the sun, and we assume the ancient Anasazi, their forebears, followed similar practices.

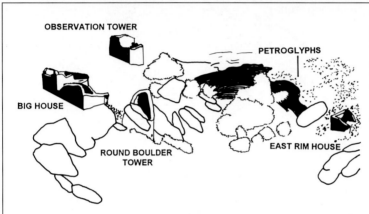

Cajon Pueblo (F-6) sur-rounded the canyon head shown in this photograph. The site is about four miles north of the San Juan River, near Aneth, Utah. Cajon is the lowest in elevation and far-thest southwest of all the Hov-enweep National Monument ruins. The country here is desertlike. Pueblo III build-ings and kivas were built all around the canyon head, mostly during the early and mid-1200s. Beneath the rim on the north side of the canyon is a spring that was used by the Anasazi and, after prehistoric times, by the Navajos.

Across the canyon from Round Boulder Tower and beneath the canyon rim, the Anasazi painted these pictographs showing a four-legged animal and an abstract painting that uti-lizes the style that appears on Pueblo III pottery.

This photograph shows the west rim of Cajon Canyon. On the left, Big House, an Anasazi great house, sits just above the oval Boulder Tower. The tower was skillfully erected around and above a huge boulder that had long been separated from the canyon rim. To the right is Observation Tower. Its south wall, facing us in this photograph, is built along an imaginary line that points exactly east and west. Inside the room, next to that wall, are portals through which shafts of sunlight mark the fall and spring equinoxes and the summer and winter solstices at sunset on those four days.

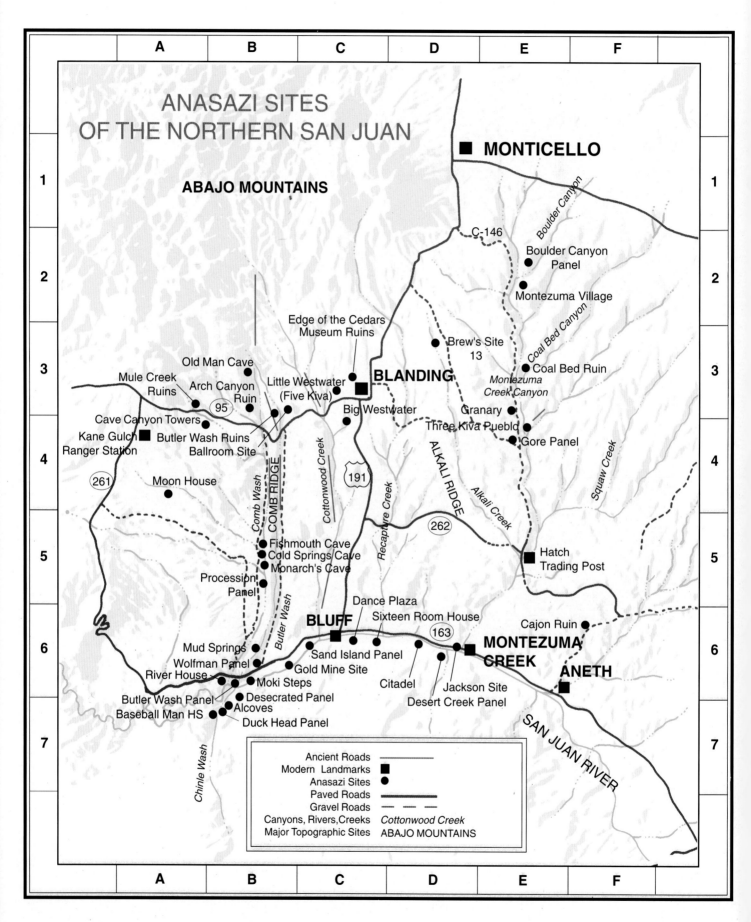

ANASAZI SITES OF THE NORTHERN SAN JUAN

■ **MONTICELLO**

ABAJO MOUNTAINS

C-146

Boulder Canyon
Panel

Montezuma Village

Edge of the Cedars
Museum Ruins

Brew's Site
13

Coal Bed Ruin

*Montezuma
Creek Canyon*

BLANDING

Old Man Cave

Mule Creek
Ruins

Arch Canyon
Ruin

Little Westwater
(Five Kiva)

Granary

Three Kiva Pueblo

Cave Canyon Towers

Big Westwater

Gore Panel

Kane Gulch
Ranger Station

Butler Wash Ruins

Ballroom Site

Moon House

Hatch
Trading Post

Fishmouth Cave

Cold Springs Cave

Monarch's Cave

Procession
Panel

Dance Plaza

Sixteen Room House

Cajon Ruin

BLUFF

**MONTEZUMA
CREEK**

Mud Springs

Sand Island Panel

ANETH

Wolfman Panel

Gold Mine Site

Citadel

Jackson Site

River House

Moki Steps

Desert Creek Panel

Butler Wash Panel

Desecrated Panel

Baseball Man HS

Alcoves

Duck Head Panel

SAN JUAN RIVER

Comb Wash
COMB RIDGE
Cottonwood Creek
Butler Wash
Recapture Creek
ALKALI RIDGE
Alkali Creek
Squaw Creek
Coal Bed Canyon
Boulder Canyon
Chinle Wash

95
261
191
262
163

Ancient Roads	
Modern Landmarks	■
Anasazi Sites	●
Paved Roads	
Gravel Roads	- - -
Canyons, Rivers, Creeks	*Cottonwood Creek*
Major Topographic Sites	ABAJO MOUNTAINS

Chapter Four

✪ *Southeastern Utah*

MONTEZUMA CREEK CANYON SITES

Southeastern Utah is gashed and crisscrossed by deep canyons. Some are forested and lined with brilliantly colored stone outcroppings; others are dry, barren, and terraced with exposed sandstone or limestone layers. Many canyons have sheer walls and are bottomed by wet-weather streams. Most of these canyons were inhabited at some time by the Anasazi. Montezuma Creek Canyon, cut by Montezuma Creek, runs north and south, beginning east and a bit south of Monticello, Utah, and extending to the San Juan River. The settlements in this canyon were close enough to the villages of Hovenweep and other pueblos of the Montezuma Valley that there must have been considerable interaction between them.

To reach Montezuma Creek Canyon, take road C-146, a reasonably good, unsurfaced mountain road that runs east from U.S. 191 five and one-half miles south of the center of Monticello and just north of Verdure. Beginning at seven thousand feet above sea level, it corkscrews with numerous S-turns for nearly six miles, beneath an electric power line, through groves of piñon pines, across cattle guards, and past a log corral, down some twelve hundred feet to Montezuma Creek at the bottom of the canyon. The canyon walls are lined on both sides with smooth gray sandstone. Normally the creek is shallow and slow running, but it can become a torrent if there are upstream rains.

The canyon system is like the backbone of a gigantic fish with numerous branch canyons that drain into Montezuma Creek Canyon from both sides. Northeast of Montezuma Creek, up Boulder Creek Canyon, is a petroglyph panel on the north canyon wall. The rock art includes circles, kachina figures, and a serpent that has been ritually killed with parallel cuts (//) across the figure. In addition, there are four-footed animals, a human figure with enormous testicles, and numerous abstract renditions. Farther up Boulder Creek Canyon, a stream pours spectacularly into a pool at the bottom of a cliff, creating a lovely green grotto. There is no evidence that the Anasazi lived in this canyon, nor are there any other signs of ancient construction near the rock art panel. The panel artists may simply have been attracted to the spot by the beautiful grotto. The ambiance of this grotto, canyon, and pool makes it easy to imagine bronze-skinned people bathing, splashing, and playing here hundreds of years ago.

Not far down Montezuma Creek Canyon, on the east canyon wall, is a spectacular series of Anasazi hand- and toeholds. This double series of toeholds winds from the brush-covered canyon floor up the gray sandstone canyon wall to the entrance of a small cavelike overhang. The cave is small, and no reported artifacts have been found there.

Another five miles down the canyon is a vineyard and a Quonset building surrounded by a new fence. Behind these improvements, adjoining Montezuma Creek, are the ruins of Montezuma Village. Some ninety to one hundred house mounds are located there. This large village is now on private land and closed to the public.

Coal Bed Canyon winds into Montezuma Creek Canyon some twenty-two miles south of where road C-146 leaves highway 191. Near the road, where the two canyons meet, piles of rubble clearly mark the Coal Bed Canyon ruin, and a narrow road branches off the main road toward the east. This side road bends sharply back to the north and into a parking area in a

The Anasazi cut these hand- and toeholds into a wall of Montezuma Creek Canyon (E-2). They are located about one-half mile down the canyon from the point where road C-146 reaches the canyon floor. This type of access up the cliff walls is common all over Anasaziland. It is said that some Anasazi steps were designed to foil the unwary—if the climbers started with the wrong foot first, they became stymied about halfway up.

grove of huge cottonwood trees. Across the creek and up a steep embankment lies the lower level of the Coal Bed ruin.

Coal Bed Pueblo was an important Anasazi site during Pueblo I, II, and III times. Situated in Montezuma Creek Canyon at the junction of Montezuma and Coal Bed canyons, it was a stopping point on the ancient road along Montezuma Creek from the San Juan River. Pueblo I and II villages were built below the mesa and, in those days, on the west side of the wash. Montezuma Creek originally ran on the east side of the mesa. Now it skirts the mesa on the west side, next to the road. The heavy green area to the south of the mesa marks the rubble from the collapsed masonry buildings of at least ten housing groups. The Pueblo III ruins stood on top of the mesa. In ancient times, on the west side of the mesa was a more or less formal gateway or entrance to the cliff-top pueblo. Only some unexcavated Pueblo III kiva outlines are detectable on the mesa top.

On the east side of the Coal Bed settlement, next to the creek, is a large circle of rectangular cut stones. This ceremonial circle is flanked on the west by a line of nine upright stone monoliths about four feet tall and four or five feet apart. In ancient times these stones stabilized the east wall of a block of pueblo rooms.

A few hundred yards south of the Coal Bed ruin, the road turns west, makes a U-turn to the east, and then continues south. On the west side of the canyon at this point is a jeep trail leading out of the canyon. To the north of the jeep trail, on the west wall of the canyon, is a spectacular panel of rock art composed of more than a dozen humanlike figures. One is an abstract figure more than six feet tall.

Nestled in the cliffs on the west side of road C-146, south of the Coal Bed ruin, framed by the patina of desert varnish, are a number of now fenced-in Anasazi masonry structures. The inhabitants of these buildings were the rural people of the area, but likely they belonged to the Three Kiva Pueblo Community two and one-half miles farther south.

Before reaching Three Kiva, the road fords Montezuma Creek and continues south on the east side of the wash. A bit farther south, at twenty-seven miles from the start of road C-146, is the partially restored Three Kiva Pueblo.

Three Kiva Pueblo was occupied between A.D. 1000 and 1300, during Pueblo II and Pueblo III times. Archaeologists from Brigham Young University have restored one of the kiva roofs and installed a ladder for visitor access. The kiva was round and had a fire pit in the center. High storage shelves were built into the walls. Stone pilasters supported a heavy-timbered, flat roof. Surrounding the restored kiva are several standing masonry walls that originally formed the sides of fourteen rooms, three milling bins, and a turkey pen.

About seven miles south of Three Kiva, cut into the west canyon wall, is the Gore Rock Art Panel, which contains a spectacular series of figures. This panel is on private land but can be seen from the road. Most of the figures are not Anasazi. One group depicts three riders on horseback, probably Navajos or Utes, following a herd of seven deer or elk and four buffalo. There were no horses in the Americas in Anasazi times. The Spaniards introduced horses to the Southwest much later. Another portion of the panel shows abstract lines, circles, and other geometric shapes as well as deer and humanlike figures. One of the most charming depictions displays two pairs of dancing cranes or snowy egrets. These birds are in the Anasazi style, but Sally J. Cole, a rock art expert, believes they were done in later times by Navajos. The Gore Panel is only about one-half mile north of the place where road C-146 ends at its intersection with road C-206, which runs east from Blanding, Utah. From the intersection, road C-206 winds south until it reaches the Hatch Trading Post. It then goes on to the Hovenweep National Monument.

Hatch is an active but isolated Indian trading post. It has a limestone south facade with protruding poles that mark the second floor. Above the poles is an undecorated limestone cornice, and above that a simple wooden sign displaying only the white, painted word HATCH. On the eastern horizon is etched the blue outline of the Sleeping Ute peak, a unique mountain because it seems to offer the same profile from every direction. The Sleeping Ute is visible from most of the Northern San Juan region.

These four-foot stone pillars made up part of a masonry wall at Coal Bed Pueblo. The stone wall that was built between the pillars has crumbled away. The remains of masonry room blocks are visible behind the pillars.

Three Kiva Pueblo (E-4) is so called because, over time, three kivas were part of the settlement.

The remains of an Anasazi stone storage granary stand against the west wall of Montezuma Creek Canyon, south of the Coal Bed ruins. The granary is now protected by a fence.

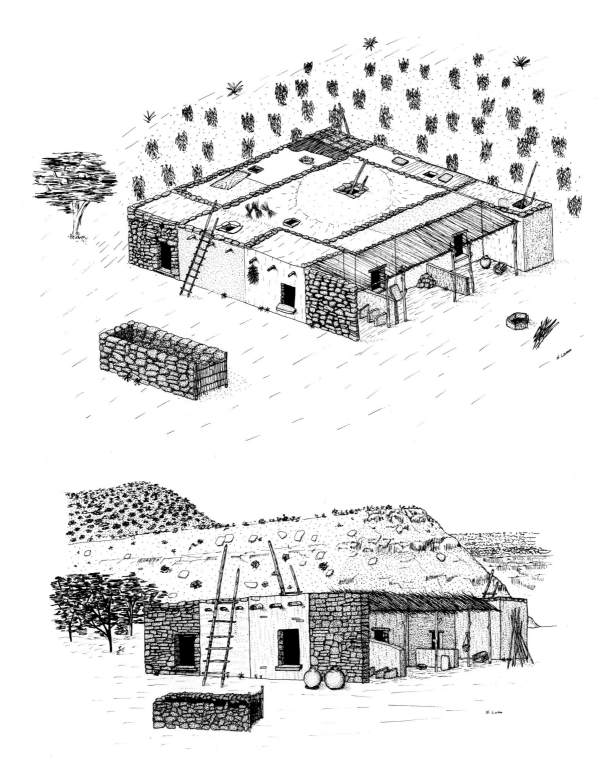

ARTIST'S RECONSTRUCTION OF THREE KIVA

Two reconstruction drawings of Three Kiva in Pueblo III times, around 1000: the first a view from the top showing how the central kiva was surrounded by living and storage units, a ramada, and a cornfield in the background. In the foreground is an open air work place. Note at the lower left a kneeling room where Anasazi women gathered to grind corn. Access to the rooms was both from the ground level and by ladder through a hole in the roof. Rooftop holes could be covered.

The second view shows the outside work areas, the canyon walls, corn fields, and the thatch-covered ramada. The Anasazi lived and worked outside, weather permitting, and in the kivas during cold and inclement weather. Drawing by Nancy B. Lamm.

The reconstruction of Three Kiva Pueblo includes a roofed kiva with an opening in the roof and access by ladder. In this photo, one side rail of the ladder is longer than the other. This was common among the Anasazi and was designed to give the older folks a handhold before stepping down to the first rung below.

This view of the restored interior of the kiva at Three Kiva Pueblo shows the entrance ladder, a fire pit, and masonry walls with pillars to support the roof. The underside of the cribbed roof consists of poles that are crisscrossed on top of each other. The bottommost poles rest on top of the pillars. The top layers of poles are covered with branches and mud to make a flat surface above. This method of construction was used both when the kiva was aboveground, as this one is, and when it was belowground, as are kivas in the Mesa Verde cliff dwellings.

These beautiful waterbirds appear on the Gore Panel, high on the west wall of Montezuma Creek Canyon, at the top of a talus slope about seven miles south of Three Kiva. The panel is located near road C–146, just before the junction with road C–206, which runs east from Blanding, Utah. The rock art is on private land, but it can be seen from the road. The birds look like Anasazi work, but because the petroglyphs are so bright, it is more likely that they were done in later times by the Utes or Navajos. It is not uncommon to find relatively recent rock art that emulates that of the Ancient Ones.

BREW'S ALKALI RIDGE SITE 13

About ten miles south of Monticello, a gravel road leaves U.S. 191 at Devil's Canyon and crosses the mesa called Alkali Ridge for about seventeen miles to road C-206, the Blanding road. The mesa runs parallel to Montezuma Creek Canyon, which lies to the east. Alkali Ridge contained some small, scattered settlements during the late Basketmaker and early Pueblo I periods. During the 700s these settlements were consolidated into a large pueblo that is now called Brew's Alkali Ridge Site 13. This site is seven and one-half miles south of U.S. 191 on the Alkali Ridge road.

On Alkali Ridge, the land was level and the soil good. But the village was not long lasting. After the land had been farmed for a few generations, it became less productive, and the villagers moved. By 900, at the end of the Pueblo I period, there seems to have been migration out of Alkali and most of the Northern San Juan region. Some archaeologists suggest that the Anasazi who left moved into Chaco Basin to the south.

Although the top of Alkali Ridge seems to have been largely deserted by 900, activity continued in Montezuma Creek Canyon to the east, where the large Coal Bed Pueblo flourished during Pueblo II times.

In 1965 Brew's Alkali Ridge Site 13 was designated by the National Park Service as a Registered National Historic Landmark. This is indicated by a bronze plaque set in a masonry pilaster at the site. The site is now overgrown with sage. A visit to this site requires a little imagination because, other than the plaque, a few sage-covered rock piles are the only evidence that a village existed here twelve hundred years ago.

Site 13, excavated by John Otis Brew, is one of the few excavated Pueblo I villages. The restoration drawings are based on Brew's work at Alkali Ridge in the 1930s. They show what a Pueblo I settlement was like in the A.D. 700s. The more inclusive drawing shows only about one-third of the original village.

Imagine this village in the 700s. People lived, worked, and raised their families here. The L-shaped buildings in which they lived partially enclosed a large plaza that contained four underground pithouses. Some of the rooms had masonry walls, others had walls of jacal. Stone slabs outlined the base of some of the rooms. The larger rooms were for sleeping; the rooms at the back were for storage.

The Anasazi were outdoor people. They lived outside whenever possible and in the pithouses during inclement weather. The pithouses were heated by a fire pit located under the roof opening. Some of the aboveground rooms had fire pits as well. Note the thatch-covered, open room. A *metate* (grinding bin) is shown on the left side of the floor of this room. Grinding corn was a daily task. In the plaza, the fenced pen was used to hold turkeys, and the slab hearths were used for cooking.

Access to the rooms was by small doorways and by ladders from the rooftops. The underground pithouses also were reached by a ladder through a hole in the roof. One side rail of the ladder was longer than the other to serve as a handhold. (The Anasazi had elderly people, too.) The rooms had no windows. The small openings shown in the drawings are doorways. Note the stone slab next to one of the doorways. It was used to close the doorway opening. The room directly to the left has its slab in place.

The methods used to build the structures shown in the drawings continued for more than five hundred years. The roofs of the pithouses and of the aboveground rooms were made of poles and branches covered with adobe. These roofs were solid and watertight. The poles were laid horizontally, and the spaces between them were filled with smaller branches and mud. Pithouse roofs were level with the plaza.

All the poles and branches used in the village were cut with stone axes. Researchers have estimated that it takes about six thousand strokes of a stone ax to fell a small tree. And that was only one part of the tedious construction process for the Anasazi.

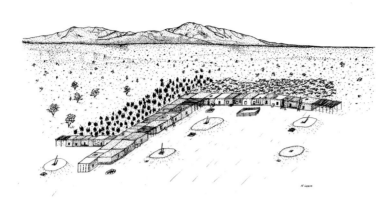

This is a drawing of how Plaza 1 at Site 13 (D-3) may have looked, based on Brew's excavation report. The Abajo Mountains rise in the background. The Anasazi began to build this pueblo around A.D. 700. It consisted of above ground rooms of masonry and jacal (brush covered with mud). The one-story rooms were arranged around a plaza in which pithouses were dug. Construction continued at the site for six hundred years. Drawing by Nancy B. Lamm.

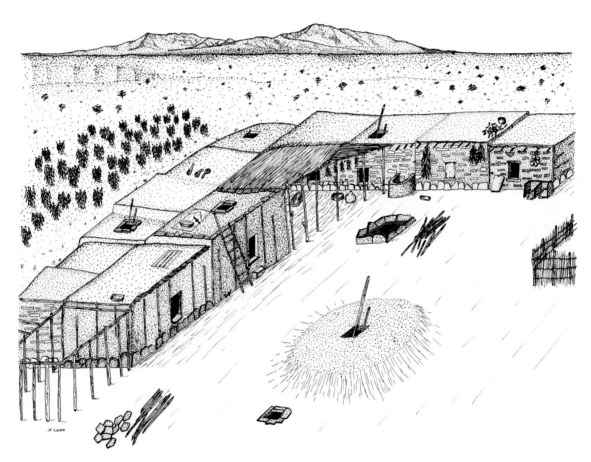

Here is another drawing of a portion of the Site 13 Pueblo I village on Alkali Ridge. Brew referred to the walls of the living quarters as having been of "post-and-adobe construction." Masonry storage rooms stood in the rear—a characteristic of Anasazi pueblo construction that lasted until 1300. In the plaza, the entrance to a pithouse is shown. The two poles protruding from the entrance are the side rails of a ladder. The pithouse design later evolved into the kiva. Brew suggests that Site 13 is one of the oldest known sites that show the Anasazi having moved their cooking and other daily activities from pithouses to places aboveground. The ramada, the arborlike room with a brush-covered roof, center, was used for grinding corn, cooking, and other activities. Some of the rooms had ground-level access, and others could be entered by ladder through rooftop openings. Drawing by Nancy B. Lamm.

SAN JUAN RIVER SITES

For thirteen hundred years the Anasazi lived on the banks of the San Juan River, and their predecessors, the Archaic people, were there as early as 6500 B.C. The Mesa Verde–Northern San Juan Anasazi occupied the banks of the San Juan and its tributaries from Chimney Rock in southern Colorado to Comb Ridge. They lived on both sides of the river. Before the river was impounded by the Navajo Dam, it was generally low enough to wade across. The San Juan served as a highway connecting the Mesa Verde and Kayenta Anasazi. Its banks were populated by Anasazi from Basketmaker times, perhaps as early as A.D. 1, to the abandonment of the region in the late Pueblo III period, after A.D. 1250.

The San Juan River is some 25 million years old. Geologic formations from 350 million years ago, in the early Pennsylvanian Period, to 20 million to 30 million years ago, in the Tertiary Period, can be seen along its banks between Montezuma Creek and Chinle Wash.

The most feasible way to see the ruins and rock art along the banks of the San Juan is to float down the river in a raft. Numerous commercial outfitters are available. One of these is Wild Rivers Expeditions, which has its headquarters at Bluff, Utah. Or you can do it yourself if you have the expertise, equipment, and a permit from the Bureau of Land Management. Commercial outfitters furnish rafts, food, and equipment and put ashore at the most interesting sites. At the flow rate of the San Juan, which is regulated by the Navajo Dam, the trip, including stops, takes five to ten hours between Montezuma Creek and Sand Island, and two to three days if you continue on down through the rapids to Mexican Hat, Utah. A useful guidebook for the river is Stewart Aitchison's *A Naturalist's San Juan River Guide*.

After the San Juan River leaves the Four Corners, it flows northwest into southeastern Utah. From Montezuma Creek to Comb Ridge were ancient settlements of Archaic and Anasazi Indians. The river here is relatively slow flowing and shallow. There is no known evidence that the Anasazi had boats, but the river and the valley were easily traversable. Settlements were built along the banks, in the cliffs, and on the terraces above. River rafters regularly run the river from Montezuma Creek to Mexican Hat, Utah.

Two interesting sites along the San Juan between Montezuma Creek and Chinle Wash are reachable without rafting: Sixteen Room House and the Sand Island Rock Art Panel.

Much of northeastern Arizona, a large area of New Mexico from Gallup north to the Colorado line, and a section of southeastern Utah are all part of the Navajo Indian Reservation. The Utah portion includes the region west of the Colorado-Utah state line, beginning south of Hovenweep and extending to the town called Montezuma Creek. Navajo land then follows the south bank of the San Juan River, Lake Powell, and the Colorado River to the Grand Canyon. The San Juan River Anasazi sites south of the river are all located on Navajo land.

Sixteen Room House

A swinging footbridge used regularly by the residents of the south side of the San Juan spans the river about four miles east of Bluff. Park your car next to the cliff by the river and cross the swinging bridge. A road leads to the base of the cliffs overlooking the river. High in the cliff on the south side of the river you can see a semicircular ring of masonry buildings known as Sixteen Room House. A trail leads up the talus slope and into the ruin.

This Pueblo III Mesa Verdean cliff dwelling sits on a rock shelf at the back of a large alcove facing the river. A curtain wall was built in front of the living quarters. There are three two-story rooms on the east side of the cliff dwelling. They are large by Mesa Verdean standards—about ten feet by twelve feet. One of these rooms had a central fire pit. Arthur Rohn suggests the room may have served as a kiva. There are no kiva depressions on the slope below the rooms. The upper floors were interconnected by doorways. Single-story rooms, probably with access through the roofs, extend to the west. Some have peepholes in the walls that look toward the river. The fortlike characteristics of Sixteen Room House are shared by many Pueblo III cliff dwellings in southeastern Utah.

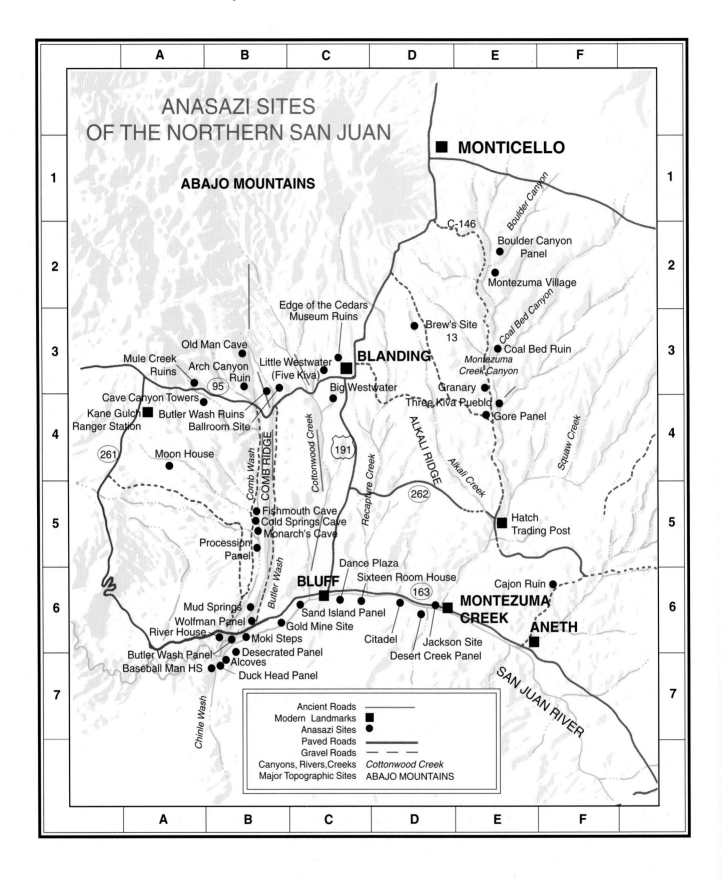

ANASAZI SITES OF THE NORTHERN SAN JUAN

ABAJO MOUNTAINS

■ **MONTICELLO**

C-146

Boulder Canyon Panel

Montezuma Village

Edge of the Cedars Museum Ruins

Brew's Site 13

Coal Bed Ruin

Old Man Cave

BLANDING

Montezuma Creek Canyon

Mule Creek Ruins

Little Westwater (Five Kiva)

Arch Canyon Ruin

95

Big Westwater

Granary

Three Kiva Pueblo

Gore Panel

Cave Canyon Towers

Kane Gulch Ranger Station

Butler Wash Ruins

Ballroom Site

261

Moon House

191

262

Hatch Trading Post

Fishmouth Cave
Cold Springs Cave
Monarch's Cave

Procession Panel

Dance Plaza

Sixteen Room House

Cajon Ruin

BLUFF

163

MONTEZUMA CREEK

Mud Springs

Sand Island Panel

Wolfman Panel

ANETH

River House

Gold Mine Site

Moki Steps

Citadel

Jackson Site

Butler Wash Panel

Desecrated Panel

Desert Creek Panel

Baseball Man HS

Alcoves

Duck Head Panel

Comb Wash

COMB RIDGE

Cottonwood Creek

Butler Wash

Recapture Creek

ALKALI RIDGE

Alkali Creek

Squaw Creek

Coal Bed Canyon

Boulder Canyon

Chinle Wash

SAN JUAN RIVER

Ancient Roads	
Modern Landmarks	■
Anasazi Sites	●
Paved Roads	
Gravel Roads	
Canyons, Rivers, Creeks	*Cottonwood Creek*
Major Topographic Sites	ABAJO MOUNTAINS

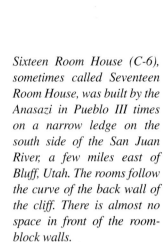

Sixteen Room House (C-6), sometimes called Seventeen Room House, was built by the Anasazi in Pueblo III times on a narrow ledge on the south side of the San Juan River, a few miles east of Bluff, Utah. The rooms follow the curve of the back wall of the cliff. There is almost no space in front of the room-block walls.

The excavated portion of Sixteen Room House consists of a single line of rooms, some of them two stories high. The rooms were constructed in the Pueblo III Mesa Verdean style. The cliff dwelling faces the north and the San Juan River. On the east side of the site are three two-story rooms that were connected with each other by doorways. The nine single-story rooms to the west, shown in this photograph, were reached by openings in the roofs. One first-floor room of a two-story dwelling has a circular hearth pecked into the bedrock, which suggests to Arthur Rohn that it might have been used as a kiva. There are no other kivas at the site.

The Basketmaker-style depictions on the Sand Island Rock Art Panel are not without whimsy—here we have a sheep playing a flute. The sheep just below the one with the flute seems to be dancing.

The crisscross lines on the petroglyph at the center of this photo are characteristic of Archaic rock art. That figure and the ones on either side of it probably date from as early as 6000 to 2000 B.C.

This section shows, center left, a hunter shooting a mountain sheep with a bow and arrow. Because the bow and arrow did not come into use until A.D. 500, in Basketmaker times, these figures likely were carved during the late Basketmaker or early Pueblo period.

On the left side of this photo, note the Kokopelli figure with an enormous phallus, playing a flute. In the center of the photo are two large "scalps with handles" and two linked, broad-shouldered figures. On the right is another Kokopelli. These petroglyphs were probably pecked during early Basketmaker times. Sally J. Cole has identified the scalp figures by their similarity to actual scalps found in the early 1900s. Scalping probably continued through Anasazi times and beyond the prehistoric period. The scalp figures are symbols of death, fertility, and rebirth.

Sand Island Rock Art Panel

Sand Island Recreational Area, the launching site for raft trips down the San Juan River, is also the location of a spectacular and varied rock art panel (C-6) that is easily reached. This view looks downriver. In the background, the dark line that extends over the river is the bridge for U.S. 191, which leads to Mexican Water, Arizona. Visible near the center of the horizon is the standing rock formation known as Mule Ear.

Drive west from Bluff for about five miles to the Sand Island Recreational Area on the river. Downriver a few hundred yards from the entrance, on the face of the cliff, is a magnificent rock art panel with a maze of petroglyph figures that have been carved over a span of thousands of years by Archaic people, Anasazi (Basketmaker through Pueblo III), and Utes and Navajos.

A short climb up the talus slope at the base of the cliff from the parking area brings you to over one hundred yards of petroglyphs. The oldest, displaying crisscross motifs that look like snowshoes, were carved by the Archaic people. An Archaic carbon-dated sandal found at Old Man Cave north of the river dates from 6470 B.C., which indicates the possible age of some of these figures. The square-shouldered figures were made by the Basketmaker Anasazi. Note the *Kokopellis* (humpbacked flute players) and the mountain sheep playing a flute. Kokopelli is the name of a Hopi kachina. The figures on the Sand Island Rock Art Panel are prehistoric figures and therefore not Hopi, but the "Kokopelli" designation for them is almost universally recognized.

This display of rock art tells us that the San Juan has been a highway since ancient times. Although rock art is scattered throughout the Southwest, much of it is difficult to reach. The Sand Island Panel contains a wonderful assortment that is easy to get to.

Jackson Ruin

The Anasazi ruins along the San Juan between Montezuma Creek and Sand Island are unexciting for many nonarchaeologists and take a little imagination to be enjoyed. The archaeologist's knowledge of pottery and masonry, however, makes it possible to read the history of these sites and bring them to life. Pottery *sherds* (fragments) are the key to determining who lived here and when.

On a rafting tour of the San Juan sites, the first stop below Montezuma Creek will probably be the Jackson Ruin, which was first reported by William H. Jackson in the 1870s. Here two small Pueblo III rooms are fitted under an overhang at the canyon head on the north bank above the landing site. The Anasazi created these two little storage rooms by digging out a space in the back of the overhang and building a wall across the front. The masonry of one of the rooms is different from that of the other. Each room was built by a different group of people, yet the structures were joined together. The Anasazi employed this technique in most of their buildings, including the cliff dwellings. Each family built its own masonry rooms for living or storage, and the rooms of different families were connected to one another. Except for the great houses of Pueblo II times, Anasazi residential structures were not preplanned.

On the plain above the storage rooms are huge piles of masonry rubble, the remains of Pueblo II and Pueblo III occupations. The Pueblo III Anasazi built a fairly large pueblo here with three-story living quarters and a number of kivas.

The pottery found at the Jackson Ruin includes Mancos Black-on-white, La Plata Black-on-red, Tusayan Corrugated from Kayenta, and Mancos Corrugated. Together with the masonry remains, the pottery sherds tell us that this area was occupied for two hundred to three hundred years.

Under the bluff next to the river are three small Mesa Verde cliff dwellings.

Desert Creek Rock Art Panel

The Desert Creek Panel, across the river from the Jackson Ruin, at the spot where the Desert Creek wash empties into the San Juan, displays beautiful and unique examples of petroglyphs and pictographs.

The Citadel

The Citadel site occupies a mesa on a narrow promontory on the south side of the river, about five miles east of Bluff. Across the canyon on the east side of the promontory is a huge mound of wind-blown sandstone rising out of the riverbed scrub. On the cliff face of this mound, a winding path of hand- and toeholds leads to the top. The cliff is of shiny, salmon-colored *slickrock* (Navajo sandstone), and the hand- and toeholds look like a series of painted black dots running up and across the cliff.

At the Citadel site itself, the Anasazi built a rectangular, multistory group of rooms. Hand- and toehold steps lead from the canyon on the west side of the site. Pottery sherds at the Citadel are a mixture of Mesa Verdean and Kayentan styles. The masonry is Mesa Verdean. Arthur Rohn suggests this site was a ceremonial shrine, because of its location overlooking the river and because there is no evidence of habitation.

Dance Plaza Site

This site sits on a high cliff on the south side of the San Juan, about two miles upriver from Bluff and about a mile and a half downriver from Sixteen Room House. The Dance Plaza is a rectangular, open great kiva measuring about ninety feet by thirty-five feet. It consists of Mesa Verde–style pecked-stone masonry. At the site are traces of room blocks with multicoursed walls. The pottery sherds are Mesa Verde Black-on-white. Arthur Rohn has determined that the Anasazi built the great kiva after A.D. 1050.

The most interesting aspect of the Dance Plaza Site is the petroglyphs carved on two large upright slabs. Rohn suggests that because the slabs fell in such an upright position, the spot may have been dedicated as a shrine, the slabs themselves representing deities similar to the twin war gods of the modern Pueblo and Zuni peoples.

Some of the petroglyphs are incised in the rock and have an Archaic look. The crablike figure is probably a broad-shouldered Basketmaker. The squiggles, mazes, concentric circles, footprint, and lizard man were done in Pueblo times. The round-shouldered figure with a round head and two antennae may be Pueblo I.

East of the Dance Plaza are the remains of a Kayenta residential site with pottery dating from A.D. 700 to 1050. The pottery includes Lino Black-on-gray, Kana-a Gray, Black Mesa Black-on-white, Tsegi Orange, Tusayan, and Corrugated. Here, too, is some Kayenta masonry. However, the site shows evidence of both Kayenta and Mesa Verde occupation. The time span, based on the pottery, extends from Basketmaker to Pueblo III times.

Gold Mine Site

By now the float trip will have passed Bluff and Sand Island. Two miles downriver from Sand Island, the rafts land on the north shore, at the Gold Mine Site. Farther downriver the rafts may stop at the Moki Steps, Butler Wash Rock Art Panel, Desecrated Panel, River House, and Great Kiva, and at the Chinle Wash locations of the Baseball Man panel, the Duck Head panels, and the Chinle Wash Alcoves cliff dwellings.

The Gold Mine Site is about two miles downriver from Sand Island. The site was mined in historical times, and some of the old mining machinery is still there. The Anasazi ruins at the site, judging from pottery found there, were inhabited from A.D. 900 to 1100, during Pueblo II times. Much of the rock art at the site, however, is probably from the Basketmaker period.

At the Gold Mine Site, a small granary may be seen under an overhang, with hand- and toeholds leading up from the talus slope below. On the ledge below the granary is a double-circle figure with legs. This image may consist of two figures, one superimposed over the other. The circle is not a shield because shields didn't appear among the Anasazi until later, in Pueblo III times.

High on the cliff face above the granary is another panel, which depicts a row of mountain sheep and a broad-shouldered, big-handed Basketmaker figure with a small round head sprouting an antenna. However, it is a tough climb to reach this high ledge.

Moki Steps

The Moki Steps (*Moki* means *death* in the Hopi language) are more than simple hand- and toeholds. They are almost actual steps that wind up slickrock to a cliff. At the base of the steps are the remains of a Pueblo I settlement with sherds of Mesa Verde Moccasin Gray, Chapin Gray, and Piedra Black-on-white pottery. This site, like so many others along the San Juan, was occupied and reoccupied for hundreds of years. The site contains sherds of Pueblo II and Pueblo III pottery: Mancos Black-on-white, Mancos Corrugated, Mesa Verde Black-on-white, and McElmo Black-on-white. The site also has some Kayenta trade ware.

Also at the Moki Steps landing are the Kokopelli Panel and Ruin. One of the most unusual images on the panel is a broad-shouldered, big-handed, and big-footed Basketmaker figure falling headfirst down the cliff face, followed by his twine bag. He is falling toward a line of Kokopelli figures. Kokopelli is the most ubiquitous rock art figure along the San Juan River, and probably in the entire Southwest. He still appears in present-day Indian art as the Navajo Watersprinkler.

The red pottery scattered around the Kokopelli Ruin appears to be Bluff Black-on-red. There is some disagreement concerning this Red ware, but the consensus seems to be that it was developed along the western portion of the Northern San Juan and then died out by the A.D. 900s. Red ware, however, continued to be made in the Kayenta region as Tusayan Black-on-red and is found along the San Juan as trade ware.

High above the Moki Steps, on a ledge near the top of the cliff, is a rock art panel cut into the black desert-varnish patina. Included on the panel are a modern-looking duck, another bird, concentric circles, and a row of little Basketmaker figures with Hopilike whorls as headdresses.

Butler Wash Rock Art Panel

The junction of Butler Wash and the San Juan River must have been significant to the Anasazi, because a superabundance of rock art is found on both sides of the wash where it enters the river. Butler Wash Canyon extends north from the junction all the way to the Abajo Mountains. Along the canyon are many ruins and rock art displays. From the San Juan to U.S. 163, the canyon is deep and filled with brush. There are several small cliff dwellings along the way. North of the highway, Butler Wash parallels Comb Ridge. This ridge is cut by numerous canyons, most of which the Anasazi occupied at one time or another for more than a thousand years. Butler Wash and Comb Ridge divided the Mesa Verde Anasazi from the Kayenta Anasazi. There was interplay between them over time, but the wash and ridge generally marked the western edge of the Mesa Verde culture.

Spectacular rock art panels were carved on both sides of Butler Wash where it empties into the San Juan. On the upriver side, to the east, are figures with big hands and big feet and duck shapes as heads. There are also broad-shouldered Basketmaker figures. One big square-bodied figure has a small round head and two antennae.

We probably will never know what these figures meant to the Anasazi who carved them. Were they real people? Were they spirits, kachinas, ancestors, or deities? It is certain that they represented something specific because rock art figures of similar form and style appear in numerous places. The form and style did change from generation to generation, however, from Basketmaker to early and late Pueblo times, over as many as a thousand years.

On the downriver, or west, side of the mouth of Butler Wash is one of the most magnificent rock art panels in the Southwest. Known as the Butler Wash Rock Art Panel, it consists chiefly of a line of heroic figures that stretches along the cliff face, about twenty feet above the top of the talus slope. The figures were formed by carving into the patina that covers the cliff side to reveal the light-colored rock beneath. This startling array of broad-shouldered, humanlike figures shows a number of different headdresses. The figures are in the Basketmaker style, and Sally Cole feels they were done before A.D. 500. Other rock art at the same site includes a figure with crosshatches on its body. This figure was carved in Archaic times, hundreds or even thousands of years before A.D. 1. Kokopellis at the site are from Pueblo times.

Near the Butler Wash Panel are the remains of Anasazi habitations, including early Basketmaker slab structures—buildings whose lower walls consist of stone slabs—and some Pueblo II stone masonry and kiva depressions. Most of the pottery at this site is Mesa Verdean.

Desecrated Panel

About a mile downstream from Butler Wash, the direction of the San Juan swings from southwest to almost due south. The sandy valley cut by the river is wide there, with cliffs on both sides. Soon the river flows west again, and there on a cliff face is another display of Anasazi rock art. It is called Desecrated Panel because some of the figures on it have been partly or entirely chiseled out

About one and one-half miles downriver from the Gold Mine Site and some three and one-half miles from Sand Island are the Moki Steps (B-6). These steplike hand- and toeholds extend upward from a Pueblo I settlement on the canyon floor. Arthur Rohn notes that the pottery at this site indicates the Anasazi there were Mesa Verdeans. The site was also occupied later, in Pueblo II or Pueblo III times.

One of the most spectacular rock art panels in all of Anasaziland, and possibly in the world, covers a vertical cliff side where Butler Wash empties into the San Juan River (B-6). The petroglyph panel lies about four and one-half miles downriver from Sand Island. The broad-shouldered figures there, shown in these photographs, were probably carved sometime before A.D. 500.

and destroyed. Many other figures, however, are still untouched. The images on the panel date from Basketmaker to Pueblo III times.

According to river lore, during the 1950s there was a severe tuberculosis epidemic on the Navajo reservation. One of the families hit hard by the epidemic lived above the cliff that bears the rock art. The singer and medicine man who was called in to diagnose and treat the illness concluded the cause of the disease was the "bad energy" coming from some of the ancient figures on the cliff below. So family members rubbed, chiseled, and hammered away portions of the panel. Thus, the figures were ritually killed to destroy their power. Along the same cliff, the Anasazi had carved an undulating serpent about twenty yards long. To kill its evil power, it was slashed across the body every few feet. Recently a portion of the Butler Wash Panel—a portion depicting two Kokopellis, one with a flute and the other with a bow and arrow—has been defaced.

River House

On the north side of the San Juan River Valley, beneath an overhang in a cliff just to the east of Comb Ridge, is a delightful little cliff dwelling called River House. As you can see in the aerial photograph, the river valley is fairly wide here and there are a number of trees between the river and the cliff. It was here that the Kayenta Anasazi passed upriver into Mesa Verde territory, and here that the Mesa Verdeans could cross Comb Ridge west onto Cedar Mesa. It was also at this point that the Mormons in the 1800s crossed Comb Ridge into southeastern Utah, where they established Bluff, Blanding, and Monticello.

River House is well preserved and has seventeen or eighteen rooms and two kivas. The kivas are Mesa Verdean in style, but the masonry at River House is Kayentan. Some of the rooms in the two-story room blocks were small and had Mesa Verdean characteristics. Others were larger and show more Kayentan characteristics. Sometimes River House is called Serpent House because of the beautiful snake painted in ancient times across the cliff at the back of the pueblo. The painting was probably done long before the cliff dwelling was built. The body of the serpent is red and outlined in white. The name River House came from the early explorers' belief that the painting represented the river. River House and some small granaries nearby date from Pueblo III times.

On a shelf on the north side of the San Juan, where the river flows through Comb Ridge, are the ruins of a settlement with pithouse depressions, pottery of Pueblo I vintage, and housing units whose lower walls consist of stone slabs. At the same site are remnants of Pueblo II and Pueblo III construction. The most significant feature of this site is a circular great kiva about fifty feet in diameter. Tree-ring dates indicate the kiva was constructed around 1050.

Chinle Wash Ruins

From River House the San Juan starts its great loop south around Lime Ridge before flowing north into San Juan Canyon. A mile and a half downstream from River House, on the south side of the river, is the mouth of Chinle Wash. The river valley is wide and sandy here, where the wash makes a sharp turn west from its northerly course and flows into the San Juan from the east. Just

This figure from the Butler Wash Rock Art Panel sports some interesting paraphernalia: lines below his face that look like a beard or ear ornaments, a three-strand necklace, two wavy lines down his chest, six bars above his head, and four bars to his left. In addition, he wears a fringed waistband and displays his genitals.

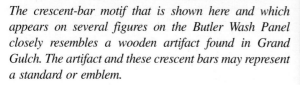

The crescent-bar motif that is shown here and which appears on several figures on the Butler Wash Panel closely resembles a wooden artifact found in Grand Gulch. The artifact and these crescent bars may represent a standard or emblem.

These two figures, one playing a flute and the other with a bow and arrow, and both with packs, were probably pecked during Pueblo II or Pueblo III times and could be referred to as Kokopellis. In 1991, after this photograph was taken, both figures were vandalized by chiseling and are probably beyond repair. They appear on the Butler Wash Panel.

Across the San Juan River from the Butler Wash Panel, and about a mile downstream, rises a cliff on which the Anasazi, over a period of hundreds of years, pecked, incised, and carved a rock art panel that, unfortunately, was partially defaced in recent times. It is called Desecrated Panel (B-7) because a number of the figures and parts of figures have been chiseled out. Local lore tells us that the chiseled figures were carefully selected for destruction to eliminate an evil and thus cure an ill patient living on the mesa above. This panel displays rock art from Archaic to Pueblo III times. The large rectangular sheep with a small head may date from before A.D. 1. To the right of the boulder, note the Flute Player, the broad-shouldered, big-handed Basketmaker figure, and the figure with the five bars above his head. The five-bar symbol resembles the emblems on the Butler Wash Panel. The destroyed figure above the five bars was a Basketmaker figure similar to the one in the lower right.

over a mile south of the San Juan, where the wash turns west, is a cliff dwelling containing some very interesting rock art. This pueblo, known as Baseball Man House, sits on the west side of the wash. On the east canyon wall are more cliff dwellings, in the Chinle Wash Alcoves.

This region is the setting for the conclusion of Tony Hillerman's novel *A Thief of Time*. Hillerman calls the region Many Ruins Canyon, but it is actually Chinle Wash Canyon.

Hillerman's Navajo Police Lieutenant Leaphorn describes the rock art on the canyon wall west of the wash: "It looked, as Etcitty had described it, 'like a big baseball umpire holding up a pink chest protector.'" The denouement of the story takes place near the cliff dwellings the Anasazi built in the canyon-wall alcoves across from this figure, which is known as Baseball Man.

Baseball Man Cliff Dwelling

At Baseball Man House, ten or twelve rooms are tucked under a narrow ledge. One of the rooms has a jacal wall. Below these rooms are the remains of more rooms and some kiva depressions.

This is an aerial view of River House (B-6) on the north side of the San Juan, some six and one-half miles downriver from Sand Island and just east of Comb Ridge. Many of the Anasazi buildings along the San Juan River have been destroyed by flooding over the centuries. River House has been spared because of its location in this cliff high above the floodplain.

This red-bodied snake, outlined in white, is found at River House. It once was thought to represent the river; hence the name River House. This painting was most likely done before the Pueblo III cliff dwelling was built. However, the large painted spirals on the cliff overhang, and the little white lizard man painted over part of the serpent, were done in the same period as the cliff dwellings, around 1200. Notice above the serpent a dark arch that was probably part of an earlier snake painting.

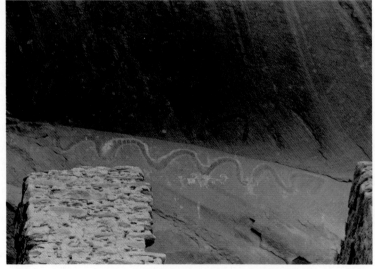

On a wall near Baseball Man House (B-7) is a rock art panel dominated by the famous "Baseball Man." This pictograph is a composite of two paintings. The first is a Basketmaker figure painted in white with broad shoulders and big hands. The second, added hundreds of years later, is a Pueblo III shield painted red and outlined in white. The combined pictograph is called Baseball Man because it looks like a baseball umpire to modern Americans.

Painted on a wall near the cliff dwelling is the Baseball Man figure, which is actually a combination of two images. One is a Basketmaker figure with broad shoulders and big hands. Over it is superimposed a shield of red and white that dates from Pueblo III times. The combination of the two figures is called Baseball Man because that is what it looks like to modern Americans.

Duck Head Rock Art Panel

Near the Baseball Man pictograph is a striking panel of figures cut into the dark brown patina of the rock. These figures, from Basketmaker times, are as clear as if carved only recently. The panel has two parts. The left part includes several figures whose heads are shaped like ducks. Two of these figures appear to be dueling with spears. Besides the duck-headed characters, there is a chicken-headed figure and a humanlike figure with birdlike feet. The other part of the panel shows a procession of figures, including a small serpent, a large bird, and a big-handed man. Near the procession is a large, reclining Kokopelli.

Chinle Wash Alcoves

Across from Baseball Man House, above a water catchment, are two alcoves in the sandstone cliff, one above the other. Each of these alcoves housed a cliff dwelling. The upper alcove had several rooms, and the lower one had a wall across the front with masonry rooms built into the wall. The defensive posture of these Pueblo III cliff dwellings was typical of such pueblos in southeastern Utah. Hand- and toeholds provided access up the face of the cliff.

The Duck Head Rock Art Panel (B-7), located near Baseball Man, gets its name from the duck-headed petroglyphs it contains. These petroglyphs appear in the upper photograph. The lower photograph shows another part of the panel, in which a big-handed figure is connected to a line that runs beneath a turkeylike bird and ends in a spiral. Beyond the spiral, note the line of small figures, each of which carries a backpack. They are going to the left, toward a small mountain sheep with bird feet and, beyond that, an open-mouthed snake. All this suggests a narrative starting with Big Hands and ending with the snake. The reclining Flute Player, or Kokopelli, is probably the most ubiquitous rock art figure in the Southwest. This one and the tiny one beneath Big Hands, as well as the big-handed man himself, were probably carved during the period in which the original Baseball Man cliff dwelling was built.

Chinle Wash flows to the San Juan River from the south, reaching it almost opposite Comb Ridge. There two cliff dwellings known as the Chinle Wash Alcoves (B-7) were built one above the other. The lower cliff dwelling had a wall across the front with masonry rooms attached to the wall. As you can see from the photograph, it was built in the mouth of a huge cave. The cave ceiling arches high above the house block. Below the Alcove sites, on a broad, flat valley floor, are the ruins of a Pueblo I and Pueblo II occupation, suggesting that this valley was more or less continuously occupied for fifteen hundred years.

As can be seen in the aerial photograph above, a broad, sandy terrace lies below the cliff face. This terrace was the site of several successive villages in Pueblo I and Pueblo II times. Pottery found there indicates both Mesa Verde and Kayenta influences. When the troubled times of Pueblo III arrived in the 1200s, flat-land settlements were abandoned, and the people moved into cliff dwellings such as the Chinle Wash Alcoves and Baseball Man House.

EDGE OF THE CEDARS STATE PARK

Edge of the Cedars Pueblo

The Edge of the Cedars Pueblo and Museum are on the west side of Blanding, Utah. The excavated and stabilized portion of the pueblo consists of a large interior kiva surrounded on three sides by room blocks. The pueblo is mainly a late Pueblo II settlement built on top of a late Pueblo I and early Pueblo II village. There is evidence of some remodeling and reoccupation in Pueblo III times. The Pueblo II construction included a great house (a structure with big rooms and an enclosed kiva) and a great kiva, which stood next to the great house. These attributes suggest Edge of the Cedars was a community center. Arthur Rohn calculates that the population may have reached 250. The pueblo was built in a beautiful spot: on top of White Mesa, in the shadow of the Abajo Mountains.

Blanding is a tranquil little town laid out on a Roman grid with exceptionally wide streets. It is said the streets were so designed to allow a wagon and team to turn around without backing up.

Edge of the Cedars Museum

The museum, operated by the State of Utah, was renovated and partially rebuilt in 1993. Around the outside are human-size, Rodinesque metal sculptures of Anasazi rock art figures. These sculptures were done by Joe Pachak, a local artist. Inside the museum building, in the stairwell, Joe has painted a startling mural incorporating regional rock art figures and motifs. The museum displays a variety of Anasazi artifacts that have been assembled over the years. Utah State Park rangers are on hand to assist visitors.

Some outstanding examples of the artifacts on display are shown in the photographs. The wooden-handled knives came from the Little Westwater (Five Kiva) cliff dwelling, south of Blanding, as did the assortment of *lithic* (stone) points.

The Anasazi were adept at making stone tools, as we can see from the hafted knives. Wood, stone, and bone were the principal materials in their tool kits. The only metal objects the Anasazi had were copper bells traded from Mexico.

The stone points represent a five-thousand-year evolution from spearheads to atlatl-dart heads to arrowheads. The small stone drill bit at the top of the photograph would have been *hafted* (attached) to an arrowlike shaft that could be spun with a bow to serve as a drill. The large piece in the center of the photograph is a knife blade that would have been glued to a wooden handle with pitch. The other artifacts are projectile points for darts, spears, or arrows.

A point's design is one of the keys to determining when the point was made and used. The big red San Jose point is an Archaic spearhead that may be up to four thousand years old. This point is similar to the famous Folsom Point, which was found embedded in the skeleton of an extinct type of bison and thus proved there were hunters in North America at least ten thousand years ago.

The largest points were for knives, the next-largest were for spears, somewhat smaller points were for atlatl darts, and the smallest were for arrows. Points are almost indestructible. They provide, along with pottery, architecture, and tree rings, a method of determining the age of prehistoric sites.

The portable loom, from late Pueblo III times, was found rolled up in a split-willow case. The Anasazi were expert weavers. Unfortunately, fabrics are so fragile that few produced by the Anasazi have survived. Weaving was done in the kivas using cotton and other plant fibers. One of the larger rods in the photograph was attached to the kiva roof and the other to the floor, creating an upright frame. The modern Pueblo blanket loom is similar to the Anasazi loom. The Anasazi weaver, who experts think was in most cases a man, sat on the ground in front of the loom and worked from bottom to top. The process is explained in detail in Nancy Fox's *Pueblo Weaving and Textile Arts*.

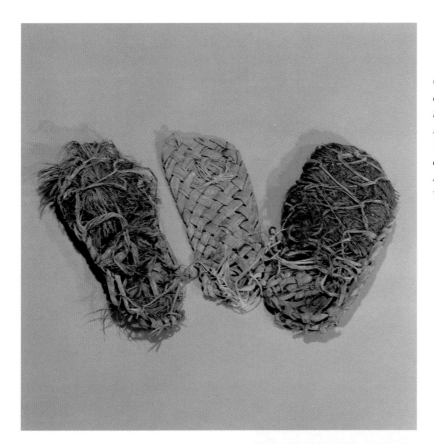

Generic Anasazi sandals, of types that were in use throughout the entire Pueblo period, from A.D. 700 to 1300. At the left and right are plaited sandals of yucca padded with cedar bark.

Just west of the Edge of the Cedars Museum building in Blanding, Utah, is a partially excavated pueblo. This late Pueblo II village was built over a Pueblo I and early Pueblo II settlement. In Pueblo II times, the site contained a great house and great kiva and at times may have housed some 250 people. The pueblo is part of the Chaco-influenced Mesa Verde Anasazi culture of southeastern Utah. This view looks to the northwest. The eastern slopes of the Abajo Mountains are visible on the horizon.

COMB RIDGE SITES

Called "The Comb" by the locals, Comb Ridge forms the east edge of an enormous *anticline* (convex upward fold) known as the Monument Upwarp. The rocks inside the upwarp have eroded away, leaving on the west side of the ridge a huge, serrated, steep-faced wall that is five hundred to one thousand feet high and runs from the Abajo Mountains west of Monticello all the way down into Arizona. The caprock on the east side of Comb Ridge is gray—sometimes almost white—*slickrock* (Navajo sandstone). Butler Wash follows the east side of the ridge, and Comb Wash the west side, from the Abajos to the San Juan River. Along both sides are unsurfaced roads that extend from Utah 95 to U.S. 163.

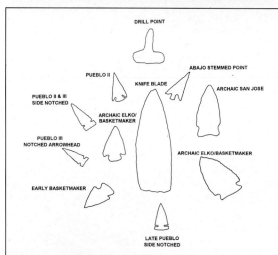

Anasazi points. The large point in the center is a knife blade found in the Natural Bridges region, about thirty-five miles west of Blanding. It would have been hafted to a wooden handle and held in place with pitch. A double-edged knife like this would have been used as a dagger or as a flesher to skin or cut up animals. Directly to the left of the knife blade is a red, corner-notched Elko point from Archaic times. The black, broad-based point at the top of the photograph is a drill bit that would have been attached to a thin shaft that could be spun with a bow to make holes in hides, fabric, or stone. Clockwise from the drill bit, the rest of the points are:

1. An Abajo stemmed point, a type that appeared first in the A.D. 700s, during late Basketmaker times, and continued into the 900s, in the Pueblo II period.

2. An Archaic San Jose spearhead that may be up to four thousand years old.

3. A corner-notched Archaic Elko point, or possibly a Basketmaker dart point.

4. A late Pueblo side-notched point used from the 1000s through the 1200s.

5. A late Archaic or early Basketmaker point that may date from 1500 B.C. to A.D. 500.

6. A Pueblo II or Pueblo III side-notched arrowhead.

7. A red, side-notched point from Pueblo II and III times.

8. A white point that probably dates from A.D. 900 to 1000, from Pueblo II times.

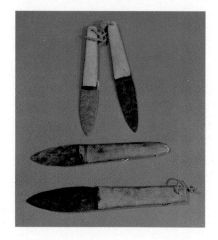

Knives from the Little Westwater (Five Kiva) ruin. These are typical Pueblo hafted knives that have a cutting edge similar to the knife blade in the photograph above. The Anasazi made a slot in the wooden handle and glued the blade into the handle with pitch.

Basket, ladle, and pot. The mat is a plaited ring basket. The Hopi still make baskets like this, though they add a willow shaft around the rim to give the basket a bowl shape. The type of basket in this photo appeared in late Pueblo times. By A.D. 1100, it was fairly common. The ladle and pot are Mancos Black-on-white.

An unusual olla (water jar) that was found under the streets, or in a field, at Blanding, Utah. Note the concentric circles at the corners—a common feature of smaller jars, but unique for a jar as large as this. The olla is decorated with a cross that resembles a Maltese cross and is sometimes called an Anasazi cross. This jar was used to hold water for ceremonies and dates from the A.D. 1000s.

This is a portable loom from late Pueblo III times. It was used to weave cotton and other fabrics. The split-willow mat at the top was used to encase the four rods shown below it. The two larger rods served as the loom's upper and lower bars. The weaver attached them to the roof and the floor to create a vertical frame. The two smaller rods were used to manipulate the shed (line across the top of the weaving). The Anasazi became skillful weavers when cotton became available in the A.D. 800s, though they did so perhaps a bit later in the Northern San Juan region.

This photo shows a nearly complete turkey-feather blanket. These blankets, used as robes, were made by the Anasazi and Pueblo Indians from Basketmaker times until after the end of the prehistoric period.

Cottonwood plates found in Westwater Creek Canyon. These Pueblo III plates are about twelve inches long and eight inches wide. Plates are not common at Anasazi sites, but others have been found at Mesa Verde.

Erosion has fractured and worn the east side of the ridge into a maze of canyons that resemble the teeth of a comb. In these canyons are the remnants of ancient occupation from Archaic times through the Pueblo III period.

Comb Ridge is bisected by the San Juan River, which cuts through the upturned beds of Mesozoic and Permian rocks, providing the only easy ancient passage from one side of the ridge to the other. Generally, the Comb marks the western boundary of the Mesa Verde–Northern San Juan Anasazi culture. West of Comb Ridge, Cedar Mesa marks the eastern end of Kayenta Anasazi

This aerial view of the west side of Comb Ridge from above Utah 95 shows Comb Wash extending along the ridge. The wash snakes its way south to the San Juan River. Cedar Mesa lies to the right of the wash. Comb Ridge tended to separate the San Juan Anasazi from the Kayenta Anasazi, though of course there was some contact. Ruins in the Comb Ridge region reveal elements of both Anasazi cultures.

country, where the Kayenta and Mesa Verde Anasazi cultures mixed. The Navajo National Monument, near Kayenta, Arizona, and Canyon de Chelly are the principal locations of Kayenta Anasazi ruins. For coverage of the Kayenta and Chaco Anasazi, see Ferguson and Rohn, *Anasazi Ruins of the Southwest in Color*. For a discussion and photographs of the rock art panel found where Butler Wash joins the San Juan River, see the section on the San Juan River Anasazi ruins.

Bluff, Utah, is a good starting point for a raft trip down the San Juan or a drive up the Butler Wash road on the east side of Comb Ridge. Bluff is a delightful old Mormon town first occupied in the 1880s. Its big Victorian houses were built by Mormon ranchers. Later, the ranchers moved north to Blanding. Bluff was settled because the gap that the San Juan River cut in the Comb allowed access to southeastern Utah from the west. The Comb was almost as impassable for the Mormons in the 1800s as it was for the Anasazi centuries before. In more recent years, modern road-building machinery has been used to create passages through Comb Ridge for U.S. 163 and Utah 95. By contrast, the Anasazi scaled the Comb from the west using hand- and toeholds.

If you drive west from Bluff on the highway that is both U.S. 191 and U.S. 163, you soon will see the white and gray wall of Comb Ridge. U.S. 191 then splits off south across the San Juan to Mexican Water, Arizona. Instead of going that way, continue on U.S. 163 for less than a mile and turn north off the highway onto a fair gravel road that follows Butler Wash seventeen miles to Utah 95. This gravel road is not bad in good weather, but it crosses several deep arroyos that empty into Butler Wash from the mesa to the east.

All the way up to Utah 95, Comb Ridge's sun-reflecting slickrock looks like a comb in the western sky. Scattered through the canyons is evidence of thousands of years of prehistoric occupation from Archaic times through the last of the Pueblo Anasazi. The banks of Butler Wash are lined with almost impenetrable thickets of trees, brush, and weeds, and throughout the eastern side of Comb Ridge the canyon bottoms are choked with undergrowth. Along the canyon walls above the washes, however, the works of the Ancient Ones remain in the form of masonry and rock art.

Mud Springs Cliff Dwelling and the Wolfman Rock Art Panel

About one mile north of U.S. 163 the Butler Wash road crosses a cattle guard. Turn west on the south side of this guard and follow the fence west to Butler Wash Canyon. From the canyon rim you can see the Mud Springs cliff dwelling under the overhang on the west cliff face. This was a Pueblo II settlement built sometime before 1100. Only a small fraction of the original cliff dwelling remains. The pueblo can be reached by crossing the deep channel cut by the wash.

From the cliff dwelling, a narrow and precipitous trail works its way down the cliff side to the Wolfman Rock Art Panel. The beautiful petroglyphs of this panel are spread along the cliff face. The panel's unusual name comes from a small square-bodied figure with huge hands and feet. The panel also includes birds, wands, lion tracks, what looks like a copulating couple, and some unidentified symbols. The most spectacular piece of art in the panel is a circular "basket" that some absolute idiot used as a target for his high-powered rifle from across the canyon!

Procession Panel

Deep in a Comb Ridge canyon five miles north of the Wolfman Panel is Procession Panel, which consists of nearly two hundred small figures carved in a line across the face of a cliff.

The first report of Procession Panel was made by Chuck LaRue and Anne and Rob Johnson, who were hiking in the region on February 4, 1990. The panel was carved on the cliff face at the top of an ancient pass across the ridge. The main part of the panel is about twenty feet across. It depicts 179 marching human figures and a number of animals and humanlike characters. The Anasazi cut the figures into the dark patina, exposing the lighter-colored rock beneath.

Most of the figures are between four and eight inches high and are at about eye level. There are other petroglyphs along the cliff side east of the main panel, but nothing there equals this incredible line of marching figures. Some of the figures are just trudging along. Others are jumping, waving their arms, dancing, or kneeling. One group is carrying a prone figure. Some of the figures are carrying staffs and wearing headdresses and are larger than the others, as if to signify that they are directing the march.

A particularly interesting aspect of the panel is that the heads, hearts, hoofs, and tails of the animals carved on it were defaced in ancient times. The animals may have been inscribed later than the marching figures. Whether this was a ceremonial "kill" or an effort to transmit the strength of the animals to human beings can never be known.

There is no evidence of settlement or habitation in the pass or nearby in either Butler Wash or Comb Wash. This indicates that the rock art figures were in some way connected with the passage across the Comb.

Monarch's Cave

Monarch's Cave, in a Comb Ridge canyon about a mile north of Procession Panel, was named in 1892 by the Illustrated America Exploring Expedition. The expedition toured the West for *Illustrated America* magazine. An inscription on the north wall of the cave, which houses the ruins of a Pueblo III cliff dwelling, reads:

I.A.E.E.
MONARCH'S CAVE
1892

These two photographs show sections of the Wolfman Rock Art Panel (B-6). The panel is found on the east cliff face of Butler Wash Canyon about one mile north of U.S. 163. The north section (lower photo) shows, from left to right, a "crook planting stick," a mask, a yucca plant, and a "basket." The south section (upper photo) shows, from left to right, a small figure, a "bag," a mountain lion or canine track, two wands, a heron or crane, another bird, a human wearing a headdress, an unknown symbol, a "twine bag," and two symbols variously called keyholes, lobed circles, or drooping eyes. Sally Cole suggests this entire panel is heavy with fertility symbolism.

These ancient carvings, which make up the main part of the Procession Panel (B-5), were first reported in 1990. They consist of 179 figures spread across an approximately twenty-foot-long section of a cliff face. The figures vary from about four inches to eight inches in height. They proceed from three directions to a circle in the center. The panel appears on the north side of an ancient pass through Comb Ridge. Access from Comb Wash on the west is through a natural gap in the ridge wall. The canyon entrance from Butler Wash road is about six and one-half miles north of U.S. 163. Each tiny figure in the Procession Panel is an individual. Many are burden bearers. Thirty-seven march in from the west (left side) and 129 from the east. A few figures approach from the lower right. The panel was probably carved during Basketmaker or early Pueblo times. It was not part of a settlement because there are no nearby habitation ruins. The only mutilation of the panel appears to have been done in prehistoric times—note the bright spots on the big animals. These figures may have been symbolically killed long after the panel was carved.

Here is a portion of the western column of figures. One of them is gesticulating, two are carrying items that rock art scholars refer to as "keyhole" objects (they may be masks), another carries an unidentified object in his arms, others seem to be just walking along, and still others carry burden baskets on their backs. Burden baskets were carried with a tumpline (band) that was placed around the forehead and connected to the basket.

Here is a photograph of the west side of Comb Ridge, showing the gap that leads across the Comb to the Procession Panel pass. The gap that leads to the pass is the one that lies closest to the viewer. This photograph was taken from Comb Wash looking south.

The cave is located in the southwest corner of the canyon. The ruins there are on two shelves, or *benches*, on a single level below the cave's sandstone overhang. A climb up to the cliff dwelling from the canyon bottom brings you first to a shelf that lies at the west end of the huge cul-de-sac that forms the end of the canyon. Only a few remnants of construction remain there. To the southwest, however, in the next alcove, stands a beautiful fortified section of the cliff dwelling. It looks as serene and pristine as when first discovered in modern times.

Between the two alcoves is about a twenty-foot span of steep, slippery rock with several hand- and toeholds chipped out of the rock face. This entryway was designed to make access to the cliff dwelling difficult.

A climb through the brush and up the loose rock on the north side of Monarch's Cave Canyon reveals Monarch's Cave cliff dwelling, which looks as pristine and picturesque as when first seen in modern times. Just below the pueblo, on the canyon floor, is a grotto with a small, sparkling pool of water. The cliff dwelling dates from around 1250, but the alcove was used by the Anasazi off and on for hundreds of years before then. The cliff dwelling is one of the larger ruins in Comb Ridge. A large defensive wall, with ports through which the Anasazi could watch all approaches to the pueblo, was constructed in front of the residential and storage rooms.

At the south end of the southwest alcove are the remains of three masonry rooms, one with a rounded front wall that may have been part of a kiva, and two that may have been habitations. The original masonry is Mesa Verdean, but masonry much less refined tops the original, suggesting it may have been added in later Pueblo or in historic times. On the north side of the alcove are several rooms with interior plaster and part of a roof still in place.

Spectacular desert varnish streaks the canyon walls above the alcoves. Below, at the base of the cliff, where a pour-over from above reaches the canyon bottom, lies a beautiful little grotto and a pool of water.

On the roof of the interior of the main cave, about a dozen red handprints and a rather large pictograph are discernible. On the cave wall to the north are two more pictographs. One is a broad-shouldered San Juan Basketmaker–style figure with Hopilike hair whorls. If this figure was painted in Basketmaker times, as its style indicates, it had already been on the wall for at least five hundred years by the time the Pueblo cliff dwellers lived there. We say this because the Basketmaker period ended around A.D. 750, and this cliff dwelling was occupied during Pueblo III times, around 1250. The other pictograph is a composition of white, abstract triangular forms. Besides the pictographs, there is a man-shaped petroglyph pecked into the cliff face. This image is probably Basketmaker as well.

The Monarch's Cave cliff dwelling reflects the disturbed times of the mid-1200s. The pueblo looks like a medieval castle protected by a defensive wall with a few peepholes. The small openings were for ventilation, but they also provided the inhabitants with views of access routes to the cliff dwelling.

Dale Davidson suggests the people of the Comb, living nearer the frontier than those of Mesa Verde, were more likely to be attacked—marauders tend to hit fringe settlements first. The raiders may have been early Navajos, Apaches, or Utes. Perhaps there were Anasazi raiders too. Scarcity of food, overpopulation, or religious zeal may have caused warfare among the Anasazi living in the Northern San Juan region, and on Cedar Mesa, on the west side of the Comb.

Cold Spring Cave

Cold Spring Cave lies at the end of a small box canyon on the east side of Comb Ridge. From the Butler Wash road, it looks like a half-closed eye streaked with desert varnish. Masonry buildings can be seen beneath the overhang. The cave was visited, and its name was incised there, by the Illustrated America Exploring Expedition in 1892.

The Cold Spring site was not a cliff dwelling. It contains a number of structures, but no residential rooms. One of the structures at the site is a curtain wall that extended across the back of the cave. This wall stands about as high as a man and is equipped with peepholes. Behind the wall is a large pond-size spring that probably measures fifty feet across. In front of the wall and along the cliff are at least seven kivas. Two were built in front of the wall. One of them is square and the other round. The others are strung along the cliff wall. The interior of one of the kivas was painted red. There are also a number of storage rooms at the site.

At the front of the cave is a crudely constructed wall that must have been thrown up as a rampart to resist attack. It is clear that older construction was torn down to make the wall because some of the boulders show bits of rock art. With the springwater and stored food, Cold Spring Cave would have been able to withstand a siege.

Part of the site was built under the overhang along the canyon wall to the northeast of the cave. Some spectacular ancient handprints were painted there on the sandstone wall—some red and some white. The prints of a child appear at a child's height above the base of the overhang. Several small masonry walls, some with adobe and some without, still stand along the cliff wall.

The absence of dwelling rooms, the number of kivas, the curtain wall, and the large spring behind the wall suggest to Dale Davidson that the cave was a ceremonial center and stronghold that may have served Monarch's Cave, Fishmouth, and other pueblos in the Comb.

Fishmouth Cave

Probably the best-known site in Comb Ridge, Fishmouth Cave can be clearly seen from the Butler Wash road, about nine miles south of Utah 95. From the road, it closely resembles the mouth of a great fish. It is also called Fisheye Cave. In the back of the cave, printed on the rock face with charcoal, is the inscription GIANT'S CAVE. In 1893 Richard Wetherill's Hyde expeditionary group designated the cave as "HEE No. 10." This Basketmaker II site contained the graves of ninety Anasazi. Wetherill noted that the skulls were not flattened in the manner of the Pueblo skulls he

The overhang above Cold Spring Cave (B-5) covered a large spring. In front of the spring, the Pueblo III Anasazi built a curtain wall and several kivas, but no dwelling structures.

had seen. He concluded that they belonged to an earlier people. Because of the number of baskets in the burials, he named the people "Basket Makers."

It is a tough climb into the cave because of the immense pile of debris that has fallen from the cave and onto the slope below. It is an exercise of "five feet up and two feet back" and a bit dangerous. Once inside, what a disappointment! The cave has been vandalized time and time again, and now there is nothing left to see but piles of dirt and rubble and the graffiti of former visitors. The cave was occupied not only during Basketmaker times, but also later, during the Pueblo III period.

Although Fishmouth Cave is a disappointment, the hike up the canyon passes two small Pueblo III cliff dwellings along the north side of the canyon. One group of standing walls with an intact doorway consists of fine Mesa Verdean masonry. At the other site, a portion of a kiva wall displays a mural with narrow double and triple bands of white paint that make large rectangular panels. This kiva was rectangular and Mesa Verdean, even though rectangular kivas are normally associated with the Kayenta Anasazi. The masonry is more refined than Kayenta masonry, and the hearth, deflector, ventilator, and banquettes follow the Mesa Verde style. Throughout southeastern Utah are a number of Mesa Verdean kivas that were not built in the traditionally round configuration. The Bureau of Land Management recently backfilled the kiva.

In a canyon to the north of Fishmouth is a beautiful little Pueblo III cliff dwelling on a shelf halfway up the canyon wall. In the back of this canyon, on the south wall, are the remains of a much earlier jacal wall. Comb Ridge canyons are filled with such buildings and artifacts. Let us hope that visitors will respect these and all other ancient ruins so that they will remain exciting and beautiful for years to come.

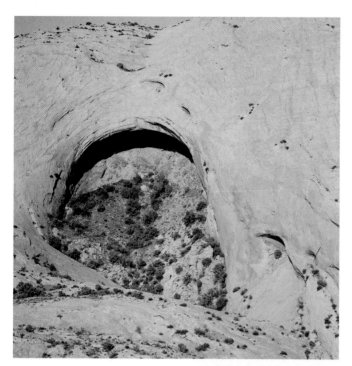

Fishmouth Cave (B-5), also called Fisheye Cave, is highly visible from the Butler Wash road, about nine miles south of Utah 95. The interior has been completely devastated by pot hunters. Only piles of dirt and rubble remain, except for several cists with vertical stone slabs joined together with mud. There is evidence of occupation from Basketmaker through Pueblo III times. Some awl- and ax-sharpening grooves in the rocks date from the Pueblo II period and later. An enormous amount of loose debris has slipped from the mouth of the cave and onto the slope below.

This picturesque, unnamed cliff dwelling sitting in the north wall of a canyon near Fishmouth Cave is an example of the many Anasazi structures hidden in the canyons of Comb Ridge. The room blocks were protected by a front wall. Such defensive barriers were common in cliff dwelling construction in the mid-1200s (during late Pueblo III times) in the Comb Ridge and western Cedar Mesa regions.

UTAH 95 SITES

Little Westwater

Slightly more than a mile south of Blanding, a surfaced road winds west from U.S. 191 for about a mile to Westwater Creek Canyon. At the end of the road is a cliff dwelling called Little Westwater by the locals and Five Kiva Ruin by archaeologists. The canyon is narrow here, and the ruins are easy to visit. A short trail from the road leads down into the canyon, up the other side, and into the ruin.

The pueblo was first occupied during Pueblo II times. After being destroyed in the late 800s or early 900s, it was rebuilt and occupied until the late 1200s.

Compare the photograph of the ruins with the reconstruction drawing and you can visualize how Little Westwater looked in the 1200s. Here the kivas were not buried in the plaza floor as at Mesa Verde but were all built like towers above the base of the cave. These people were Mesa Verde Anasazi, however, not outliers from Kayenta to the west or from Fremont to the north.

The canyon, on both sides, was occupied at various times from the Basketmaker period through Pueblo III. As you climb back up the east side of the canyon to the parking area, notice the remains of masonry structures in the cave above. The principal construction there was done between 1212 and 1214.

Big Westwater

Three miles downstream to the southwest from Little Westwater Pueblo is Big Westwater. This ruin was excavated for the Bureau of Land Management in 1979 by L. W. Lindsay. The excavation produced some very striking evidence of the Anasazi's problems in this region during both Pueblo II and Pueblo III times. The pueblo was originally occupied in the early Pueblo II period and was burned around 900. It was rebuilt between 1150 and 1200 and was again burned sometime after 1207. The last construction was in the uncertain times of the mid-1200s. At that time, the residents built a protective wall with numerous observation ports. The facts indicate that there was trouble in the Northern San Juan region at the end of Pueblo I and again in Pueblo III. The most active period of construction was during the sixty-year span between 1150 and 1210, even though that was a period of recurring drought.

Big Westwater was built in a canyon head under an overhang. The pueblo faces south and is about 130 feet wide. The remains of two room blocks can be seen: one is a block of two rooms on the east side, and the other consists of larger rooms and a curtain wall on the west side. Big Westwater has six well-preserved rooms and a kiva. The observation ports in the walls allowed surveillance of approaches to the pueblo. Lindsay's report says, "Various ports, taken together, provide nearly full coverage of all accesses, . . . including from both east and west rims of the alcove where descent to the site is possible and south up the arroyo." Dale Davidson has pointed out that the ports also provided ventilation.

Butler Wash Cliff Dwelling

The Butler Wash cliff dwelling is easily reached. Take Utah 95 west from its junction with U.S. 191 just south of Blanding. About eight miles west of the junction, stop at the parking area on the north side of the road. This area consists of a paved drive that leads to the trail entrance. At this point you can see, to the west, the huge shape of Comb Ridge extending south as far as you can see. The cliff dwelling was built in the ridge. From the parking area, a well-marked trail leads across the mesa to an observation platform opposite three alcoves that house the Butler Wash cliff dwelling.

The cliff dwelling was a small Pueblo III village of late vintage, built and occupied not long before all the Anasazi left the Northern San Juan region. The chief part of the village was housed in the northernmost of the three alcoves. Along the front of this alcove, the Anasazi built four kivas above ground level. These structures were Mesa Verdean in their masonry and design. The

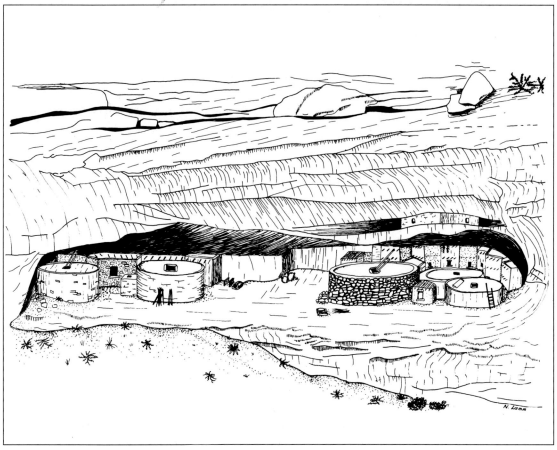

The drawing shows how the kivas at Little Westwater (C-3) were built above the plaza floor—not into it, as some of the kivas at Mesa Verde were. Access was generally from the roofs. Living and storage rooms were built behind the front row of kivas. Although the construction differs from that of Mesa Verde, the masonry and design are similar enough that the Anasazi here are considered to have been part of the Mesa Verde Anasazi culture. This settlement is typical of many Pueblo III (A.D. 1100 to 1300) cliff dwellings built in the canyons of southeastern Utah. The photograph shows how the Little Westwater site looks today. Drawing by Nancy B. Lamm.

Big Westwater Pueblo faces south and was designed to catch the low southern sun during the winter and yet be in the shade of the cliff overhang during the summer. This canyon-head settlement is similar to those at Hovenweep inasmuch as it is close to a water source and has Mesa Verdean masonry.

rectangular kiva on the north side shows Kayenta influence. Behind the kivas, the Anasazi built rooms for sleeping and rooms for storage. The sleeping rooms stood in front of the storage rooms. In front of the kivas lay a flat rock plaza. Below the cliff dwelling, the Anasazi cultivated the can-yon bottom to produce corn, beans, and squash. They probably also raised turkeys.

The other two alcoves were probably for storage of food, although the center one may have been used for ceremonies. In the troubled times of the Pueblo III period, the settlements included more space for storage than they did earlier. The three alcoves, high above the valley floor, were chosen as building sites to protect the people from outside aggressors.

This aerial photograph was taken from the east, overlooking the Butler Wash cliff dwelling (B-3). Three alcoves in the east side of Comb Ridge house the cliff dwelling. They contain residential rooms, kivas, and storage rooms. In the foreground of this photograph, you can see the cliff dwelling overlook. The overlook lies at the end of a foot trail that begins at a parking area off Utah 95. Visitors can enter the ruins by hiking up the canyon floor, starting north of the highway, and then climbing the canyon's western slope to reach the southernmost alcove. The plaza in front of the ruins allows easy access to all three alcoves.

Along Utah 95, eleven and four-tenths miles west of U.S. 191, are parking areas and a sign that reads BUTLER WASH INDIAN RUINS. The short trail to the ruins is marked by small stone cairns and several marked stakes. Much of the trail crosses a slickrock area where special attention must be given to locating the next cairn. The hike to the ruins gives a good idea of the enormous amount of effort the Anasazi had to expend to construct these masonry buildings without any tools except stone axes and ropes. The size of the task can be imagined by looking at the remaining structures and at all the debris that has fallen out of the pueblo since it was abandoned. This drawing gives an idea of how the cliff dwelling looked when it was occupied. The main part of the settlement was in the north (right) alcove. Residence and storage rooms were in the rear of the alcove, behind a front row of kivas. The exact use of the two other alcoves is not clear. However, the southernmost alcove was probably used for storage, and the middle one may have been used for ceremonies. The masonry wall in the center alcove was built without mortar. In the other walls of the pueblo, the Anasazi utilized a mud or clay mortar to bind the stones together. Drawing by Nancy B. Lamm.

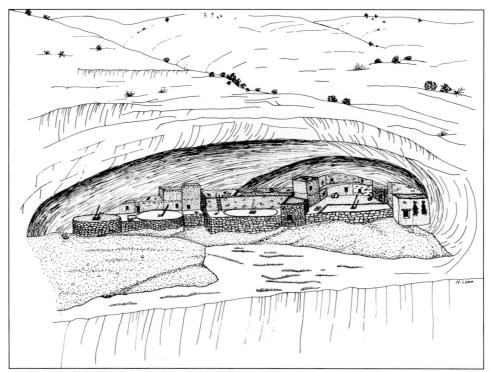

The photograph above is a telescopic view of the north alcove of the Butler Wash cliff dwelling. The drawing shows how the alcove looked when it was occupied. Note that kivas were built across the front of the settlement, except at the north end. A rather wide plaza lay between the kivas and the cliff edge. In the drawing, a mixture of Kayenta Anasazi and Mesa Verde Anasazi cultural influences can be seen. For example, a rectangular Kayenta kiva lies next to three round Mesa Verde kivas. All four kivas are aboveground, and not set into the rock base of the plaza as is the case in some of the Mesa Verde cliff dwellings. Drawing by Nancy B. Lamm.

Ballroom Site

The canyon just to the northeast of the Butler Wash cliff dwelling houses the Ballroom cliff dwelling. Ballroom is a delightful little ruin built at the end of a small, now shrub-filled box canyon. The "ballroom" from which the pueblo gets its name is a dry cave that extends back into the slickrock for nearly one hundred yards. At the mouth of the cave is a curtain wall about six or seven feet high. The front of the cave is strewn with huge boulders that have become dislodged from the ceiling of the overhang. Some may have fallen in prehistoric times and others more recently.

The Ballroom cliff dwelling is especially interesting because the site includes two almost intact masonry rooms with several of the roof beams still in place. On the sandstone wall above the room blocks are three painted stickman figures—one red, one brown, and one gold.

CEDAR MESA SITES

Arch Canyon Ruins

West of Blanding, Utah 95 cuts through Comb Ridge, makes a dramatic turn to the north, drops down the west side of the Comb, and crosses Comb Wash. One mile west of the Comb is a Bureau of Land Management sign reading ARCH CANYON 2 MILES. Here a sandy, unsurfaced road leaves Utah 95 and wanders up the canyon for two and one-half miles to the mouth of Arch Canyon. The road is bounded on the east by the Comb Wash Valley and the Comb Ridge escarpment, which consist of miles of horizontal layers of red and white sandstone. At the mouth of Arch Canyon, the road enters a towering grove of old cottonwood trees. Park there.

Follow the trail from the cottonwoods along the south side of Arch Canyon Wash. Soon you will reach the Bureau of Land Management registration box for hikers who wish to explore and camp in Arch, Texas, and Butts canyons.

The principal ruin in Arch Canyon was built against the north canyon wall, a few hundred yards farther up the wash. It is fenced and is identified by a sign. Green vegetation covers the debris from the pueblo. The cliff is striped with desert varnish.

Large multicoursed masonry walls are still standing next to the cliff. Part of the construction is in the Mesa Verde style, with loaf-shaped stones held in place by mud plaster. Another portion is Chacoan, with carefully laid tablet-size stones. The village was occupied during both Pueblo II and Pueblo III times. A Bureau of Land Management sign at the site suggests the pueblo was abandoned following the drought that began in 1276.

At one time, the village had room blocks built against the face of the cliff. They stood from one to four stories high. The Anasazi removed a number of buildings from the edge of the cliff, and some rebuilding took place. Large stone piles in front of the standing walls are the remains of collapsed buildings.

Rock art at Arch Canyon includes both pictographs and petroglyphs. There are paintings of buffalo there that were probably done by the Utes long after the Anasazi abandoned the pueblo. But a splendid brown lizard-man pictograph, a classic of Pueblo times, has Anasazi counterparts everywhere in the Northern San Juan region. Also still visible are excellent Anasazi petroglyphs incised in the cliff face during Pueblo II and Pueblo III times, including several spirals. One of these spirals is large and meticulously carved. There are also connected spirals that look like modern goggles. The walls of some of the rooms were painted in ancient times. Swatches of white paint show on the cliff now that the rooms are gone. You can also see holes in the sandstone where the roof poles were inset for room ceilings.

Across the canyon to the south, on a large boulder high on the slickrock slope, is a rock art image of a warrior with a shield and a spear. This is one of the few Anasazi depictions of battle gear.

Around the canyon to the northwest, in an alcove high on the canyon wall, are several storage rooms. During the troubled times of the 1200s, food was scarce and thus carefully protected in rooms like these.

Boulders from the roof of the cave have crashed down and destroyed portions of the Ballroom cliff dwelling. The rooms and wall to the rear survived, and a few rooms in the front can still be seen. This photograph shows some of the debris that fell from the roof, and portions of the surviving room blocks.

At one time, Arch Canyon Pueblo (B-3) had four-story room blocks backed against this cliff wall. Massive wall segments still remain. This is a big site, as large as Spruce Tree House at Mesa Verde. For unknown reasons, most of the buildings were torn down by the Anasazi themselves and the debris moved to the front of the site. This is a view up Arch Canyon to the northwest. The rubble that once was the Arch Canyon Pueblo lies beneath the cliff overhang.

Anasazi Roads

Along Comb Wash to the east of the Arch Canyon ruins is a clearly defined segment of an ancient Anasazi road. The map at the beginning of this book shows several of the known Anasazi roads in the Northern San Juan region. In the hundreds of years since they were built, most have been obliterated by erosion or by modern farming. The aerial photograph shows a small portion of the Anasazi road mentioned above. It has been traced along Comb Wash from the Abajos almost to the San Juan River. Anasazi road segments have been identified in the Montezuma Creek Canyon, Butler Wash, and Cottonwood Creek. Others fanned out from the Lowry and Pigg ruins, connected Sand Canyon and Goodman Point, and followed the Mancos River at the Ute Tribal Park. One extended west from Wallace Ruin, near Cortez, Colorado.

Chaco Canyon is the center of a number of identified Anasazi roads. The roads there have been easier to identify than some others because northwestern New Mexico is barren and has not been farmed. The roads at Chaco connected the canyon to at least thirty outlier sites. The "Great North Road," which led to Aztec, New Mexico, may have continued north toward Mesa Verde. Kathryn Gabriel, in her book *Roads to Center Place*, suggests the Chacoan road system included roads in the Northern San Juan region.

The Anasazi roads were not invariably straight; they followed the terrain. They were, however, planned and laid out. They were not just trails that became roads by constant use. However, the purpose of Anasazi road building is still something of an enigma. The Anasazi did not have the wheel, so they had no wagons. Nor did they have horses, oxen, llamas, or any other beasts of burden. People and their feet were the only mode of transport. Human beings carried everything.

The roads must have been multipurpose. We know they led to ceremonial complexes: the great houses and great kivas. We also know that they had a certain religious and social significance of their own because shrines dotted the routes, and so, perhaps, did overnight hostelries. And of course the roads served as trade and communication routes. Dale Davidson points out that there were Anasazi roads throughout the Northern San Juan region. Unlike the roads in Chaco Canyon, most of the ones that ran along level ground have been obliterated. The ones that ran along the cliffs tend to be the ones that are still visible.

Mule Canyon Ruins

This little Anasazi settlement was excavated and partially restored when Utah 95 was constructed. It is an interesting site because it makes a Pueblo II Anasazi village easy to visualize. Note the masonry walls of the room blocks, the kiva (which has been covered by a protective roof), and the tower.

At this site, a pithouse was built about A.D. 750 as part of a Pueblo I occupation. The site was eventually abandoned and later reoccupied during Pueblo II and early Pueblo III times, from 1000 to 1150. This mesa-top village was Mesa Verdean in character and does not show much influence from the Kayenta region, even though it is on Cedar Mesa west of Comb Ridge. The twelve masonry rooms at the site formed a single-story building and housed two or three families. These rooms were used primarily for sleeping and storage. Entrance was by ladder through an opening in the roof of each room.

Mule Canyon is an example of a *Prudden unit* or a *unit pueblo*, terms used by archaeologists to refer to a particular type of village layout. In this layout, the room block stood on the north side of the pueblo, the kiva lay south of the room block, and farther south lay a trash dump. T. Mitchell Prudden recognized this building arrangement during his research in the Northern San Juan region in the late 1800s.

The room blocks, kiva, and tower at Mule Canyon were connected by tunnels. One tunnel led from the room blocks to the kiva and another from the kiva to the tower. The kiva's roof was level with the plaza.

Only recently have archaeologists come to realize that the Anasazi in the Northern San Juan region of southeastern Utah were road builders. This photograph shows a segment of an ancient road that has been traced from the mouth of Arch Canyon, two and one-half miles north of Utah 95, to as far south as the old Mormon trail on the other side of Cedar Mesa. The road is about nineteen miles long. Here the road appears as a faint, straight line that cuts diagonally across the center of the photograph.

Here is an aerial view of Mule Canyon Pueblo (A-3) from above Utah 95. This view shows, in the center, Mule Canyon and, in the background, the Abajo Mountains. A Mesa Verdean kiva is seen beneath a protecting roof. The base of a tower lies to the right of the kiva. The kiva was connected to the tower and to the room blocks on the left by tunnels. Mule Canyon Pueblo was a Mesa Verde–style Pueblo III settlement. It was excavated during the 1970s when Utah 95 was constructed. The ruins lie on the north side of Utah 95, about five miles west of Comb Ridge.

The tower stood two stories high and may have been designed for communication with the Cave Canyon Towers, a group of masonry structures about a mile to the south. Kiva-tower complexes are common in the Northern San Juan region. Another one can be seen, for example, at Mesa Verde's Far View settlement.

Cave Canyon Towers

This group of Pueblo III buildings is also called the Five Tower Site because it consists of five towers. The towers stand near a water source at the head of Cave Canyon. These structures provide a forceful argument for the idea that the Anasazi built towers for reasons other than to protect their villages and homes, because no settlement lies next to them. The towers may have belonged to Mule Canyon Pueblo and other small settlements in nearby canyons. Cave Canyon branches off the west side of Mule Canyon.

If the towers were not built for defense, they must have been built for religious purposes. Water was scarce in this area, and preserving a nearby source was critical to the survival of the Anasazi in the region. The towers may exemplify the special obeisance and recognition the Anasazi gave to their water sources.

Each of the towers is several stories high. No reconstruction has been done on them; but they were well built, and so many of the walls are still standing.

Moon House Cliff Dwelling

Moon House cliff dwelling is one of the most interesting ruins in the Cedar Mesa region. It sits at the head of Owl Creek Canyon, north of the Old Mormon Trail. The Mormon Trail was the route taken south by the Mormons in early days to cross Comb Ridge at the San Juan River. North of Moon House, on the horizon, is one of the spectacular landmarks of the Southwest—two peaks known as the Bears Ears. The road into the Manti–La Sal National Forest passes between the ears.

Moon House is a fortified Pueblo III cliff dwelling named for a pictograph of the moon painted on a wall of one of its rooms. From across the canyon, all that can be seen of the cliff dwelling is a rose-colored curtain wall, with small doorways, following the canyon overhang. The top of the curtain wall does not quite reach the overhang and thus leaves a few feet of space for ventilation. This fortresslike design reflects the growing fear felt by the Anasazi. No longer did they build open, unfortified villages on the mesa tops. Here on Cedar Mesa, as at Mesa Verde, in Comb Ridge, and in the canyons of southeastern Utah, concern for security became a way of life and a way of architecture.

OLD MAN CAVE

Old Man Cave is situated at the head of a small canyon off Comb Wash, north of Arch Canyon. Bureau of Land Management archaeologists Dale Davidson and Phil H. Geib reported that part of an open-twined sandal from Archaic times had been found there in 1984. The sandal was carbon-dated at 6470 B.C.! The cave had been looted before the bureau excavated it, but the priceless sandal was left behind. The bureau determined that there were two occupations of Old Man Cave at widely separated times. The first occupation began about 7,800 years ago, during the Archaic period. The Archaic people abandoned the site more than 1,500 years later, about 4100 B.C. About 4,000 years later, it was reoccupied by Anasazi Basketmaker II people.

Basketmaker II Occupation of Old Man Cave

Basketmaker II artifacts found in Old Man Cave include portions of baskets, rabbit-fur blankets, slab-lined cists mortared with fiber-tempered clay, and a burial pit that was in use during Basketmaker occupation of Cedar Mesa—from A.D. 200 to 400. The Basketmakers did not live in the

Moon House (A-4) is a spectacular cliff dwelling built into the wall of a small canyon that is a tributary of Owl Creek Canyon. The pueblo gets its name from a painting of the moon in one of the rooms behind the pueblo's exterior wall. This photograph shows the wall, which was built for defense. Most of the openings in the wall are designed to ventilate the rooms behind it. Defensive walls like this one are more prevalent in the Comb and on Cedar Mesa than they are to the east in Montezuma Creek Canyon, the Montezuma Valley, and Mesa Verde. The pueblo is reachable by a trail from the Old Mormon Road. The entrance to the Old Mormon Road is south of the Kane Gulch ranger station on Utah 261.

cave. Instead, they used it for storage and burials. The four-thousand-year period between the Archaic and the Basketmaker occupations suggests that the Archaic people were not the ancestors of the Anasazi. However, as Douglas Bowman has demonstrated, the Archaic people and the early Anasazi did occupy the Northern San Juan region simultaneously until around A.D. 500.

A cradle board found at the cave, made of reeds and held together with yucca cord, exemplifies the skills that these people had very early in the Christian era. Unlike the Pueblo Anasazi, the

This piece of an Archaic sandal, found by a Bureau of Land Management ranger in Old Man Cave, has been carbon-dated at 6470 B.C. It is part of an open-twined sandal, a type made and used by the Archaic people who lived in the Cedar Mesa region.

Dale Davidson, standing, and the Bureau of Land Management excavation team are shown here working at the south end of the Old Man Cave site in 1992 (B-3). The worker on the left is holding the dustpan at the level the cave floor sat during Archaic times. After being first occupied around 7,800 years ago, the site was used by the Archaic people for about 1,500 years. It was not again occupied until the Basketmaker II Anasazi began living there around A.D. 200.

Basketmakers did not use a hard cradle board. As a result, their skulls were not flattened in the back. The Pueblo Anasazi flattened the backs of their babies' skulls by securing the children to a hard-surfaced cradle board. The skulls remained flattened for life. This difference in the skulls differentiates Basketmaker remains from those of their descendants, the Pueblo Anasazi. The difference was first noted by Richard Wetherill in 1893 at Cottonwood Canyon Cave 7, on the east side of Comb Ridge. The difference in the skulls revealed that the cliff dwellers had been preceded by the Basketmakers.

Wetherill also noted that the cave in Cottonwood Canyon held ninety-seven skeletons of Anasazi who had been massacred there. So much for the concept that the Anasazi were not a warlike people. They probably were as mean as any other people, a conclusion that is also supported by the rock art images of scalps and by the evidence of cannibalism near the Mancos River.

The early Basketmakers were traders. The delicate beads found at Old Man Cave came all the way from the Pacific Coast. There is still disagreement among archaeologists about whether the trade was sporadic or whether the Anasazi had regular markets. The ancient Maya, Zapotecs, Aztecs, and other peoples had the same kind of regular markets that flourish among the Indians of Mexico and Guatemala today. The Spaniards reported markets in the villages of northern Mexico. The Pecos Puebloans had a flourishing trade with the Plains Indians. However, some archaeologists argue that the egalitarian Anasazi families made everything they needed and that there was therefore no need for trade except to get jewelry and a few other exotic items. Others disagree. Dale Davidson feels that markets were part of the Anasazi culture and that these people regularly traded among themselves and with others. Salt had to be acquired from the Zuni and Colorado River regions to the south. Other known interregional trade items include obsidian, jet, jewelry, shells, feathers, hematite, chert for arrowheads, and pottery. Kayenta Red wares were a hot item. East of Comb Ridge and north of what is now Utah 95, the Anasazi built an entry road into a plaza at Cottonwood Falls, suggesting that they had a market there. The humpbacked Kokopelli may represent a trader with a pack. Trade among the Anasazi is discussed in Ferguson and Rohn, *Anasazi Ruins of the Southwest in Color.*

■

/// Glossary

ANASAZI: Descendants of Asians who crossed the land bridge between Siberia and Alaska during the last ice age. Often called the *cliff dwellers*, they represent a continuous culture, beginning with the early Basketmakers (1500 B.C.) and continuing through the Pueblo periods, which ended around A.D. 1300 in Mesa Verde and the Northern San Juan region. Modern Pueblo, Zuni, and Hopi peoples are descendants of the Anasazi.

ANASAZILAND: The area of the Southwest that was occupied by the Anasazi. Centered on the Four Corners, it extended from the Rocky Mountains to the Grand Canyon and from the Little Colorado River in the south through the Northern San Juan region in the north.

ARCHAIC PEOPLE: Nomadic hunters and gatherers of the Southwest that generally preceded the Anasazi but were not their ancestors. Their culture covered the period from 6500 B.C. to A.D. 500.

ATLATL: Throwing stick used to propel a spear or dart. Replaced with the bow and arrow sometime around A.D. 500.

BANQUETTE: A benchlike masonry wall built around the inside periphery of a kiva. Masonry *pilasters* (columns) were built on the banquettes to support the roof.

BASKETMAKERS: Anasazi so named by early explorers for their fine baskets. The Basketmaker II and Basketmaker III periods extend from 1500 B.C. to A.D. 500 and A.D. 500 to 750, respectively. The Basketmakers were followed in the Northern San Juan region by the Pueblo Anasazi.

BOX CANYON: A canyon with nearly vertical walls on both sides.

CAPROCK: A sedimentary rock plate overlying other rocks. A caprock is usually visible on a canyon rim.

CHACO CANYON ANASAZI: The ancient Indians of the Chaco Canyon region of northwestern New Mexico, the region that produced the "Chaco Phenomenon" between the late A.D. 1000s and the mid-1100s. The Chaco Canyon Anasazi built spectacular great houses, pueblos, and roads. They strongly influenced the Northern San Juan Anasazi during Pueblo II times.

CLIFF DWELLING: Anasazi masonry pueblos constructed beneath cliff overhangs. They were used primarily in the Northern San Juan region during Pueblo III times (A.D. 1100 to 1300), but some were built during the Pueblo II period (A.D. 900 to 1100/1150).

CRIBBED ROOF: A beehive-shaped kiva roof made of logs layered on top of each other. Each log in the bottom layer extended from one kiva pilaster to another. The logs in each of the rest of the layers were crisscrossed on top of the logs immediately below them, creating concentric rings of decreasing size. The openings between the logs were filled with mud and small branches.

DANCE PLATFORM: An open platform used for ceremonies. The term is often applied to unroofed great kivas.

DESERT VARNISH: A brown or black stain that appears on boulders and cliff walls in desert regions, caused by rainwater carrying manganese oxide or iron oxide.

DRY WALLS: Stone masonry walls built without mortar.

FOOT DRUM: In the floor of kivas or great kivas, a recess covered with wooden planking, producing a drumlike sound when danced upon.

GREAT HOUSE: Large, multistory masonry structures with built-in kivas, constructed initially at Chaco Canyon and, later, in Pueblo II times in the Northern San Juan region. Lowry Pueblo and the Far View ruins at Mesa Verde are examples. Great houses may have been centers of political power.

GREAT KIVA: Large round or rectangular structures used by the Anasazi from Basketmaker through Pueblo times for ceremonies and community gatherings. Some were roofed, and some of the round ones had a diameter of forty-five feet.

JACAL WALLS: Walls consisting of a framework of posts interlaced with woven branches and covered with mud. Also known as *wattle and daub*. The word *jacal* is pronounced *ha-CALL*.

KACHINAS: Modern Puebloan spirits that are associated with the Puebloan origin myths and that teach and guide the modern Hopi and Zuni.

KIN KIVA: Generally a subterranean, circular room about twenty feet in diameter and eight feet high, utilized by related family groups for rituals, toolmaking, weaving, storytelling, and the instruction of children.

KOKOPELLI: A Hopi term often applied to the hunchbacked flute player depicted in Anasazi rock art and on Anasazi pottery.

LAND BRIDGE: Dry land that connected Alaska and Siberia during the last ice age. This land is now covered by the Bering Sea.

MANO AND METATE: Terms derived from Mexico for the handheld grinding stone and stone receptacle used by the Anasazi to pulverize corn and other seeds into meal.

MESA: A tableland or flat plateau, generally bounded on one or more sides by steep cliffs.

MODERN PUEBLO PEOPLE: Modern inhabitants of the pueblos near Santa Fe and Zuni, New Mexico, and the Hopi mesas of Arizona.

OLLA: Pottery jar with a bulging base and wide mouth, used for cooking or water storage.

OUTLIER: Any of a number of Chacoan settlements connected with or controlled by the Chaco Canyon Anasazi, usually by means of specially constructed roads.

PECKING: A method of shaping or dressing masonry stones by striking or pitting them with a hammerstone.

PETROGLYPH: Figure pecked or incised into a rock wall.

PICTOGRAPH: Figure painted on rock.

PILASTER: In a kiva, a rectangular, upright masonry column built on a banquette and upon which the roof timbers rested.

PITHOUSE: Living quarters of the Basketmaker Anasazi. These structures were partially underground, had flat roofs, and were circular or rectangular.

POINTS: Sharp chipped-stone tips for spears, darts, and arrows.

PORTICO: Covered colonnade across the front of a building.

PUEBLO: A cluster of single- or multistory, flat-roofed, masonry or adobe living quarters built by the Anasazi on mesas, in canyons, or in cliffs. In most cases, the living quarters were connected to one another. *Pueblo* is the Spanish word for *town*.

RAMADA: A roofed room without walls, constructed in front of walled Anasazi living quarters.

RIMROCK: A ledge of rock that forms the natural boundary of a mesa or other elevated landform.

ROCK ART: Figures painted on—or carved, incised, or pecked into—rock surfaces.

ROOM BLOCK: A group of connected or adjacent masonry rooms within a pueblo.

SHERDS: Small pieces of broken pottery.

SIPAPU: Small lined hole in the floor of pithouses and kivas, symbolizing a connection to the underworld from which the Anasazi's ancestors emerged.

SLICKROCK: A colloquial term used in the Southwest to describe the smooth, light-colored sandstone that covers the sloping areas between canyons.

TALUS SLOPE: Rock debris at the base of a cliff or below a cliff dwelling.

TRASH DUMP: The area near Anasazi pueblos—usually in front—where trash was deposited.

TREE-RING DATING: A method of determining the age of logs used in pueblo construction. The annual growth rings that appear in the timbers can be matched and correlated to calculate the date the tree was cut. Tree-ring dates in the Southwest extend back to the beginning of the first century A.D. Tree-ring dating is also called *dendrochronology*.

UNIT PUEBLO: A standard pueblo design with storage and living rooms on the north side, a courtyard and kivas in the middle, and a trash dump on the south side.

/ / / Bibliography

Aitchison, Stewart
1983   *A Naturalist's San Juan River Guide*. Pruett, Boulder, Colo.

Akens, Jean
1987   *Ute Mountain Tribal Park: The Other Mesa Verde*. Four Corners Publications, Moab, Utah.

Atkins, Victoria M. (ed.)
1993   *Anasazi Basketmakers*. Papers from the 1990 Wetherill–Grand Gulch Symposium, Cultural Resource Series No. 24. United States Department of the Interior, Bureau of Land Management, Salt Lake City.

Breternitz, David A., Arthur H. Rohn, and Elizabeth A. Morris
1974   *Prehistoric Ceramics of the Mesa Verde Region*. Museum of Northern Arizona Ceramic Series No. 5. 2d ed. Interpark, Cortez, Colo.

Brew, J. O.
1946   *Archaeology of Alkali Ridge, Southeastern Utah, with a Review of the Prehistory of the Mesa Verde Division of the San Juan and Some Observations on Archaeological Systematics*. Papers of the Peabody Museum of American Archaeology and Ethnology, No. 21, Harvard University, Cambridge.

Cassells, E. Steve
1990   *The Archaeology of Colorado*. Johnson Books, Boulder, Colo.

Castleton, Kenneth B.
1987   *Petroglyphs and Pictographs of Utah*, vol. 2. Utah Museum of Natural History, Salt Lake City.

Cattanach, George S., Jr.
1980   *Long House, Mesa Verde National Park, Colorado*. U.S. National Park Service Historical Research Series 7-H, Washington, D.C.

Cole, Sally J.
1990   *Legacy on Stone: Rock Art of the Colorado Plateau and the Four Corners*. Johnson Books, Boulder, Colo.

Ferguson, William M., and Arthur H. Rohn
1987   *Anasazi Ruins of the Southwest in Color*. University of New Mexico Press, Albuquerque.

Fox, Nancy
1978   *Pueblo Weaving and Textile Arts*. Museum of New Mexico Press, Santa Fe.

Gabriel, Kathryn
1991   *Roads to Center Place*. Johnson Books, Boulder, Colo.

Houk, Rose
1994   *The Four Corners Anasazi: A Guide to Archaeological Sites.* San Juan National Forest Association, Durango, Colo.

Hurst, Winston B., and Joe Pachak
1992   *Spirit Windows: Native American Rock Art of Southeastern Utah.* State of Utah, Division of Parks and Recreation, Edge of the Cedars State Park, Blanding, Utah.

Jernigan, E. Wesley
1978   *Jewelry of the Prehistoric Southwest.* University of New Mexico Press, Albuquerque.

Lange, Frederick W.
1989   *Cortez Crossroads.* Johnson Books, Boulder, Colo.

Lange, Frederick, Nancy Mahaney, Joe Ben Wheat, and Mark L. Chenault
1986   *Yellow Jacket: A Four Corners Anasazi Ceremonial Center.* Johnson Books, Boulder, Colo.

Lindsay, La Mar W.
1981   *Big Westwater Ruin: Excavation of Two Anasazi Sites in Southern Utah, 1979–1980.* Utah State Office, U.S. Bureau of Land Management, Salt Lake City.

Lister, Florence C.
1993   *In the Shadow of the Rocks: Archaeology of the Chimney Rock District in Southern Colorado.* University Press of Colorado, Niwot, Colo.

Lister, Robert H., and Florence C. Lister
1978   *Anasazi Pottery.* University of New Mexico Press, Albuquerque.
1983   *Those Who Came Before.* Southwest Parks and Monuments Association, Globe, Ariz.

Malville, J. McKim, and Claudia Putnam
1989   *Prehistoric Astronomy in the Southwest.* Johnson Books, Boulder, Colo.

Martin, Paul S., and Gerhardt von Bonin
1936   *Lowry Ruin in Southeastern Colorado.* Field Museum of Natural History, Publication 356, Anthropological Series 23(1), Chicago.

Matlock, Gary
1988   *Enemy Ancestors.* Northland Publishing, Flagstaff, Ariz.

Mays, Buddy
1982   *Ancient Cities of the Southwest.* Chronicle Books, San Francisco.

McGregor, John C.
1982   *Southwestern Archaeology.* University of Illinois Press, Chicago.

Morley, Sylvanus G.
1908   "The Excavation of the Cannonball Ruins in Southwestern Colorado." *American Anthropology* 10, no. 4 (Oct.–Dec.).

Nickens, Paul R.
1981 *Pueblo III Communities in Transition: Environment and Adaption in Johnson Canyon.* Memoirs of the Colorado Archaeological Society, No. 2, Colorado Archaeological Society, Boulder, Colo.

Nobel, David Grant
1981 *Ancient Ruins of the Southwest.* Northland Press, Flagstaff, Ariz.

Nobel, David Grant (ed.)
1985 *Understanding the Anasazi of Mesa Verde and Hovenweep.* School of American Research, Santa Fe.

Nordenskiold, G.
1979 *The Cliff Dwellers of Mesa Verde, Southwestern Colorado.* Reprint of 1893 edition. Rio Grande Press, Glorieta, N.Mex.

Oppelt, Norman T.
1991 *Earth Water and Fire: The Prehistoric Pottery of Mesa Verde.* Johnson Books, Boulder, Colo.

Rohn, Arthur H.
1971 *Mug House, Mesa Verde National Park, Colorado.* U.S. National Park Service Archaeological Research Series 7-D, Washington, D.C.
1977 *Cultural Change and Continuity on Chapin Mesa.* Regents Press of Kansas, Lawrence.

Smith, Duane A.
1988 *Mesa Verde National Park: Shadows of the Centuries.* University Press of Kansas, Lawrence.

Thompson, Ian
1993 *The Towers of Hovenweep.* Mesa Verde Museum Association, Mesa Verde National Park, Colo.

Veile, Catherine W.
1980 *Voices in the Canyon.* Southwest Parks and Monuments Association, Globe, Ariz.

Watson, Don
N.d. *The Cliff Dwellings of the Mesa Verde.* Mesa Verde Museum Association, Mesa Verde National Park, Colo.

Wenger, Gilbert R.
1980 *The Story of Mesa Verde National Park.* Mesa Verde Museum Association, Mesa Verde National Park, Colo.

Williamson, Ray A.
1984 *The Living Sky: The Cosmos of the American Indian.* Houghton Mifflin, Boston.

/// Index